As
a Tale
That Is
Told

We spend our years as a tale that is told.

PSALM 90 : 9

As
a Tale
That Is
Told

The
Autobiography
of
R. M. MacIver

THE UNIVERSITY OF CHICAGO PRESS
CHICAGO & LONDON

Library of Congress Catalog Card Number: 68:15632

THE UNIVERSITY OF CHICAGO PRESS, CHICAGO & LONDON
THE UNIVERSITY OF TORONTO PRESS, TORONTO 5, CANADA

Author's Note

Many of those who figure in this personal history are happily still potential readers of it. In order not to give needless offence or cause undue embarrassment I have in a very few instances changed a name and the scene of an incident.

I gratefully acknowledge the careful scrutiny the typescript received from my wife and the suggestions made by my son-in-law, Robert Bierstedt. I am much indebted to my son, Donald, for the skill with which he deciphered my minuscule penmanship and prepared typed copies for me.

I have benefited also by the observations of my friend, John Lageman, who, among other services, pointed out several places where the narrative needed some amplification to be effective.

The writing of this book brought me an unexpected reward in the freshened remembrance of old times and of friends and good neighbors many of whom do not figure in this tale but enrich my sense of the days that were, of times the good and the evil of which were blurred for me until I relived them in the record.

R. M. M.

Contents

Contents

Illustrations

1

The Setting

When I had reached the age of gray-haired reminiscence and was told I should write my autobiography, I swore I never would. No one told the truth about himself and no one knew the truth about himself. Everyone is a prejudiced witness of the events in which he participated and of the situations in which his lot was cast. The story he relates is always contrived to create an image of what the writer fondly believed himself to be, to create a coherent impression, to magnify achievement, to rationalize his slanted impressions into the preconceived pattern of a life. Memory is capricious, especially in the old. It colors the past, above all the remoter past, in retrospective hues. It gives false salience to selected episodes. It is particularly partial in portraying the author's relationships with other folk. It is inept in the analysis of the influences that have shaped his attitudes and ways of life. No, I would never write what is optimistically called an autobiography.

And now, under the illicit persuasion of the fullness of the years, I am doing just that.

In the courts they swear to tell the truth, the whole truth, and nothing but the truth. They never do; they never can. But without honest witnesses the story would never be known.

The place of my birth and earlier youth was the little town of

Stornoway on the island of Lewis, the most northerly and much the largest of the Outer Hebrides. It is a land where the winters are never very cold and the summers never very warm, where rain is more frequent than sunshine, drizzly rain blowing in from the Atlantic, where the changing seasons make only a minor difference in the treeless landscape, except for the purpling of the autumn heather, the early darkness in winter, and the summer day so long that in June night is no more than a passing shadow over the sky.

It was a quiet sleepy-looking town, with its staid rows of gray-slated stone houses. In my youth there were no automobiles, only the occasional jogging country cart coming to buy or to sell. But for two months in summer it presented a very different scene. Stornoway was the center of the west coast herring fishing. The population swelled from about four thousand to seven thousand, and the streets along the piers resounded with bustling activity. For the rest of the year the only noise was an occasional brawl outside one of the three hotel bars the town possessed at that time.

My parents were a union of town and country. My father, Donald MacIver, came from a line of crofters and small farmers, independent self-respecting folk who made a modest livelihood by participating in the herring fishing in addition to cultivating their crops of barley and oats and potatoes. Their women also spun the wool for the making of Harris tweed. Country-bred himself, my father held to the strict religiosity characteristic of his people and followed without questioning the old mores. My mother, Christina Morrison (often spelt "Morison" by members of her kin), was town-bred, more sophisticated, less tradition-bound, adhering in a rather liberal way to the prevailing Presbyterian religion. The Morrisons were a widespread kin-group that had some quite distinguished members and was well represented in the town. In our home there was a massive brass-bound family Bible, on a free front page of which the family tree of the Morrisons was neatly drawn. As a boy I used to ponder over it, gazing at the alliances and their offspring as they moved down from generation to generation, ending with my own.

Although their temperaments and attitudes were so different, my parents got along together reasonably well, an accommodation due mainly to my father's meekness and my mother's *savoir-faire*.

My father migrated as a young man from the village of Shawbost to the town. His forebears had been evicted from their land in the southeast district called Uig, when much of that part of the island was converted into salmon-fishing and deer-hunting preserves, a vicious practice that depopulated large areas of the Highlands. Once every summer the whole family made a pious excursion in a coach and pair to visit our relations in Shawbost, my grandmother, uncles and aunts. I do not remember my grandfather, who died while I was still very young. The drive over the rough gravelly road took around two hours and a half. Most of us walked up the small hills on the road to ease the horses. The distance was eighteen miles. I remember my grandmother, a comely well-set-up lady with a resigned face, wearing a fine shawl over her shoulders and a white mutch on her head. We would sit down to a too-bounteous meal piled on a large table in the long and dimly lit living room of the thatched cottage and be pressed on all sides to eat more than was good for us of the fish, usually trout from a lake nearby on the edge of the sea, and chicken and pies, with great plates of warm fresh scones and, of course, the inevitable tea. After the meal one of my uncles would take me down to the lake while he fished for trout with an illegal many-hooked contraption called an otter.

Like quite a number of our country folk, my father was well educated for one who had not gone beyond the public school. He was quietly intelligent, though lacking the imagination my mother possessed, and he took much interest both in local and national affairs. He became a rather successful merchant, being one of the first to trade on any scale in Harris tweed (a misnomer, since this superior cloth was mostly produced on Lewis), the making of which became an important island product. At that time it was all hand-made, the spinning, dyeing, and weaving, though later the weaving and often the dyeing were taken over by the mills. He was a pleasant-looking trim-bearded man, of gentle ways, a man of peace, and withal a good man of business. He had wanted to train for the ministry of the Free Church of Scotland, but his obligations had prevented him. His greatest devotion was still for the church. He was still at heart a preacher, as we youngsters had good reason to know. In spite of his mild manner he would wax fervent over the sins of the folk. He had high respect for education and a good library that contained, besides a collection of devotional works, the more respectable classics of the nineteenth century—the Brontës, Walter Scott, Dickens, Thackeray, Ruskin, Tennyson, Browning, and so forth.

My mother was of a very different cast. She was impetuous, high-spirited, strong-minded, with a sharp tongue at times and a neat way of summing people up, without having in that respect any of the inhibitions of my father. She saw through to the motivations of people and had no compunction in expressing her opinions. My father did not escape her critical comments, mostly on his tendency to believe the professions of the unctuous. In my very early years I secretly resented these comments. I would say to myself: When I'm big I'll marry a woman who'll never fuss at me; I'll be the boss and let no woman nag me. At that stage, when I was five or six years old, I respected my mother, but I could not say I loved her.

She never complained but went about her many tasks with quiet assurance. She was skilled in all household arts. For all our minor complaints she had her own prescriptions. No pills for her, no nostrums out of a bottle. We would be given hot lemon drinks, plenty of fluids, hot foot baths or sitz baths, vigorous rubbings with olive oil, and so forth. She had one guide, a series of small red books on health by a certain Dr. Kirk.

She was slight, spare, alert, with a sense of swiftness, with beautiful but sometimes sad eyes. When she was gay she would sing to herself with a happy lilt. In a different mood she would recite some poem or hymn that had a melancholy note. One of her favorites was a poem on the burial of Moses that began as follows:

> On Nebo's lonely mountain
> On this side Jordan's vale,

and her voice would swell as she came to the lines

> That was the grandest funeral
> That ever passed on earth.

It's curious but I can remember nothing of what my father said, while snatches of my mother's words still echo in my memory.

My mother always held herself erect, always showed a brave face to the world. She was always trim and tried to keep the rest of us so. Usually she wore a tight-fitting front-buttoned bodice that enhanced her slimness. I little knew then of the many burdens she had to carry. It was only later, when I was myself learning not to take everything at its face value, that I began really to appreciate my mother. I came to admire her independence, her forthrightness, the way she gave a flavor, a pithiness, a bite sometimes, to what she said. My father by contrast seemed tame, too ready to echo the views of the paper he approved, especially the religious *British Weekly,* or of the parson who Sunday morning and evening proclaimed the eternal truth to us.

My mother was herself. She didn't make "goodness" the principle of life, the way my father did. She was a woman of decision, a personality. In the course of growing up I came to hug the thought that I inherited more from her. "The woman makes us most," our then favorite poet Tennyson said.

Such was the way I knew my parents, but I am fully aware that the very relation of child to parents instills in the former an angled view of the latter, not without prejudice and screened from some of the more full-blooded manifestations of personality that tend to be inhibited by the responsibilities of parenthood. One speaks of what one owes to one's parents, but how can one reckon it? We owe our existence to them, and the biological inheritance we possess all comes directly from them. But they do not fashion us as the sculptor creates the statue. They did not foresee what we would be. We are the creatures of the sex urge and, beyond that, of the inextricably complex meshings of the genetic threads in each specific act of conception. For one thing I am grateful to the powers that be that I inherited a body of such steadfast healthfulness that it has thus far resisted the enemies that lie in wait to lay us low. For the rest I am grateful I had parents who lavished on me their loving care, though I have departed a long way from the instruction in which they sought to bring me up.

We lived at first in a two-storied house on North Beach Street, looking out on the inner bay. Across the bay Stornoway Castle, an imposing Tudor structure, stood on a plateau in the midst of spacious grounds well planted with low trees, practically the only woods on the whole island. The one-sided street broadened out to a line of piers, where troughs stood in summer into which the fisher-girls threw the gutted herring and where rows on rows of wherries were moored alongside. Between the street and the pier there was a space that was covered during the fishing season with barrels and coiled ropes and nets spread out to dry.

The harbor is as commodious as any in the United Kingdom. Nearly landlocked, its encircling arms offer safe shelter to great ocean-breasting ships. One arm extends from the lighthouse along a coastline indented by pleasant, quiet coves giving access to heather-covered slopes. The harbor narrows into a bay along the townside of which there is a spread of wharves and piers. Then the bay stretches a long finger to its shallow end, bounded on one side by the high walls of the castle grounds and on the other by a low parapet, behind which, across the roadway, runs the residential area of Bayhead.

The town itself is situated in the nook of a peninsula that juts into the Minch, the windy sea between the island and the mainland. A mile or so across the peninsula there is a great sandy bay, Broad Bay. We boys loved our occasional excursions to Broad Bay, at first permitted only in the company of elders, since under certain conditions there were quicksands hidden in the expanse. Sometimes strange fish drifted on to the sands, and every few years there was an amazing phenomenon, the news of which brought hordes bearing bags and baskets to the scene. The sands had "broken," it was announced, which meant that vast quantities of shellfish—razorshells, we called them—had erupted and were waiting for the pickers.

Southwest from the low-lying town an expanse of moorland opens up, diversified by peat bogs and numerous brown lochs, in many of which trout lurk. Beyond that, to the southeast, the hills of Uig rise, where most of the land had been converted into deer preserves for the sportsmen who annually arrived around the twelfth of August.

Such were the scenes amid which my youth was passed. To the stranger it might seem a remote and rather forlorn habitation. To us boys it was the center of the universe, as his homeplace is to the member of a primitive African tribe or to the resident of a metropolis. But I still find it hard to imagine any place that would have more to entice and delight the adventure-loving youth than my little town, with its great harbor, its quays and its bays, its variety of landscapes and seascapes, its opportunities for boating and fishing and exploring the endless variety and teeming life of the shore.

Visitors complained of the frequent rains, but the weather seldom mattered to us. We were inured to the drizzle that blew in from the Atlantic, sometimes for weeks on end. The rain was rarely a deterrent to us when we went fishing on the sea or on the moors, when we played our school games of soccer, or when at a later age we biked a few miles to play golf on the local links. But there were times when the Atlantic sent us gales instead of drizzle, and to us who lived on its edge and thought of the boats at sea, the howling of the wind had its awesome aspect. The tragedy of fishing vessels that never returned was experienced in every village of an island where fishing occupied so large a proportion of the male population. I remember how I used to lie awake on winter nights when the storm rattled the windows and whined around the gables, and now and then a vicious gust seemed to shake the house itself. And I would breathe the Sunday-school hymn beseeching mercy "for those in peril on the sea."

The sea was always changing, always exciting, and there was always danger. In the course of my schooldays more than one of my fellow pupils were drowned bathing or falling from a dock or while fishing in a rowboat. I was still very young when strolling near a pier I saw the shrouded body of a drowned youth being lifted from a rescue boat, and it left a deep impression on me. But I loved the sea, as one might an unpredictable mistress.

2

Childhood

We are no more aware of the wonderful ways our bodies change and our minds stir from their slumber as we pass through our early years than the plant is aware of its sprouting and budding. We sense first bodily pains and pleasures and the crude distinctions of smell and sight and touch and sound and taste. On that basis, modified by the instructions and prohibitions of our elders, we build our first little wonderlands of myth, our little nightmares of disturbed nerves. It is a world of fleeting memories and dimly apprehended experiences.

Out of these first years of dawning consciousness a few images, moments, impressions, print themselves enduringly on the memory when all else is blankness. My first recollection goes back to a sheer moment of infancy, a blur of crawling in the night over the grateful warmth of my mother's body. Clearer recollections of earliest childhood are of a narrow dimly lighted entrance hall, with a flight of stairs only a little way from a big front door, between which I toddled, feeling around the lowest side railings and rattling a little stick between them, making my own rhythms. I recall, when I was a year or two older, scrambling up the dark brown bannisters, sliding down a few feet and dropping off, and the stern reprimand I received. Several of my childhood recollections are of situations when I got into trouble. The strongest belongs to the days when I still played at the foot of the stairs and was accused of being rough to my baby brother. I denied the charge and was most severely taken to task for telling a lie, which was an awful sin in the eyes of God and man. The shock of it reverberated in me for hours. I began to be afraid of God.

Aside from such pinpoints of remembrance the memories of early childhood, its feelings and probings and sensings and lustings and learnings, have all merged into the overlay of later perceptions. The event that stands out most clearly came with my fifth birthday, in 1887, when I entered school, our Nicolson Institute. I was the first-born, which made the occasion the more momentous. I had a new suit, a real suit made for the occasion by tailors employed by my father, and was carefully groomed by my mother with a topknot in my hair. The great event was signalized by a professional photograph, showing a slim eager-eyed boy all agog for the adventure. I was delighted with the stumpy photographer, because he used a bird whistle to hold my attention. Before long, I was taking on my own the daily trudge to the school, which was situated about half a mile away on the outskirts of the town. I proved a quick learner and, having a pleasant little lady as teacher, was quite happy to be at school and mix with my co-agers. I was a rather shy type of social animal, but the fact that I could beat them at reading and spelling gave me confidence among them.

At this time I was left more to my own devices than usual. It was because my mother had given birth to a fourth child and was unable to lavish her care on me. We had a short, apple-cheeked, bustling "amphibious" assistant who worked in the house and also helped out in the store. We had also a nursemaid, but I paid little attention to her. And my father, devoted as he was to us, simply had no facility for entering the world of childhood. He would ask in a vague way how I was doing at school, and he would tell us the importance of being "good" and being diligent. But he couldn't enlist our interests, couldn't meet us on our own ground, couldn't play with us or tell us bedtime stories.

We had moved from our first house to a new one near the head of the bay, a more commodious stone house in a more agreeable situation, with room enough for our growing family. We had a view in front into the castle grounds, since there were no houses on the other side of the street. Instead there was a parapet, below which a shallow stream flowed into the bay, with an exposure of the stony bed and its low pool-strewn sides when the tide was out, and many feet of water when the tide had risen. Opposite our house was an opening in the wall giving access at low tide to a line of stepping stones beyond which a path led to a little lodge where one could usually enter into the castle policies. This situation was most convenient for me. I loved to paddle in the stream, looking for flukes and elvers under the stones, darting after minnows with a butterfly net, or digging in a patch of mud for a kind of clam we called a "brollock," and besides there were strange creatures that occasionally turned up, curious snails or baby rays or even a rare sea trout that had allowed itself to be imprisoned in a pool. The life of the seaside is endlessly varied. I never tired of the fun of it, and unless I was compelled to desist by the rising tide I would often have to be summoned home by urgent command. I was nearly always alone on these adventures.

We were never a very coherent family or, on the other hand, a very contentious one. My brothers did not share my interests, though I could occasionally persuade one of them to accompany me and in the very earliest years we all joined together in some naughty bedtime pranks. But we soon went our separate ways. My nearest brother, Donald, was very recessive, extremely quiet-mannered, very good-natured, diligent, even-tempered. My next brother, Jack, was slow to develop, was impish and unreliable and rather inert. It was only later, when my youngest brother, Keith, was old enough, that I found a real companion at home for my fishing and boating excursions. He was always ready for adventures. He did not share my liking for books and my school ambitions. On the other hand, he was the only member of the family who developed any skill with his hands, who was good at jobs, fixing and mending things, finding bait and putting the fishing rods in order.

As I think back to my earliest recollections I realize the more how the traits we evince through the course of a lifetime are inherent in our particular being from the first. Experience evokes what was latent at the beginning, however much later thwartings and compulsions may temper, repress, or twist it, aggravating some tendencies and restraining others. I still see myself in the young boy whose tale I tell, though nearly eighty years have intervened.

In childhood one takes the way things are as the natural state of affairs. Nothing is peculiar or bizarre or not-to-have-been-expected. I had no conception that the inclusive menage in which I lived had some unusual and unhappy features. I was free from the burden of them, but they weighed on my father and more particularly on my mother. The house next door to our own on Bayhead Street was occupied by my two maternal aunts and one uncle. It was a fairly spacious house, but each of them used just one room, turned it into a kind of cell, and there was little communication between the three. My older aunt had frequent fits of utter depression, when she would lie moaning in bed. She was beset by religious fears, the judgment day, the wrath of God, and the fires of hell. What this poor virgin woman could have done to justify such fears remained mysterious. My other aunt I can see only as a peevish, bent little creature in a shawl, poking about her cluttered room or feeding the chickens beside a messy little henhouse she ran in the yard. There was a spacious common yard for our two houses, and beyond it a long garden, with black currants, red currants, and gooseberries, many rows of all kinds of vegetables, and flower borders. I frequently roamed around it, and I would pay mischievous visits to my henhouse aunt who loved to gossip. My uncle, like my older aunt, rarely left his room. His dark hair, which was not characteristic of the family, and dark bristles of a moustache gave him a rather swarthy appearance. He did no work whatever, did not appear to have any interests, but liked to crack some silly joke, which he kept on repeating with hoarse guffaws.

My mother presented the most absolute contrast to her sisters and brother. She was so efficient, so much in command of everything. She was constantly trying to keep a semblance of decency and order in the house next door and to dispel or at least to restrain the black fears of her older sister. I once happened to be near when, everything else having failed, she emptied a pitcher of cold water over that unhappy woman's head, and it actually seemed to be effective, for a time, in reducing her to quietude, so that she listened to what my mother was saying. But the task was endless, and as her family grew the burden of it all began to tell on my mother's health. But she never gave up, never flinched.

Such was the environment in which my childhood was passed. Its problems did not touch me. There was a treasure house of attractions outside, and the ways of that jangled household next door were merely the curious features of new experience. The school soon ceased to be the focus of my days. The teaching was so repetitive, and I was already ahead of it. But I kept on learning more about the world around me, about the rich life of the seashore, about the doings of the folk. I learned to swim and dive, to cast for trout with a rod, to scout the purpled hills for blueberries.

I had no real pals at this stage, though I liked to play the rough-and-ready games young boys played in the street, treasure hunts and a variation of cops and robbers. I had the reticence that characterized our whole family. We rarely discussed our concerns with one another. We were chary about giving expression to our emotions. Kissing was taboo. We rarely told our parents what we had been doing—if they insisted, they had to drag the story out of us. We could be talkative, but nearly always in a chattering, inconsequential way.

The atmosphere of a home is something you feel but find it hard to describe. Ours was never noisy or obtrusive. It was dominantly sober-minded. We played no games at home together. It was partly because we were so dissimilar in temperament and interest—for myself I used to curl up in my room with a book. But it was largely due to the influence of our father. He was far from being morose. Often he was quietly cheerful, as he believed every Christian ought to be. But the tone was set by the daily religious ritual, by my father's morning prayer after breakfast and his scripture-reading and somewhat lengthy prayer after the evening meal. These were practically the only occasions when we met as a family, and there was a brooding solemnity about them that descended on us, imposed over our boyish moods. My father conveyed the impression that we all lived under the Great Taskmaster's eye. I seemed to be particularly sensitive to it. Somehow I could not share my father's spirit. It made me uneasy. I did not question it, but it secretly disturbed me. If those rigorous demands for abstinence and "holiness" were the law of God, no doubt I would have to be "converted," but I shrank from pledges of abstinence and would find it most unpleasant to be "holy"—so please not yet! My mother was quiescent on the subject and did not participate in his pleas to us. Only my nearest brother seemed in any way responsive. None of us ever mentioned the subject among ourselves.

Our house was a meeting place where not infrequently an uncle or aunt or cousin would drop in from the countryside to share a meal or two, and they would often talk in Gaelic so that we youngsters were unable to follow the conversation. Later on I did pick up enough Gaelic to gather the drift of what was said. Sometimes my father would usher into our evening meal some peripatetic evangelist or some traveling salesman who professed great interest in religious matters—I had an instinctive distaste for such people—and then the conversation would be equally unregarded or meaningless to us youngsters.

In my early boyhood the admonitions and inculcations of home seemed to have remarkably little effect on my outlook, though no doubt it influenced me in ways I did not suspect. The unconscious influence of home indoctrination strikes deeper than the conscious acceptance or rejection. The pervading ethos of puritanism may well have had something to do with my bashfulness with respect to sex, which remained until well into my college days. But I reacted against my father's attitude toward what I regarded as merely pleasant recreations and counted among the joys of living. I had a capacity for finding quiet enjoyment in all kinds of experience, in companionship and in the changing scene of the out-of-doors, savoring the sounds and sights and motions and smells of the seashore. My father was an ardent teetotaler and of course held smoking to be a curse, but these matters did not affect me then. It was his taboo on dancing, on card-playing, on festive gatherings of boys and girls together, that I secretly resented. And when he linked these taboos with the commands of God I didn't see how I could reconcile it with what I read in the Bible. I was not yet a rebel, but I had ceased to be a conformist. The kind of life portrayed in the various novels I read was less confined, less inhibited, than the life around me, and I responded to their more congenial influence. Sometimes on a Sunday afternoon—for the Sunday prescriptions forbade "promiscuous" reading and play of any kind—I would skip out into the garden or cross the street to gaze at the rising or falling tide below and feel that I was back in the real world, so much more convincing than the heaven and hell they talked about on that long and somber day. This feeling came to me at a very early age, before I was able to give it any expression.

My first uneasy impression of a world ruled by an awesome judge who recorded all we did, followed by a growing feeling of undue restriction, of resentment against being forbidden to do what one enjoyed doing, when the doing was not manifestly harmful to oneself or to others, was a strong formative influence in the shaping of my social creed. In this way I became a restive, questioning nonconformist. Compulsive orthodoxies I came to regard as destroying the salutory principle of "live and let live," in defiance of the diversity of human beings with all their varieties of temperament and taste and outlook and urge for self-realization. I took delight in books or plays that protested against the cramping of human nature. Even in much later years a neat protest of this sort would give me a little thrill of a satisfaction—when, for example, I was attending a good musical comedy, and it broke into a ditty, as in "South Pacific" or "Annie, Get Your Gun" or "No Strings," that proclaimed the desirability of welcoming difference or of "doing what comes naturally."

3

Growing Up

The growth process is an eternal miracle, as it moves through the subtle emergence of form, temperament, capacity, character, into the autonomous adult, affected for better and worse by the range of opportunity, the impacts of the near environment, the quality of training, the nature of the indoctrination, that direct, evoke, and suppress the intrinsic potentialities of the growing child. Thus he becomes at length the personality who toils and struggles and flounders and loves and begets and, after turmoils and troubles, reaches the dignity and indignity of age. Complex beyond reckoning is the process, and the story can never be genuinely told, as the changing youth meets the thrusts of family and mates, of schooling and neighborhood, of custom and habit, of the powers low and higher that rule us, of chance happenings, of failure and success and all the emotions they variously elicit. The observer may trace the signs and stigmata of change, but the change is within, beyond scrutiny, rooted in the unconscious being.

Growing up means acquiring the double-edged sense of time. The infant is keenly aware of pleasure and pain, its first conception of good and evil. But its time span is minimal, it lives in the moment, for the moment. Slowly the sense of the future invades the feelings and thoughts of the hour, and memories teach what to avoid and what to welcome. I seem to have lived through my first ten years before I acquired any incentive to envisage and pursue any long-term goal. I was eager enough to succeed in whatever I was doing at the moment, whether at work or at play. I might cherish vague ambitious dreams, but I had no presages for the future, beyond the general belief that some day I might become somebody. Pains and delights were alike sharp and soon forgotten, with new boyish experiences and adventures. The tasks imposed on me I took in my stride, the day-by-day trudge to school, the routine lessons by uninspiring teachers, the fetching of the afternoon milk from the farm on the hill, the prescribed time for being home in the evenings, the compulsive solemnity of Sunday (we always called it "the Sabbath"), with its round of church services and Sunday school. I was easygoing, companionable in a shy way, overtly obedient, though not unwilling to evade the rules. I would sneak some "profane" book for private Sunday reading, and I was remiss at remembering to be home at the prescribed time. When my father gave me an Ingersoll watch to eliminate my excuse that I didn't realize it was so late, the watch would happen to go slow on special occasions. Our evening meal set the limits for outings, usually six o'clock and never later than half past. It was not known as dinner or supper but as "high tea." Tea was indispensable at every meal, but "high tea" meant such concomitants as kippers or "red herring" or "finnan haddies" or possibly a shepherd's pie, with piles of new-baked scones, and for dessert some kind of starchy pudding, tapioca or corn flour or currant pudding, with occasionally a change to baked apples or apple pie.

The impact of changing conditions on children during the early stages of their growth is incessant, subtle, and crucial. There is the rapidly changing interaction between the children themselves as they develop their capacities and modes of expression. Being the oldest sibling I had a quiet sense of superiority without becoming bossy, a tendency enhanced by the gentle recessiveness of my brother Donald and the fecklessness of Jack, whom we always discounted. I was the leader in the trips we made into a bit of park we called "the Plantation," not far from our Bayhead home. There we engaged in run-arounds and romps and occasionally in nasty little pranks.

When not yet in my teens I would sit round the fire in the living room with the others and tell them little bedtime stories, eking out my own reading with imaginative flights. But I had no real fellow feeling with any of them until Keith, six years my junior, was a bit older. Keith was ever ready for adventure, unsparing of himself, cheerful, outgoing, and ingenious.

At the same time changes were occurring in our relations with our parents. Our father played a smaller role in our lives. He seemed unable to interest himself in our doings, in spite of a few fumbling attempts. He liked to know in general terms how well we were getting on in school, and above all he inculcated in an abstract way the paramount importance of being God-fearing and moral, but not in a way that reached our hearts. He was stern to punish our transgressions of the code, and if they seemed to him flagrant he resorted to the good old-fashioned way of taking us across his knees and vigorously applying his bare hands to our bare bottoms.

My mother was our preceptor, guardian, and tidier-up. She sought to make us proud of ourselves, to bear ourselves well, to be neat and mannerly. She was ambitious for us without seeking to spur us unduly. She took us for what we were, but she could be sharply sarcastic if we were slovenly or careless. My aptitude at school was a great satisfaction to her. She taught us snatches of poetry and loved to recite her own favorite pieces. In earlier days she would sing ditties to us in her high lilting treble, ringing clear but not infrequently with a touch of melancholy. She was a lady of high valor, though it took me a long time to realize how much she herself had to withstand.

It was not until I was nearing my teens that any significant change came into my life. In a desultory way I had already begun to have ideas about what I would like to become. My interest in books began to vie with my interest in fishing and in school games. I found not only delectation in them—they opened up so many worlds that were more appealing to me than the small world I lived in—but also the stimulus to become a writer myself. Sometimes, however, on reading books by H. G. Wells and Jules Verne, I opted instead for the life of the scientific explorer, with leanings toward astronomy.

17

There was nothing at school to arouse my incentive. During these years the school had been descending from bad to worse. Our Nicolson Institute had been the leading school in the outer islands and had acquired a fine reputation over the north of Scotland. But it was under a headmaster who had been gradually deteriorating. He was then a scrubby reddish-bearded man with rheumy eyes, who was morose at times and had fits of capriciously singling out some culprit for punishment. He had a curious range of punishments. Sometimes he would condemn a boy to work after hours in his garden, but a favorite penalty of his was to clutch the offender and thrust a dose of "sneeshum"—snuff—up his nostrils. It was irritating and could be somewhat painful, but he would watch with glee the contortions of his victim. When he was really angry, he would administer a severe caning on the outstretched palm, while making unappreciated pleasantries about the virtues of the cane. We feared him but did not hate him. There was something pathetic about our headmaster. Often enough he was practically indifferent to our goings-on, kept his head down, and muttered some lesson. In later years I felt a retrospective sympathy for him. He was a widower, rather warm-hearted except in his blacker moods, but reserved, a man who must have been lonely. He did not seem to have friends. In that little town there were few outside interests for such as he. Radio and television had not yet arrived to provide their temporary distraction for the unfilled hours. The winters were bleak enough for people whose only outdoor interest was their gardens, what with the driving rains and the whistling storms and nightfall around four o'clock. Our headmaster took to bouts of drinking, and in between he was a tippler though not really an alcoholic. But the future seemed to hold nothing for him.

Suddenly, as it seemed to us pupils, the whole situation was changed. One Sunday evening, when I was strolling about our garden, a girl from the house beyond the garden wall showed her head over the top and called to me: "Have you heard the news?" Maggie's news was that the school had been placed under a new administration. When I went to school on Monday the old headmaster had disappeared. There was a new head and there had been a general shakeup. Two new teachers had arrived with him. One was a red-headed upstanding man of a most kindly disposition. He was to be our teacher for the classics, Latin to begin with and later on Greek. The other was the teacher of mathematics, a big loose-limbed man who took no particular interest in us but was a reasonably efficient teacher without being in any way inspiring. The new headmaster was a neat pale-faced dark-bearded man who himself taught English to the upper grades. He was a thorough disciplinarian, and at the start he set us all on edge, used as we were to the slovenly haphazardness of the old regime. But he certainly knew his job, and once he had reformed the system everything went smoothly enough. We all came to respect him, though he did not evoke any warmth of feeling.

The changeover was a turning point in my life. There was now something to strive for. Paths were opening to the future. When I heard there were going to be prizes for excellence, I felt it was a call to me, and I was eager to respond. The new discipline was an uncomfortable shock to our school habits. Our listlessness met with sharp reprimands. Punctuality was insisted upon. Homework, negligible before, was imposed, though not excessively. But once the initiation stage was over schooling became meaningful to most of us. Something had been missing from my life, and now I knew what it was. I owe a great debt to this headmaster—W. J. Gibson—and in retrospect I realise that I never properly acknowledged it. In youth we take so many gifts as though they had dropped from the sky.

The headmaster taught my class in English. I began to appreciate the fine art of writing, the matter of style, the aptitude of words. I had always had some feel for rhythm, since I first listened to my mother repeating some of her favorite verses. We read in class Chaucer's *Prologue to the Canterbury Tales*, dwelling on the picture of the various assorted characters from the romantic knight to the earthy miller. I had some advantage from having already been an ardent reader, not only of the standard works in the home library, but also tales of adventure and exploration, not to speak of an occasional "penny dreadful," the rigorously tabooed, lurid little paperbacks about Buffalo Bill and the Wild West that we schoolboys used to smuggle from hand to hand. For the first time I had to write compositions on class subjects. I recall how I wrestled in the attempt to describe in my own words one of Chaucer's characters—for some mysterious reason I chose the Nun Priestess—and tore up several tries and was not at all satisfied with the last one. But I was thrilled when the headmaster bestowed some praise on it.

The kindly redhead worked hard to teach me the rudiments of Latin. He was gentle, amiable, and painstaking. He was not a great teacher, nor was he very much of a scholar, but he was so friendly and so anxious to be helpful that I hadn't the heart to let him down. It was an uphill task, that first struggle with Latin grammar, but under him I did get a fairly decent grounding in an elementary knowledge of the language, and it stood me in good stead in later years.

The third of the new teachers I held in no esteem. He was a teacher by profession but not by vocation. He was neither prepossessing in appearance nor outgoing in manner, but he knew his subject and brooked no nonsense. In those days in nearly all schools mathematics was taught in a traditional routinized fashion in which you had to learn by heart the propositions delivered by Euclid. The teaching gave no inkling of the beauty of mathematical reasoning or of its significance for some understanding of the spatial framework of all that exists.

The difference between good teaching and poor teaching is like that between a clear-shining lamp and a smoky, flickering flame. I had the best of reasons for appreciating the difference. The new school dispensation changed the climate of my life. Ever since, I have recognized that teaching is a high art, the most essential, the most socially significant of all the arts, and the prime utility of civilization. With education now the prerogative of every youth, we are still wasting this most precious asset by the undervaluation of the teacher's role, by our failure to elevate the standards of the profession, by our willingness to rank the teacher at the bottom of the professional ladder, thus squandering the potencies of youthful talent and aptitude, endeavor, and opportunity. There has been some notable improvement in recent years, but we pay the majority of teachers such meager salaries that our country schools are mostly staffed by women, some good but many deplorably mediocre. We make candidates for school jobs go through a tedious year of pedagogical training, so uninviting that our better college graduates balk at taking it. If, nevertheless, there are good public schools with devoted and effective teachers, it is in spite of the system rather than because of it.

The school began to occupy more of my time but by no means to the exclusion of other interests. I had scope enough and plenty to occupy my free time. It was a propitious period for the little town. Most years the herring fishing season was prosperous and the east European markets for the salted fish were wide open. The Harris tweed industry was growing, and my father's business was flourishing accordingly. Many pleasure yachts dropped anchor in our beautiful safe harbor, and nearly always their people visited my father's shop to buy webs of tweed. We boys used to be quite excited when some particularly munificent yachtsman bought large quantities of the material.

In these more prosperous times the town had a livelier aspect throughout the summer, and there was always something doing to keep me on the move. I seem to have been endowed with a rather excessive curiosity about what was round the next corner or what the hammers were nailing in the shed across the street. I was always assuming that the bigger fish would be swimming below the farther rocks or that the trout would bite better in the next brown loch. I visited the lofts where they repaired sails, the boat-building yards, the spaces under the docks where they worked on the piles, the smoky pungent-smelling line of sheds where the herring was kippered.

I recall one occasion during these days which made a curious, uneasy impression on me. There was a naval reserve training station on the outskirts of the town, and not infrequently the boom of the guns on its artillery range sounded through the town. Many of the island fishermen were enrolled in the reserve and called up at convenient seasons. Among the queer characters of the town there was a harmless monomaniac who went into a total panic when the guns were being practiced. He used to go around buttonholing people, particularly us boys, asking in fearsome tones, "Will they be firing today?" We knew nothing of the history of "John the Battery," as he was called. With the thoughtless cruelty of boys we made fun of him. But one day I was reading a history of the Napoleonic Wars, and I had a sudden consciousness of the brutal fury of destruction it brought on hundreds of thousands of innocent people who were compelled to fight as well as on the families and homes of those who lived in its range. I began to wonder if our quivering John had somehow been exposed to its merciless wrath. I had my first intimations that the paeans to honor and triumph and victory that were scattered through our school readers—"The Revenge," "The Burial of Sir John Moore," the laudations of the glib poet Thomas Campbell, "Sing the glorious day's renown," and so forth—were at best only one side of the story. Sometimes a flotilla of Her Majesty's Navy would visit our harbor, and on one such visit around this time the captain of a torpedo-boat destroyer entertained our class aboard his vessel. The various mechanisms of destruction were explained to us, and we were even invited to pull the trigger of some relatively small weapon pointed at a target. I brooded over these things, and when one evening soon thereafter the sun set in a fiery red glow over a large stretch of the horizon, I imagined I was looking toward a ravaged countryside beyond the skyline after the invaders had passed through, where burning towns and villages alone lit up the night. No doubt it was a reminiscence of Campbell's description of the scene, after Nelson's victory over the Danes, when the last fires of battle "in conflagration pale lit the gloom."

When it comes to imagining things, I have always been better at picturing dire events than at presaging happy ones—in spite of which tendency I have no inclination to melancholy. The particular vision cited made a strong impression on me, and though it was soon dissipated, it came back vividly after many years, in a world where the fore-imagining was but the pale ghost of the horrendous reality.

Meantime we lived in the great age of peace and regarded such thoughts as nightmares derived from an obsolete and barbarous past. There were minor wars, far from our shores, troubles with a colony or two, but these were merely unhappy incidents in the inevitable expansion of empire.

4

Early Adolescence

I was sixteen when I left our island to attend the University of Edinburgh, and the three preceding years were increasingly focused on that objective. It was not merely a question of gaining admission to the university. No island boy went to any of the Scottish universities unless he was successful in getting placed in the "bursary competition." It was for us the test of fitness to proceed to a degree and for nearly all of us the necessary financial provision for the academic training. From schools, academies, and coaching institutions all over the country the most promising youth were preparing for the crucial test.

It was easier on our island particularly, and it was generally easier everywhere in those days, to concentrate on schooling when the need arose. We had none of the modern devices that bring to the country areas the entertainments of the city. On our island we did not even have electricity till near the end of my schooldays, and telephones were slower still to arrive. My own folk had little use for social entertainment. There might be a "Grand Concert" in the Drill Hall to raise funds for some worthy cause or to celebrate an anniversary. On such occasions some volunteer would play one of Mendelssohn's "Song without Words" on the piano or the "Air on a G String" on the violin. There would be a few Gaelic songs, which always received enthusiastic encores. A miniature military band would trumpet out a march, and a bagpiper would entertain with "Lochaber No More."

And some one would probably recite a patriotic ballad. But it mattered not what was offered. Everything was received equally with resounding applause.

The prospect of a bursary sharpened my ambition. I began to feel and think like a scholar. The university was for us islanders not only the main avenue to a career but also the place where the light of knowledge evoked our capacities and enriched the spirit. The belief in education as a value in itself, a most precious value, was characteristic of the Highland folk. I know of no other area, certainly in my time, where so large a proportion of youth, coming mostly from quite poor families, found their way to the seats of learning. To become a teacher, a doctor, a lawyer, a preacher, meant not only to enter a desirable vocation but also to attain the high esteem accorded to a man of learning. The teacher, the dominie, was a leading figure over the countryside. The village folk brought to him their personal difficulties and their local problems, and when a crew of fishermen acquired a new wherry, they would call on him to give it a name. It was notable that classical names were frequently bestowed not only on boats but on children, names like Aeneas, Augustus, Caesar, Leander. The bursary competition—offering scholarships most of which were open for any of the four universities, Aberdeen, Glasgow, St. Andrews, and Edinburgh—brought academic training within reach of any really bright Scottish boy. There was less regard for the schooling of girls, but a few of them did make the grade.

So long as the crucial test was years ahead I carried on my studies with moderate assiduity but with no excessive effort. I have always been a steady worker rather than a hard one. I have never been guilty of burning the midnight oil. Only one class aroused enthusiasm in me, the course our headmaster gave in English. I had an aesthetic delight in reading plays and essays and poems that beautifully wed meanings to words. The rhythm of language was then to me the finest music. I had a remarkable memory for poetry and without any effort at memorizing could recite such poems as Milton's *Lycidas*, Gray's *Elegy*, Tennyson's *Lotus-Eaters* and *Ulysses,* and various odes of Keats and Shelley and considerable passages from

Hamlet and *Macbeth,* to mention only a selection. And after all these years, in spite of all the inevitable forgetting and the burial below recall of so many memories, most of these lines still come to me as easily as when I learned them first. There were occasional passages or phrases that gave me a strange delight. They would keep echoing in me for days on end. Their sheer felicity spellbound me. It happened when I read, for example,

> All our yesterdays have lighted fools
> The way to dusty death

or Keats's

> Thou still unravish'd bride of quietness,
> Thou fosterchild of silence and slow time

or Wordsworth's

> The sounding cataract
> Haunted me like a passion.

I became more and more determined to become a writer of some kind. I became more interested accordingly in my Latin and Greek assignments. I didn't like struggling with grammar and syntax and I found Caesar's *Gallic Wars* pretty boring. But Horace's *Odes* attracted me, and I began to have some feeling for the language, with consequent improvement. I merely endured the mathematics class, since neither the teacher nor the teaching was of the kind to arouse any interest. I had also a class in French, but of it and of the unhappy lady who presided over it, silence is the kindliest comment.

In that period there was no real training offered in science, only some general lectures with a few simple table experiments. My interest was whetted to go farther, and I regretted later the lack of opportunity to study some part of this vast area. Our curriculum, as was usual in most of our schools at that time, was very much along the old established classical line. But it was a good discipline, for me it did foster a sense of accuracy and style in expression.

The school was my playground as well as my seminary. At school and still more at college I have associated with some students who in their eagerness to succeed disregard sports altogether and at most take an occasional walk for exercise. I have always felt the need to relax in some sport or game after a spell of concentration. I like to play almost as much as I like to work, and I enjoy working after playing just as I enjoy playing after working. Eager students not infrequently blunt their clarity and perceptiveness by excessive periods of concentration, especially as examination time approaches. Before sitting for my finals in "greats" at Oxford, the most grilling examination I ever took, I helped to induce three of my pals to go with me to the beautiful Huntercombe golf course for the immediately preceding week, much to the surprise of our acquaintances. We played two rounds a day, and the only studying we did was an hour or two of revision in the evening. But three of the four of us got firsts. As a teacher I used to advise my own students to unbend and take time off before the ordeal but never met with any response.

Soccer was the great school game, and being a fast, elusive runner though quite lightweight, I made a decent showing and became a regular member of the team. Immediately school was out we were off to the adjoining playing field, unless the weather was totally prohibitive.

The school provided me also with two good pals, who were my rivals for school honors. One was a handsome black-haired, red-cheeked country boy, my chief competitor. The other was a tall lanky sprawling town youth, who had an observant eye and made quaint homely reflections on the ways of men. The three of us would occasionally meet for a Sunday afternoon walk into the countryside, discussing matters near and far in a desultory fashion. Donald, my first-mentioned friend, was the more restrained and conservative of the two—while I was much less conservative and quite apt to let myself go on causes dear to me. The other, Malcolm, was quietly critical with a turn for sarcasm. He was the only one of the three who ever directly raised the subject of sex. It was not that the subject was taboo for us, but for my part I had not succeeded then in breaking away from the conspiracy of silence maintained by our elders. So when the silence was broken by others, it gave me a curious feeling, a mixture of curiosity and retreat. I remember the first time Malcolm broached the topic. "Have you ever thought," he began in his quaint way, "about the progenitor you carry?" But it was too portentous a gambit for us, and after a would-be flippant remark or two the conversation took another turn.

In passing, I should observe that while Sunday strolling had been disapproved by my father there was coming about in our home some modest measure of relaxation from the rigor of the code, or perhaps rather some tolerance of nonconforming behavior without actual approval. I have known of families where the growing children, if reasonably well behaved, have softened the attitude of puritanic parents, whereas in other families where the children really kick over the traces, such parents tend to be all the more confirmed in their vain insistence on full obedience to the code. At this time I joined freely in mixed picnic or evening parties, though there was always on the home front a jealous lookout for danger signs.

One curious incident did occur that precipitated quite a flareup. A girl from the south of Scotland had come to run some kind of service for the summer fisherfolk, a mixture of teashop, first aid, and "Christian Endeavor" mission housed in a temporary shed near the quays. My father was always to the front in welcoming people who came with missionary zeal, and so the young lady was introduced to the household. She was a buxom redhead with a throaty and I thought rather affected voice, toward whom I felt not the least attraction. One day she said to me she would very much like to look round the outer bay—which has an interesting series of coves or inlets—and would I mind taking her in our rowboat. Being entirely free at this holiday time, I arranged accordingly. As I rowed she kept looking at me with embarrassingly soulful eyes, and as we were on the way back she stretched out her left hand, showing me a ring and saying it was her engagement ring. I murmured my congratulations and that was that. Or so I thought.

Two evenings later, when I came in for supper, I met the most frigid reception. My attempts to communicate were wholly in vain. I felt like a pariah. When I left the table I was exceedingly perplexed to know what was the matter. Finding no answer I went down to the room where my parents were sitting. They did not once address me or look at me. I waited. They passed ominous remarks about youths who made fatal mistakes. "He'll regret it once, and that's all his life," said my mother as though to herself. "A foolish son," quoted my father, "is a grief to his father and a bitterness to her that bare him." So it went on in the most mournful tones. I could stand it no longer and burst out, "What's taken you? What *have* I done?" It was some time before the story became clear, but it appeared that our precious redhead, Marla, had approached my father and in confidential whispers informed him that I was in love with her. She had tested it by showing me a pretended engagement ring, and I had been so upset that she could not doubt it. Of course she knew I would have to wait several years, and so on. The tale was grotesquely far from the truth, and I knew by this time that the lady was, to put it mildly, not well balanced. My indignant, outraged denials had some effect, and the social atmosphere improved. But weeks passed before I was thoroughly cleared of suspicion of at least flirtatious conduct. I never saw Marla again.

Actually, at this period of my life, girls were for me a very remote interest, a mere romantic potentiality. I was quite exceptionally slow in this respect. I was shy of them, and none of those I met touched the still silent chord. No doubt this was partly due to the hidden working of home indoctrination. Besides, I was becoming more ambitious to succeed at school, and beyond that there was the love of the out-of-doors. There my dominant interest was in fishing. Often I'd go fishing in the bay in our rowboat, with a brother or some companion, letting down my line for whatever might come along, and sometimes there were real surprises, such as the curious-looking creature we called a "shoemaker." But my biggest triumph was a cuttlefish, a big one that, as I hauled it in, squirted brown fluid around the boat and then threw a long tentacle over the gunwale, clinging fast with its rows of suckers. It succeeded in tearing the hook out of its mouth. Nobody would have believed our tall fish story had I not hewed off the length of tentacle clasping the boat, an indisputable trophy. But I enjoyed most roaming the moors from one loch to another, where on good days our rods took tribute of the speckled trout they contained. Very occasionally we were tempted to sneak into the forbidden territory of the large streams and estuaries, all the area being rented in parcels to the wealthy sportsmen who arrived regularly on the twelfth of August for the opening of the salmon-fishing season. Once, when I was plying a smallish protected stream along with my oldest brother, we were spotted by the gamekeeper who came chasing after us. We made the wall bordering the roadway and clambered over. He wasn't so quick getting across the wall, and spotting our bicycles cached nearby on his side of the wall, he flung them violently across. Happily for us they weren't much injured, and we made our getaway. But he evidently had recognized who we were, and in his chagrin, he made arrangement for a court case against us. Fortunately my father did not regard poaching as one of the more deadly sins, and through his influence the charge was dropped.

These were the years when the herring fishing boomed. All through the summer there would be gathered as the evening fell, cluttering the docks in triple or quadruple rows, as many as seven hundred or more wherries (the name applied to the one-masted fishing vessels of the time), each with its complement of six men and a boy. It was a beautiful sight to see the lines of boats with red-brown sails streaming out of the harbor at early morn or returning in a long straggle through the late afternoon. The fishing industry brought into the town hundreds of people besides the fishermen—curers, salesmen, dealers, coopers, carters, carpenters, fish-girls to gut the fish, and auxiliary workers of various kinds. The smell of tar and brine and the smoke of the kippering sheds pervaded everything. All was noise and bustle in the normally placid town, the shouted commands as the herring were being unloaded, the Gaelic songs of the fishergirls at their vats, the teasing and ribald comments of the carters as they rattled by, the orders to wherry skippers as they eased into the piers.

There was plenty to interest a youth in the thronging life of the inner bay. I liked to watch the fishermen as they sorted out the herring from their nets, throwing overboard most of the other victims of the catch. Sometimes a big fish would get caught in the coils, messing and tearing the net. The brown nets were spread to dry or for minor repairs over every available spot. The gulls would be screaming and squabbling as they dined on the rejected fish. I would listen to the bidding in the fish market and the tattle between the dockers. I watched the swift operations of the fishergirls as with one thrust of the knife they gutted a herring and threw it in the big vat. I listened to the carters calling to the fishergirls they passed.

They spoke mostly in Gaelic, and I had picked up enough elementary knowledge of the language to understand what they said. Frequently their salutations were bawdy, and my innocent ears were surprised at the bold freedom they took. I was learning about ways of life very different from my own. I still recall the momentary shock I received when I interpreted what seemed to be their commonest greeting. It was: "Did you get it last night?" And I was hardly less surprised at the saucy rejoinder of the girls. I liked to stand around in the Post Office Square on Sundays and listen to the hot evangelical appeals and the robust hymn-singing of the east coast fishermen gathered there, with all the accents of Buchan and the Moray Firth.

I was then both very ignorant of and rather curious to learn about the way people really behaved. It was not a snoopy or gossiping interest but a genuine curiosity about folkways. People were proving to be so different from what I had thought they were. I had acquired a vague pity for all older folk. I had gathered from that rather unreliable source of information, the hymnal at church, that older people were burdened down with cares and liable to all sorts of grievous pains and ills. There were also the words of the Preacher that after youth came "the evil days, and the years draw nigh when thou shalt say, I have no pleasure in them," the days "when the grasshopper shall be a burden and desire shall fail." The poetry of these gloomy forebodings sometimes obsessed me. Yet when I observed grow35nups in action I began to distrust the indoctrinations I had received. Occasionally I felt as though I were emerging from a thought-prison. I no longer believed some things I had accepted on authority, without positively disbelieving. It made me rather uncomfortable, chiefly on Sundays. On Monday morning I went back to what was for me the real world, the evidential realities. My father was so utterly sincere and wholly assured in his beliefs that it was impossible for me ever to expose any questionings at home. Unbelief was a primal sin.

In later years I have reflected on the remarkable distance between what I was taught to believe and what I came to hold as true or right. It wasn't in religion alone that the divergences lay. It was also in morality. I could not share my father's fervent belief in total abstinence or regard certain frivolities as sins. I could not divide men into sheep and goats, the good and the bad. The black-and-white distinctions proved to me to be mostly varying shades of grey. Even in politics the lines were similarly drawn. The "grand old man," William Ewart Gladstone, was regarded as the supreme champion of righteousness in high places—and had he not written *The Impregnable Rock of Holy Scripture?*—and Joseph Chamberlain as the devil's advocate. I did in fact admire Gladstone and I had not much regard for Chamberlain, but I thought Gladstone a bit pompous and rhetorical, whereas Chamberlain, if misguidely, was seeking a solution for an important economic problem. I refused, in short, to put God on one side of every alternative and the devil on the other. My father thought our parson a prophet of the Lord, whereas I came to regard him as a fervent but narrow-minded man. One difficulty for me was that my opinions were tentative, somewhat timidly held, while his were the expression of profound conviction.

On the actual problems that beset young teen-agers, the teaching I received was in large measure either vague or misleading. Concerning sex particularly, all our instruction was a series of strong but general negations, in effect that we must rigidly exclude all thoughts about sex from our minds until the period of marriage approached, that we must not form any intimacy whatever with girls, that we must never do anything to stimulate sex feelings in ourselves. These admonitions were uttered in muted tones, and spoken at rather than to us, as a sort of commentary on evil behavior, nearly always on a Sunday afternoon when the elders and some of the juniors happened to be together in the sitting room. The "facts of life" were not supposed to be divulged to the young, and the elders closed their eyes to the likelihood that the young would try to find out for themselves. It may seem curious that although I liberated my mind from religious fears at a relatively early age I retained a degree of sex apprehension that in my later teens caused me a considerable amount of needless worry.

At this point it may be appropriate to present a broad review of the ethos in which I was indoctrinated during my upbringing on that countryside I was now preparing to leave for ever.

Queen Victoria was still for us the great and glorious queen, and Great Britain was the ruler of the greatest and most beneficent empire the world had known. She was the mistress of the seas, which meant she was the guardian of the peace, the balancer of power, the arbiter of the destinies of nations. In those days the newspapers were more comfortable reading. One could ignore them for weeks and not feel that some crucial decision in world affairs might have occurred in the interval. We blessed the narrow seas that kept us apart from the national enmities and outworn traditions of Europe. Britain, with its democracy that respected persons according to their place in the scheme of things, with its lead in industry and commerce, with its banking and its fleets on every sea, was the acme of civilization. History was the epic of the long bitter struggle for freedom that culminated in our parliamentary democracy, and in the course of it our brave little island under Providence had become great and strong and at length the warrior keeper of the peace over all the earth. Other empires had flourished and failed, but ours had enduring foundations in the loyalty of its peoples, who enjoyed the blessings of prosperity and peace and were partners in the liberties it bestowed. Such was the over-all social environment of my youth.

The nearer environment was dominated by a cloudy religiosity. Its spirit was narrow and divisive. In particular there was the rift between the "Wee Frees" and the "Big Frees." The issue was a theological one, with social-class undertones. Most of the townspeople, especially the more well-to-do, including our own family, belonged to the United Free Church, the Big Frees. There was also controversy, though rather less heated, between the Big Frees and a more conservative minority who did not break away, at the Disruption, from the old Established Church. The last-mentioned had a jingle that deprecated the bare colorless and usually organless edifices of the Free Church, "the kirk without the steeple." The Frees in turn characterized the Established Church as

> The auld kirk,
> The cauld kirk,
> The kirk without the people.

I remembered the latter jingle because my mother sometimes repeated it with gusto. Perhaps one should explain that the word "cauld" (cold) referred to the lack of evangelistic zeal imputed to the Establishment.

The Wee Frees espoused strict Calvinistic tenets. They upheld the doctrine of predestination, which signified that "the saved" were predetermined for salvation from all eternity by the decree of an all-wise God. At the same time they painted lurid pictures of the fires of Hell in which "the lost" would burn forever. I wonder whether any more nightmarish theology was ever conceived, even in the blackest mood of some guilt-crazed priest. I can trace the beginnings of my critical doubts about man's eternal truths to my early exposure to such doctrines.

My own church did not accept the doctrine of predestination, but in other respects it held to the rigidity of the code. The result was that I became thoroughly uncomfortable about the whole business of religion, as I knew it. Every Sunday, in a most unpleasant way, it thrust before me again the dire alternatives of outer darkness, eternal damnation, with no escape hole to purgatory, or dedication to a way of life I found wholly alien, cramping to mind and body alike.

I was by no means epicurean in my outlook, for I had a serious cast of mind and was an eager reader of all forms of literature. But I enjoyed the relaxation of fun and games and gay parties, and I regarded the Puritan creed as a denial of the pleasures life bestowed. If only this theology had left Jesus alone, as the friend of publicans and sinners, I would have felt differently about religion.

I have dwelt on this topic because my lonely brooding resistance to the religious code that laid seige to my youth had a powerful effect on my outlook. I passed at length from questioning and doubts and lingering fears to the rejection of all dogmas.

My painful struggle against these authoritarian pressures, guarded as they were by the dread sanction of final damnation, had the effect of weakening my confidence in other kinds of authority. I did not become a rebel against authority, but I began to view with a more critical eye its claims and pretensions. I began to surmise the self-centered interests and prejudices that frequently lie back of the noble professions and high-minded principles so easily proclaimed by power-hungry leaders. I had not in these years any inclination to take an active interest in public affairs or join any "movements." I was beginning to learn the ways of the world, an aspect of education not contained in any schoolbooks. I remember how much I was impressed when I came across the saying of a seventeenth-century Swedish statesman (Count Oxenstierna): "Don't you know, my son, with how little wisdom the world is governed?" Little did I dream that in the course of my own lifetime the truth of that saying would be so devastatingly exhibited.

A Testing Time

My last two years of schooling were a testing time in more ways than one. I was determined to get away from home, to leave the island. The feel of it, the smell of the ebb-shore, the breath of the moors, was in my blood. I felt the sorrows of my mother. I had a real respect for my father, but his religious zeal put difficult pressures on me. His first ambition had been that I would become a parson, as he had wanted to be himself. But I was totally unresponsive. Then he became anxious to have me join the communion of the church, and although I desired to please him I shrank from making a commitment against the grain. I could not sit at the communion tables, to drink in public the wine (unfermented), which the parson said was transmuted into the blood of the Lord, and to eat the bread, which was His body. I could not bring myself to it, despite the terrible curse they said would fall on anyone who ate or drank unworthily. It all made me very uncomfortable, not least the quiet brooding way in which my father showed his disappointmnet.

I longed for a freer air, and there were other conditions that stimulated my yearning to get away. I wanted to live where I could feel the pulse of the times, be near to thinkers and scholars and artists, men of many minds and ways. I wanted to belong to this greater world, away from the inhibitions and prohibitions of home. I wanted new opportunities and challenges. I had so far left the island only for a visit to Glasgow, this in the company of my father who took me with him around warehouses in Sauchiehall Street all day. On some pretext, offering to do a little business for my father, I was able in my final school year to take a fleeting trip to London, where I went to a theater for the first time and had a big, brief thrill exploring Soho.

Living at home had lost much of its appeal. My mother was overburdened by cares. After the birth of my youngest sibling, my only sister, a gentle, pleasing, but somewhat delicate girl, she had lost strength. The house next door, with its melancholy crew of her sisters and brother, was more lugubrious than ever. My mother did everything possible to keep them all in decency and order, but the strain was heavy. Even with her failing strength she kept her brave spirit, her independence and sagacity, and her shrewd sallies on the ways of the world. Since I was the only obvious scholar of the family, she had a strong ambition for my success. She remained aloof from my father's concern over my failure to commit myself to the church. She was never more admirable than in the conduct of affairs in these darker years, and my admiration and love for her were deep within me. I could not help her with her problems, and I could only hope that I would justify her belief in me and become a credit to her.

The last two years of schooling would determine everything. I stood high in my classes, being always first in English and either first or second in Latin and Greek. My mathematics varied from very good to moderately fair. My competitor for top honors, Donald, was my senior by a year, and it worked out nicely when he became "dux" of the school for our next to last year and I did for our last. The heat was really put on when one day, near the end of our next to last year, the headmaster held a conference with the two of us. In earlier years boys from our school had found their way to the university, but always after they had spent a final year or two in some high-grade off-island institution, such as Gordon's College, which prepared them for the bursary competition. No boy had ever gone directly from our island to the university. The better bursaries provided a bare sufficiency to see the frugal scholar through his four university years, say some £40 for each rather short academic year.

The proposal of the headmaster was that Donald and I be the first to enter straight from the Nicolson Institute—it was a prime ambition of his. We agreed to try, and the upshot was that both of us won good places in the bursary competition list.

Meanwhile I worked steadily, but without any excess or hardship. It was work I really enjoyed and took in my stride. The only subjects I had no devotion to were mathematics and French. Mathematics had been mostly a meaningless memorizing of theorems and problems, working out logarithms without knowing what it was all about, and so forth. French had been taught by a schoolmarm who had learned a pitiful smattering of the language at some college, possessed neither interest nor competence in instruction, and made no effort whatever to evoke interest in her pupils. The poor lady seemed distracted, forlorn, a moody misfit who had lost any hope of making good. She was given to occasional bursts of running wildly at nighttime around the piers, and the boys would tell us gleefully next day, with the unwitting heartlessness of youth, that Miss X was on the run last night.

I have always been one who liked to be active all the time, and besides my studies, I still enjoyed school games and boating and fishing. If I worked a bit harder, I gave up none of my usual activities. We spent some holiday weeks living at a fine farmhouse in the district called, for obvious reasons, Lochs, at a place right on the bay, where for the first time I became acquainted with the ways of cattle and of horses.

I have a vivid remembrance of an evening when I sidled away to sit in at a *ceilidh,* the nighttime get-together so characteristic of the landward villages. At the agreed-on rendezvous cottage neighbors, men only, began dropping in, casually seating themselves on the long settle that flanked one side of the main room (there was a shorter settle on the opposite side). In the middle of the clay floor a peat fire was burning, the smoke ascending freely to the thatch of the ceiling, the inner side of the thatched roof. A single paraffin lamp was ensconced on a wall bracket, and the room was shadowy outside the central glow of the fire. When the party was assembled, the casual conversation turned gradually into storytelling. One of the company had heard a new angle to a story about "Kenny the Seer," a famous folk hero renowned for his remarkable soothsaying. There was some dispute about it, and then someone gave his account of how a villager, who some months before was found dead on the side of the road, had met his death. It seemed that the victim had had a premonition of evil. He was returning in his country cart from the town, where among other activities he had paid a rather prolonged visit to the "pub" and so had not set out until night had fallen. On the way he saw a strange reddish light shaped like an arrow that seemed to hover in mid-air ahead of him and to keep moving ahead of him as he advanced. He was giving a lift to a young boy bound for another village along the way, and he said to him, "Do you see yon light? I'm no so easy about it." The boy saw it, too. And when he let the boy out on the path to his village, the driver said: "It's still beckoning, Holy Jesus! I wouldn't be knowing." Those were the last words he was ever heard to utter. There were no signs of injury on his body. The story was followed by remarks on the peculiarities of the deceased, but all in a compassionate vein. The group spoke of other dire premonitions that had come true, with comments on the unknown dark powers that surround us. By midnight a hush had spread over the company. The peat fire had become a core of red embers, and in the semidarkness, with muttered "good nights," the men slowly filed away.

The ways of the countryside, the attitude of the folk seemed very different from those of our little town. One scene I well remember was the "waulking" of the Harris tweed cloth woven on a cottage loom. Two rows of sturdy women sat facing each other on a hillside with the web spread between them, and they pulled it back and forth with a rhythmic motion, chanting lustily all the while a special "waulking" song.

The villagers were nearly all crofters, cultivators of oats and barley and potatoes on strips of peaty soil, who engaged also in fishing and whose women toiled hard on the crofts, carried creels of peat from the cutting areas, and often also worked the spinning wheel. They were mostly dignified and for their status remarkably well educated. The village was a kind of little democracy. Our town had its class distinctions clearly enough marked, with its middle class of leading merchants, fish curers, professional people, headed by the "factor," the agent of the laird of the island who owned the big castle, and one or two well-established property owners, with a lower class of small craftsmen and workers of various sorts. The village was homogeneous, without class demarcations. Its leading men, the parson and the dominie, or schoolmaster, were themselves men of the folk, respected and consulted but mixing on equal ground with everybody else.

I enjoyed listening to the folktales of the countryside. Many of them dealt with eerie apparitions, dire forebodings, and tragic happenings, with a very occasional story of miraculous escapes. Every village had experience of the disasters that befall those who go down to the sea in ships. A majority of the men had been fishermen and had also been in the Royal Naval Reserve. My best pal, Donald, was full of the country lore and inclined to believe in premonitions, in the strange intuitions that came to people, in what was called "second sight." I was the sceptic who regarded these things as the work of the overwrought imagination, and we had many an argument on the subject. "There are more things in heaven and earth, Horatio"—he would quote at me. Some of his tales were highly circumstantial, and I well remember the one that impressed me most, since he informed me he had it at first hand.

It came from the schoolmaster of a nearby village called Bach. There had been a heavy storm at sea, and he dreamed he was standing on the shore below the village, looking out over the broad Atlantic bay. As he watched, he saw seven figures emerge from the waves, clad in their oilskins, and walk slowly past him. As they went, they turned their faces toward him, and they were the crew of a wherry belonging to the village, six men and a boy. He knew them all very well. He awoke in a sweat. It was the middle of the night and he fell asleep again. This time he dreamed he was standing at the door of a carpenter's shed in the village. There was great activity inside, sawing and planing, and he observed they were making coffins. He looked outside and there were the same six men and a boy, still in their oilskins and dripping wet, slowly moving past, turning their faces toward him. But the strangest part of his dream was that in a corner of the same shed a wedding ceremony was taking place, and that was something quite unprecedented. In the morning he had planned to take a trip to Lochmaddy, a port on a lower island of the outer Hebrides, on a little steamer that plied between that port and Stornoway. The morning after arriving there he rose betimes to meet the steamer then due, being anxious for news. As the vessel was being eased into the dock, its captain recognized him and called across: "I have bad news for you. In the recent storm three fishing boats were lost, and one was from Bach." "It was skipper so-and-so's boat," the schoolmaster shouted back. And it was.

What made the story much more remarkable was that a wedding did actually take place in that carpenter shed. It was a runaway couple. The parents of the young man belonged to the village, and since they were wholly opposed to his choice, the local clergyman had refused them a church wedding. It seemed a bizarre coincidence.

The story caught me. I could not doubt the schoolmaster's veracity. But I was not convinced. I know how easily such tales are unconsciously improved, and how the process develops as they pass from mouth to mouth. I have myself had one or two premonitions, but none that came true. The most direct came to me many years ago. Sitting at my desk one morning I had a sudden arresting inner message that my brother Donald, who was then on active service in Mesopotamia during the First World War, had been killed at that very time. I put down the date and the hour, but happily my brother came through the war unscathed. One out of how many such intimations proves true, but who speaks of those that don't?

Outside of my friendship with my two school pals, social life consisted of occasional picnic parties. It was a favorite mode of recreation among the younger folk to organize picnic groups, usually on a Saturday. We would row out in one or two boats to some harbor bay, where we would land, set out the provisions we respectively contributed, and after the spread indulge in a frolic game or two. I was beginning to have an appraising eye for the girls and a new interest in their company, but without "falling" for any of them. While I enjoyed their company I still feared and shrank from any approach to intimacy. It was only during my last school year that I felt the first sting of love for a girl. One day in the classroom, during a brief interval, a girl who was sitting right in front of me in the next row of seats turned round and said, "You have beautiful eyelashes, Bobby." That was all. It was certainly the kind of thought that had never occurred to me, and it awakened a curious disturbance. The young lady was a tallish, rather pale, dark-eyed brunette whom I had chatted with before and whom I regarded as one of the few interesting girls around. But all at once there was something more than interest. I was still rather shy—an attitude that stayed with me for quite a number of years but that at length was completely enough overcome! I thought of her every day. When I walked the streets, I looked always for the chance of her appearance, but in vain. But actually to seek her out was beyond the range of conceivable behavior. It happened in the latter part of the winter term, and other matters had become very engrossing.

The time arrived when Donald and I set forth to sit the bursary competition that was held annually at each of the four universities. We went to Aberdeen, in hope and much trepidation, sat with hundreds of other aspirants through the grinding week, and spent our evenings in our cheap lodgings comparing notes. The waiting period after our return was tense. I felt my whole future hung in the balance. And then the good news—we both stood reasonably well up the list, assured of a good bursary. I decided on Edinburgh University, and Donald was to go to Aberdeen. I was sixteen years old, somewhat below the usual age of entry. The prospect made an amazing difference in my attitude. The feeling that I was shut in, pressured, cramped in spirit, had been growing in me. I dared not express my thoughts, my feelings, at home or even to my friends. I had lost sympathy with the neighborhood ways. It was essentially an intellectual rebellion, one I could not proclaim without causing pain to those I respected and perhaps also to her I loved. I cherished no thought so dearly as that of the new independence that awaited me. That summer was a time of high expectation, with dreams of a future as a scholar but most of all as an author. English was much my favorite subject. I wrote short stories and even a would-be poem or two by way of practice.

The great day came. That night I was taking the little steamer that every day plied between Stornoway and Kyle of Lochalsh, to the mainland port, from which I would have an all-day train journey to Edinburgh. My mother was ambivalently happy and proud, facing the thought of my prolonged absence. My father was serious and concerned over my losing the home influence but still had some touch of pride in my achievement. We had a big supper spread, and the parson was in the company. Before I left he prayed over me at length, and then came his parting words: "Never mind the fringes, my boy, never mind the fringes. First get right with God." The remark rankled in me. What he meant by the "fringes" was what he called "book learning"—the knowledge of the arts and sciences and languages that I was so eager to acquire.

After the last good-byes on the dock that blustery night of middle September, I stood for a long, long time at the stern of the steamer, watching the receding lights, staring at the foamy wake, wistfully thinking of those I was leaving behind, far behind, dreaming of the future. At length, as the sea roughened in the open Minch, I went below to the extremely narrow shelf cot of an inner cabin that smelled of rubber and fried fish. Of one thing I was sure, I would never make my home on that island again, beyond my summer visits. There was a touch of melancholy in the resolve.

The Seat of Learning

Nothing is what we anticipate it will be, and the disparity is all the greater if the anticipation has been cherished long and ardently. I had let my imagination run free on what my academic life would mean to me, the enlightening instruction from the chair, the opening-up of ever new horizons, the race for academic distinction, the evening get-togethers with stimulating pals, the exposure to the fine arts, the entertainments, the free life of the city, the Athens of Scotland. Actually my first year was humdrum, laborious, without inspiration.

In the first flush of arrival, it was different. Living by myself, I felt emancipated, adult, independent, supported mainly by resources I had won for myself. I could wander where and when I wanted to, and there was a wonderful city to explore. I roved around in delight, crossing the Meadows from my lodgings for trips to Holyrood and the castle and Arthur's Seat and along the beautiful Georgian squares beyond Princes Street, with an occasional excursion to the Braids, the great bridge, and all around. I happened to have a week for such wanderings before classes began. I felt I was living in history.

I boarded in a cheap but quite decently kept rooming house for students. All meals were included, simple but respectable meals—and the whole cost ran to about fourteen shillings a week. Occasionally I would indulge in the luxury of a lunch at a small hotel near the Old University, and that never cost me more than a shilling. I had two student neighbors where I lived. One of them I knew because he was a brother of one of my former school teachers, who hailed from Kingussie. The other came from the same area of Perth-shire. The former, Kenneth, was a pleasant, quiet-spoken youth of moderate caliber; the other, John was a somewhat reticent, extremely ambitious, tall, ruddy youth. I became quite friendly with Kenneth, but we saw very little of John. So far as we were concerned, he kept very much to himself. He was a voraciously hard worker. No matter how late I might be in retiring, I could still see the light of his lamp beneath his door.

I did not realize then how unsophisticated I was, and Kenneth was equally a simple small-town youth. I wanted to join in affairs and make new acquaintances, but the proud bashfulness of a country boy who knew he had little social experience was too strong. It took quite a number of years before I began to feel at ease with people who belonged to other strata or affiliations. The result was I revolved in a little circle that brought me fewer associations than if I had still been living in my own little town.

The university itself did nothing to promote the social life or well-being of the student. You registered for subjects, attended large classes where the professor delivered a formalized lecture. There was never any discussion; there were no seminars, no tutors. Nobody advised you which courses to take or how to plan your program. Nobody knew or cared whether you attended the classes or not. You might be absent for months, but since there was no roll call nobody would be aware of it. You might be ill, but no medical office gave attention or advice. You rarely, if ever, saw your professor after class was over. Very few of them read the class paper you were asked to prepare, since that task was usually given to an assistant.

In my first year I took Latin and Greek, which was the usual procedure. I was planning to go on to an honors program in later years, but I expected to do so in English literature. The professor of Latin was a quiet retiring person, with broody eyes, meticulously learned, methodical, ready always to instruct, but rather dull, without any animation. He did nothing to convey the significance of what we read, being concerned with the form rather than the substance.

But he was exceptional in that he himself read the exercises of his students and was conscientious in correcting their compositions. The professor of Greek was a fastidious gentleman who specialized in Homer, and was fond of translating it for the class into an ornate stilted prose. He pronounced Latin and Greek in the characteristic English style, using vowel sounds that in all probability the Latins and the Greeks would not have recognized. It is peculiar that although the English have developed a language unexcelled in expressiveness and flexibility they have—or had—little feeling for other languages and have a special facility for mispronouncing them. Our professor of Greek kept his distance from his students. Although I stood very high in the class, I do not recall ever having an interview with him.

Within the university system, the only other activities with which I had any association were meetings of discussion or debating societies run by student groups. My neighbor Kenneth was a member of the Celtic Society, and induced me to attend a meeting or two; but it had little liveliness and a good deal of clannishness, and so I soon ceased to attend. I did get into another society, the Diagnostic, which carried on more spirited debates. I went to its meetings but on the whole remained an outsider.

I did not get to know any of the city folk. During all my years in Edinburgh, I was not inside a city home more than two or at most three times. I had therefore to find my recreation otherwise, on my own. I took up golf and became an avid but inefficient and untutored player, cutting—and replacing—the turf on the course on Blackford Hill, where it cost me only a few pennies a round. Sometimes I played by myself, sometimes I found another neophyte to accompany me.

I took a special delight in my initiation to the performing arts. The theatre at Edinburgh occasionally had visits from travelling troupes. The first show I saw was a popular musical comedy of those days, *The Belle of New York*. It was frothy stuff, and I sat open-eyed, enjoying with a question mark the display of dancing legs and beckonings and slithery songs. It was different when Henry Irving and Ellen Terry came with *The Merchant of Venice*. I became wholly engrossed in the histrionic posturings of his Shylock no less than in the perfect grace of her Portia. My first taste of opera was Tannhäuser, and the fact that it was a second-rate company did not dilute my untutored total absorption in the sonorous roll of the Wagnerian chords. But the highlight of my first season was a two-week visit by the D'Oyly Carte Company, and I went the limit in extravagances by paying them three visits for *The Gondoliers, The Mikado,* and *H.M.S. Pinafore.*

If I felt disillusioned over the lackluster quality of the light of learning, my introduction to the world of the arts, which included a modest acquaintance with paintings and a symphony concert or two, brought a degree of compensation. The halo my youthful enthusiasm had placed over the professorial head had dimmed, but possibly, I thought, I should not feel too disappointed. It made it easier for me to aspire to be a professor myself, since I certainly had no halo around my own head. In this frame of mind I returned home for the summer, finding everything pretty much as when I had left.

That long summer passed quietly enough. I no longer had the feeling of moral oppressiveness in our home atmosphere. I did not belong any more, and my father had evidently decided that nothing could be done about it. Actually I was on somewhat more easy terms with him than before. There was now a tolerable golf course within some two miles of us, and he showed an interest in taking up the game. So we not infrequently played together and, being about equally bad, made a good match of it. I spent a fair amount of time reading in preparation for my second year. My main subject was to be English. I was still confident it was my best subject and that I would specialize in it. I would sit at the feet of the famous authority, George Saintsbury, whose histories of English and French literature were cram-full of information.

Fate willed it otherwise. Again my high hopes were dashed. I ardently enrolled for Saintsbury's lectures, which actually consisted of rather patchy, fastidious notes on our texts. He would intersperse sarcastic worldly-wise remarks on the follies of men, especially those who wanted to change the sacred ordering of things. I recall, for example, the tone of contempt in which he lambasted the member of parliament, William Willett, who year after year introduced a bill to establish daylight-saving time: "The dear gentleman thinks if we all pretend it's an hour later it will be an hour later."

The first class exercise was to write an essay on a Shakespearean character. Saintsbury said it should not exceed five hundred words. I strove for weeks trying to cut down to length what I wanted to say about Miranda. I wrote it and rewrote it. When the results came out, I got a pretty average *B*, a mark I had not received in any other class. Was I wholly wrong in thinking I had written a pretty good essay? Was I utterly mistaken in thinking I had some talent for writing? Perhaps I could prove it when I had a second chance. When that came at length, I was awarded the same mediocre grade. It was much the sorest disappointment I experienced in a long academic career. For a time it shook my belief in myself. I read over and over again my unhappy essays with a critical eye but still could not see why they didn't rate. I had an opportunity to read one of the essays accorded an *A*. I thought it good but not so superior. It differed in that it played around the subject, but that called for a considerably greater space than we were allotted, and actually that essay ran to several thousand words. I felt cheated.

Saintsbury was a curious mortal. He was a connoisseur of words and phrases, a kind of literary taster (he was in fact also well known as a connoisseur of wines). He did not seem concerned with anything but style in a narrow sense, not with the nature and development of the theme or with the commentary on society or on life it contained. His class ran into the hundreds, since English was a subject taken by practically everybody, and it was uncommonly rowdy. Scottish university students at that time were notoriously given to unruly class demonstrations when the professor was ineffective or disliked. Such demonstrations usually took place before a holiday or at the end of a term. In Saintsbury's class they might break out on any occasion. They most often consisted of loud foot stamping in rhythm, and sometimes a student at the back would be picked up by his fellows and passed by waiting hands from tier to tier. The front two or three rows were occupied by girls, and the "passed" student would often be dumped among them.

Saintsbury was quite incapable of dealing with these disturbances. A testy man at best, he would immediately lose his temper. I have a vivid picture of his head and shoulders above the lectern placed on a table on the dais, his whiskered cheeks glistening between two gaslights bracketed at the ends of the table—his class was held at four and the dark began early on winter evenings. He would glower at the unruly students, shout something inaudible into the uproar, wrap his gown close to his shoulders, and sweep out of the room.

Once every three years there was a general saturnalia. An honorary official, the lord rector, was elected for this period to represent the students. His only official responsibility was to deliver a lecture to the whole student body some time during his tenure. The election was the occasion of a traditional campus fight between student factions. The ammunition was little bags of powdered ocher of various hues. The statue in the middle of the old quadrangle was boarded up, and various other protective precautions were taken by the authorities. The students came for the fray dressed in any old garments, and soon they looked like many-colored savages. But the casualties were not serious as the storm swept back and forth across the quadrangle. In the evening the students went in bands through the town, and many ended up at a bonfire, round which they danced. I took part in the affair on the one occasion when it occurred in my time, behaving utterly unlike my normal self, exulting in the primitive call. In the evening I was caught up in a roving band of students. We sped along the streets singing student songs, pulled in two passing girls who seemed not too reluctant to be impressed, and presently ran into a bigger group proceeding toward the bonfire. In the mix-up I got detached and decided to call it a day.

I had another class that gave me a degree of satisfaction during my second year. For the first time I had a teacher of mathematics, Chrystal, who was a master of his subject and could convey to his students some sense of the significance of the intricate patterning of lines and numbers. He was a cheerful robust man with a sense of humor, with a highly articulate way of making his points. I enjoyed his course, but for me it had to be subsidiary, and it could not dispel the heaviness of spirit that possessed me.

It was a dismal session for me. My hopes had been upset, and my mood discouraged any social gaiety. What made it worse was a foolish obsession that took hold of me. In retrospect it seems to me well nigh incredible that a false echo of the puritanism of my upbringing should have had such power over me. Like other youths of my age I had an occasional nocturnal emission, and usually it came as I wakened from a nightmare in which I was making frantic efforts to escape from some dire pursuit or was feverishly trying to keep some very important engagement but was frustrated by horrendous obstacles. It so happened that in my father's library there was a pseudo-medical dictionary written by someone whose piety was more potent than his knowledge. And although I seldom had any success in finding useful information on its pages, I had come across an article that expatiated on the debilitating effects of uncontrolled emissions, In my ignorance I became haunted by that fear. I wonder if anyone at the age of seventeen today is so curiously ignorant as I was then. But it took me some time before I shook off the obsession. It was no doubt fundamentally due to the deep impression of the perils of sex that the hushed and solemn attitude to the subject at home had inculcated in me.

So I returned for the long vacation to my native isle, not having enough incentive to do anything else. If my first university year had been somewhat below my expectations, my second seemed by comparison a complete failure.

7

The Rising Tide

All living is a patterning and change of patterning, woven by the rhythmic processes that are inherent in organic existence, subtle internal rhythms, rhythms as regular as the succession of night and day, recurrent and non-recurrent rhythms that are evoked in response to favorable or unfavorable circumstances. My Edinburgh years were characterized by a cycle of the last order.

My second summer at home began at the depth of the downgrade. I had thoughts of quitting academic life and preparing myself to become a writer. I would go around and gain experience of how people feel and struggle and suffer and think in their hearts. I would get over my callowness and mix freely with people of all kinds. Perhaps the decisive factor against this new course was the shock it would have been to my mother. She stoutly believed in me and in my scholarly future. My father would of course have been outraged. So I said practically nothing about my sore defeat. I was destined to an academic career, certainly for the nearer future. I would go through with it.

The freedom of the summer, the tang of the sea, the breath of the windy moorlands, the distractions of golf and fishing, enabled me to shake off in time the depression I had carried home. I became impatient for more serious activity. Somewhat to his surprise, I offered to reorganize my father's inadequate system of keeping accounts and, having done so, devised and set in motion a policy for the collection of old debts. Being generally inclined to optimism, I concluded that my lack of success in an academic course in English was no real criterion, that I could succeed equally well in spite of it. Why should I accept the judgment of some hack graduate who wearily toiled over his pile of essays? There were many roads to Olympus. So, with fresh incentive, I set about studying in preparation for my return to the university. Since I had done well in the classics I would concentrate on the honors courses in that field. In this spirit I returned to Edinburgh.

My later university days were much happier than the earlier ones. I knew what to expect, and I knew the conditions of success. I would become a university professor. I might not write the novels I had dreamed of but instead would make contributions to learning. The prospect seemed clear, and the position would be comfortable and reasonably honorific. I had overcome in a measure my native reticence, and I had no obsession to discomfit me. I made some good friends among my classmates, and I soon began, for the first time, to feel really at home in the university.

I went to occasional parties. I learned to dance, a performance I greatly enjoyed, especially as I proved to be a good performer. In those days the waltz was still supreme, interspersed with polkas and two-steps and fox trots and occasional reels. I delighted in the company of attractive girls, and I found I could be on easy terms with them. But at that stage I had no thought of going beyond passing companionship to sexual relations. The implications, the involvements, the disturbances, the sheer demands of intimacy were sufficient deterrents. Most of the time I was not conscious of any lack on that account. Nor did the abstention cause me to have any Freudian dreams. If at long intervals the urge of sex became intolerable, it demanded only the most fleeting of relationships, the yielding to which ended in revulsion.

Much that at a later period I read on the subject of sex I did not find applicable. It was said, for example, that when the urge is less imperative in youth it diminishes in adulthood, a statement I could not endorse. Perhaps I was luckier than many youngsters, in that I was relatively undisturbed in youth by the unsolved dilemma of sex. For youth, at least male youth, has had to face what is for many a cruel choice, to remain chaste in spite of the most powerful of urges at what is usually its most powerful stage or to incur the censure of society and risk the violation of its laws, not to speak of the possibility of other undesirable consequences. The young men of today are often less restricted than those of my time and in some circles the girls are more compliant and at the same time know how to protect themselves—but the dilemma is still far from being resolved.

In my idle brooding on the subject of girls, I classified them into four categories according to the degree in which they made any sort of appeal to me, and I amused myself occasionally by assigning girls I met to one or other of these categories. My top category, however, remained empty. I made a jingle about my categories that ran as follows:

> For whom would I wait
> As my own soul mate?
> Whom would I pass
> To my honors class?
> Who would make do
> *Faute de mieux?*
> Who might beguile
> On a desert isle?

My social life did not interfere with my studies but rather gave impetus to them. While doing some work in the classics, I also took a course in logic under the distinguished Andrew Seth Pringle-Pattison. He and his brother, James Seth, a fine gentleman who helped me at a crucial juncture in later years, practically monopolized the teaching in the field of philosophy, the latter being professor of moral philosophy. The older brother had added the name Pringle-Pattison as a condition of an inheritance. P.P. was a man of imposing appearance, statuesque, with high, broad, classical features and long, trim grey whiskers. His lectures were lucid and beautifully organized. He made his subject very attractive to me, and I found myself making top-grade marks. Toward the end of the academic year it became a contest for first prize between myself and a student named Handyside, and we ended equal first. I enjoy a keen competition, and as H. was a formidable candidate, of quite unusual philosophical acumen, I was indeed gratified by the result, when we were bracketed equal first. Later on we were contemporaries at Oxford, where his philosophical penetration was even more apparent. But he never made the contribution his gifts promised. He was killed very early in the hideous folly of the First World War, and of its uncounted victims no one could have been more grievously miscast for soldiering than that gentle scholar.

Most of the friends I made were specializing in the classics. They became and remained my good friends, whether near or far away. Alike we went from Edinburgh to Oxford to finish our preparation for an academic position. Fifty years after leaving Edinburgh University I revisited it to receive an honorary degree, and three of them, Lothian, Robinson, and Giles, joined in my welcome back on that occasion. Time had been kindly to them also.

By the end of my third year I had to make an important decision. I had done reasonably well in my classical studies but had not given them adequate concentration, having been interested in other subjects and not having been sufficiently motivated in my first two overcast years. I had in consequence no assurance of winning first-class honors, an important qualification for superior academic standing. I was also giving some consideration to sitting the examination that would qualify me for the higher civil service, since I had begun to feel that a lifetime devoted to the classics was not my proper goal and would yield, so to speak, diminishing returns. Should I then postpone my graduation for a year to better my chances? I was younger than nearly all the students of my year. There were possibilities of a special one-year scholarship. If that didn't work out, I might find some way to earn my keep by working in the summer. I would not want to ask my father for money. I decided to take the chance.

It worked out, with the aid of a scholarship. My final years at Edinburgh went very smoothly for me, so much so that they have left few traces in my memory. I had my work well under control and won top grades in my classes, without the midnight oil that some students assiduously burned. I seem incapable of working more than a modest number of hours. Some internal regulator says "stop," and after that signal my work becomes quite ineffective. I mentioned earlier my fellow boarder whose light shone far into the night. Midway in his university career, all that ended in a dangerous brain fever—I don't know the technical name for it. Happily he made a complete recovery after some months, but he studied hard no more. His ambition took a new direction, with much greater success. He debated in the Student's Union, joined a political club, cultivated social relations and at length became a member of parliament, rising to a position in the government. If you have an aptitude for something, you don't gain by forcing yourself with excessive toiling over it.

I made some new friends in addition to my classical companions. Friendship has always been for me a source of warm cheerfulness. One friend, who for a time became my closest pal, was a slim unmuscular youth with cultivated tastes and no particular flair for scholarship. We were very unlike in most ways but somehow complemented one another. However, he clung to me rather more perhaps than I did to him. I went at vacation times to London to stay with his family—his mother and his three sisters—and had jolly times going around with the girls, visiting the theaters and places of interest. He in turn spent part of one summer with me in Stornoway.

During these years my interest in social and political affairs was quickened. My studies took me into the history of Greece and Rome, but I was becoming eager to explore what was happening in the world in which I lived. It was, like all times, a time of transition. The revered Queen Victoria, the symbolic embodiment of an age that was already fulfilled, the long and increasingly prosperous Victorian age, the time of the British Empire's greatest range and might, had passed away during my third year at Edinburgh. I recall arguing with some of my pals who shared the general veneration of the queen as a great and wise ruler. I held she was a great symbol, a remarkably successful promoter of the spirit we call Victorianism, and an imperial unifying influence but not great in her own wisdom as a policy-maker. Now the sporting, prodigal Edward was on the throne, in a measure reflecting the changing times. The Boer War

54

was still being waged, and I was among the dissidents who distrusted Cecil Rhodes and the imperialist ambitions of his supporters. In my visits to London I occasionally came in contact with people, more frequently women, who had a stupidly snobbish class and racial sense of superiority that I particularly detested. I was developing a stronger interest in social movements and issues. Much as I felt I had benefited from my classical studies, I began to wish I could enter the unexplored and still academically slighted social sciences.

It was in this spirit I ended my happier years at Edinburgh University. It had become for me the home of treasured memories. I took first-class honors in classics, with one or two special awards, and accepted an opportunity to proceed to Oriel College, Oxford, with a good-sized scholarship masquerading as a Bible clerkship. The expression had come to mean a scholarship with the obligation of reciting a Latin grace several days a week after the gong had sounded for dinner in the college hall.

Oxford

The two great English universities were very different sixty years ago from what they have now become, and they were also most unlike the Scottish universities. In the latter, nearly every student was there to study. In the former, more than half the students were the children of privilege, and very few of them showed much interest in the pursuit of knowledge. If they wanted a degree at all, they took the "pass" course, a conveniently easy road for the young gentleman who spent most of his time at sports and parties, with days off for the races and other affairs. The serious students took one of the "honor" programs. They were mostly "scholars," whereas the others were nearly all "commoners." Class distinctions were dominant in university society. The elite students came from the great public schools, and it made a difference whether you had been at Eton or Harrow or Winchester or came instead from one of the less famous public schools. A few of the dons were "gentlemen," and most of the others were at least good middle class. There were elite societies and there were societies or clubs of the non-elite. The difference was obvious in every direction, even in the way you addressed your "scout," the man who prepared your morning tub and served your particular staircase.

Another difference was the ecclesiastical ambience. The colleges had mostly been pious foundations, partly for the training of future clerics. Morning chapel attendance, averaging so many days a week, was obligatory, though a student might plead off as being, say, a Moslem. A number of the dons were in holy orders. We had a long Latin grace before dinner and on very special occasions an even longer one "after meat." A large proportion of the university voters were clergymen of the Episcopal Church. To have a vote it was necessary to possess the M.A., but that degree was acquired in a very unusual way. All it called for was the passage of three years after the B.A., together with a fee. It was predominantly clergymen who were interested in it.

Again, there was a quaint disparity between certain of the time-honored regulations and the character of the students they regulated. The university of ancient days had been a finishing school for grown-up boys more than an institution of learning for young men. But the rules were mostly unchanged, even if some of them were consigned to oblivion, such as the prohibition against playing marbles on the steps of St. Mary's. If you were out in the streets after 9 P.M. and did not wear the short rag that passed for a gown, you were liable to a fine and reprimand. The proctor, one of the dons, roamed the streets with two "bulldogs," his apprehending men, and they would chase and bring before the "prog" any offender, who was duly reported to the dean of his college. You needed a pass to be out after eleven, and since the gates were closed at 9 P.M., you had to gain admission at the porter's lodge, where that worthy noted your time of entry. Such regulations were regarded by the average student as sporting hazards to be eluded or bypassed with a bit of luck or ingenuity.

The whole manner of life was different. Each of us belonged to a particular college. My Edinburgh companions were at Trinity and Balliol and Queen's. Each of us had his assigned tutor, who supervised our work, suggested courses to attend in one or another college, prescribed essays to be handed in, and gave each student at least half an hour's causerie each week. Nearly all lectures were given by the colleges, though there were a few "professors" who gave university lectures. The tutorial dons chatted with us in a very informal way. Nobody was in a hurry to get anything done. The theory was that you did most of your studying during the long vacation. You attended classes if you liked them—except your own tutor's. There were no examinations to speak of, outside of the big university examinations that took place in your second year and at the end of the fourth.

Four years was a long spell for those of us who had already been through some Scottish university, too long I sometimes reflected in later years. I had many other things to learn, many other experiences to share, beyond those that are purveyed within academic walls. Four years taken from one's youth in order to learn, perhaps only a little better, the kind of learning he already possessed—was that not wasteful excess? Since my first ambition was to be a writer, wouldn't it have been more rewarding to have found a job, perhaps in a publisher's office or as a researcher for a periodical, something to bring one into the world of affairs? But these were much later afterthoughts. At the time I was perfectly content to follow the traditional road. And these Oxford years had their own quality. The might-have-been was alluring, but the actualized alternative was less hazardous, was pleasant withal, and there was the strong prospect of an assured future.

For a Highland Scot, England, in its most traditional enclave, was like a foreign country. Attitudes, codes, manners, showed distinctive differences. The English public schoolmen were more sophisticated, had a style of their own, made frequent use of class clichés, were much more outspoken about sex and bodily functions, were very sure of themselves, and conveyed the impression that their folk were the lords of creation. Their mode of life, their codes, their shibboleths, their manners, their outlook, had a clear-cut finality, as though they had been ordained from all eternity. They had no need to achieve anything to justify their position. They were so sure of their place in the scheme of things that they did not display any condescension toward the outsider. They did not exhibit the overt discrimination so many Americans adopt. In my occasional meetings with them, at games or other activities, I found them all courteous and ostensibly friendly. But it was the kind of courtesy you extend to foreigners.

The scholars lived a life apart from the commoners. The latter took the academic aspect of the university with the same insouciance with which they wore the rag of a gown they had to don at times. They gave mighty little attention to classes, and the only spell of work most of them did was a bit of cramming before the soft "pass" examinations. Nor did it matter much to them whether they made the grade. In spite of their greater *savoir-faire*, I thought of them as more big-boyish, less adult, than our own youth.

My Oxford days were remarkably untroubled. I seemed to be active all the time, but I rarely worked hard. I had always my Edinburgh friends with whom to forgather. I made a number of new friends. One for whom I had a particular admiration was a fellow scholar at Oriel, a year senior to me, George Gordon. His field was English, and he had a great flair for apt expression, sometimes earthy and always penetrating and realistic. We belonged to the same literary club, one in which I delighted. From a paper or two he wrote for it, I expected him to become a great writer, and although he contributed a few good things, he never reached the goal. His academic career was broken by active war service, and then his health became impaired and he died young. He was a man of rich and wonderful spirit. Gordon and my Edinburgh competitor, Handyside, were the two most notable students I knew at Oxford, and both were cut off before they could fulfil their promise.

In comparison with my Edinburgh days, my life at Oxford had at times a trancelike feel, a serene remoteness from the world of affairs, from the ordinary concerns of existence. In these later days of the Great Peace, no international crisis was obtrusive enough to disturb the spell. I spent a few hours every day playing tennis with some acquaintance or getting my ankles bruised at hockey or, in my first year, rowing in the college fours. We had to show up at the college chapel two or three times a week, for the ten-minute morning service. Somehow I caught the eye of our provost, and not infrequently the nice old factotum who checked our chapel attendance would have a message for me that the provost expected me to walk round the meadows with him. Provost Shadwell we regarded as a rather formidable personage, an imperious gentleman who observed meticulously the time-hallowed rituals of the college, a scholar learned in many ancient lores. My pre-breakfast walks with him proved nevertheless to be pleasant and entertaining. On one occasion, arising out of a discussion with him, he decided to enlighten me on the portraits that hung in the college hall. He sent a messenger for the bursar, who had a key to the vaults where the historical records were guarded, and this aloof and somewhat musty celibate had forthwith to appear. After being instructed on the role of the notables whose portraits we viewed, I was taken to the vaults and the bursar was asked to read to us extracts from the Latin deeds that conveyed to the college its charters and endowments. I didn't remember much of this information and so got caught out when late in the term the provost gave a breakfast—his favorite way of entertaining us—for a group of students in which I was included. After breakfast he buttonholed me and pointed to a portrait above his mantelpiece, saying, "You know who he is." I didn't, and was duly reproached. A characteristic story about Shadwell concerns another breakfast over which he presided. Near the beginning of the meal his face suddenly blanched, and with a look of horror he stood up at the head of the big mahogany table and cried: "My God, I've been serving the bacon on cold plates!"

Shadwell was succeeded by a very different kind of provost, Phelps, "the Phelper" in our Oxford jargon, a breezy upstanding man with longish grey whiskers who had distinctive ways of his own. He was quite a spectacle speeding down the High on his bicycle, with his whiskers streaming behind. He liked to take a group of us on long Sunday walks, say ten to twelve miles each way, stopping at some village inn or tavern for lunch. Keeping up with his brisk stride, we covered the ground in very good time. On our return he would invite us in for tea, and I never saw anyone prepare tea with such fastidiousness. He would have two teapots warming at the fireside. From one he would pour a cup for each of us, having warmed the cups as well, and then would discard it. In due course he would infuse the tea in the other teapot and pour it at the right moment for our second cups. During our walks and at teatime he stimulated a running discussion on one topic after another, most frequently on the ways of different peoples or of particular groups, including the folklore of Oxford and its colleges. The Phelper was popular with the students, even though they occasionally made fun of him. A favorite story about him took place on a wintry morning. When ready for his cold bath—which he took like the rest of us—he was overheard to exclaim, "Be a man, Phelps, be a man!"

Most of the work I did was in the morning hours, when the only interruption was occasional attendance at a class. One usually made one's own breakfast, over a small fire in the study. Daily I prepared my scrambled eggs and tea, left it to the scout and the bedmaker to tidy up—our vigilant authorities saw to it that the latter was always an unattractive old dame—and then set to work. The afternoons were for the river, the field, or the tennis court or a countryside excursion, or occasionally a punt on the "Char." There was something most evenings to distract one, a debate at the Union, the meeting of a club, a get-together in someone's rooms, perhaps with a bottle or two of wine, the Balliol concert on Sunday nights. It was surprising that some of us were able to get a fair amount of work done in-between.

I was taking the curriculum leading to the honors degree under the ancient rubric of *Literae Humaniores*, commonly known as "Greats." It involved two major examinations. The first part was mainly concerned with classical subjects, and the second had a philosophical orientation, with a variety of optional subjects. Fortunately there were various subjects you could take on the side. I say "fortunately" because I was getting more restive to break out of the study of a bygone world to get a better understanding of the world I lived in. The more we studied the social and political life of ancient times, the more eager I was to learn about the doings and troubles of our own tangled society. I took a delightful course on Greek sculpture from a great authority, but I knew nothing about the modern development of the arts. There were great changes going on all around us. Industrial and technological developments were causing social transformations and disturbances. There were troubles in the Balkans and mutterings between the power alliances of Europe. But we were wholly immured within the walls of a dead age. Except for the debates in the Union there was rarely an occasion when the living present, so pregnant for the lives of us all, was brought to our attention.

This is no animadversion on the particular curriculum I followed. One has to specialize, and I had chosen to go this way. It seemed the only sure road. We had fine men as lecturers and tutors. Lit. Hum. had been and still was then the most honorific program offered by the university. From the classics I had gained firsthand knowledge of great literature and the thinking of powerful minds.

Were I seeking to find fault with the Oxford of my days, it would be on other lines. We studied Aristotle's *Politics* and Plato's *Republic* and Cicero's *Letters,* but the subjects these authors mainly dwelt on, society and government and economics and sociology, were given practically no recognition. The social sciences were regarded as upstarts in the academic world, fringe subjects hardly deserving the devotion of the true scholar. In the Scottish universities the situation was not much better.

I was unhurriedly ambivalent at first as to my future direction. I was doing very well in the view of my tutor and presently won the university award for the best showing at a special scholarship examination in the literature of Greece, Rome, and England. Nevertheless I came to an irrevocable decision. I decided that a lifetime dedicated to the classics was not for me, that my deeper interest and my vocation lay elsewhere. It was incumbent on me to follow to the end the "school" I had entered, but I planned to take in addition any instruction that had any bearing on the social sciences. There were, for example, courses in political theory and social philosophy. In addition, I spent a fair amount of time in London, reading in the British Museum recent French and German works in sociology, being especially interested in the writings of Simmel, Durkheim, and Lévy-Bruhl.

After the intermediate examinations my time had come to leave my college quarters. I found comfortable lodgings in Long Wall Street, where I had as neighbor my Edinburgh pal, Lothian of Trinity College, whose good humor and cheery laugh made him a most agreeable companion. I had a new tutor, E. D. Ross, a sturdy circumspect Scot who was a distinguished Aristotelian scholar—but, I must confess, rather dull as a lecturer.

For the rest, my Oxford days were punctuated by a series of minor events that blend in recollection into a pleasant blur. They included a small European tour, visits in London, sometimes with my Edinburgh friend Charles and his family, and periods back on my native island during the summer.

So came my finals, the long examination stretch for Greats. Rightly or wrongly, I thought my future depended on the result. I followed, however, my theory about preparation for the intelligent type of examination we would undergo—that it is unwise to pore over books and cram one's memory at the end in feverish urgency. So I persuaded three of my friends to spend the last week with me on a golf course, with only brief intervals for review of subjects.

Mine was a long apprenticeship. I owe much to it. I am grateful for what it did for me and for the opportunity I was given to go through with it. But gradually the conviction has been borne in on me that our established mode of training scholars is wasteful and roundabout. Oxford was better in one important respect than most universities. It didn't harass you with a multiplicity of niggling examinations, and it did make some effort to assure quality and evoke initiative. But for many of us who went there, the process was needlessly long. Later, when I taught in a postgraduate faculty at Columbia University, I was conscious of the same needless lag. Lecturing *at* students is the traditional way. It is not enough and it is not good enough. Nor is there any merit in the laborious process necessary to arrive at the goal of a doctorate, often resulting in the lapse of several years before the candidate has completed all the requirements. We should teach our abler students to educate themselves, and that requires a different approach altogether. The situation is, I understand, better than it used to be, but it is still far from what it should be.

9

Beginning of a Career

Through the good offices of my tutor I received an invitation to a lectureship in political science at the University of Aberdeen. I had committed myself to the life of a teacher and scholar. It was the least remunerative of the professions. To many people it seems a dull, restricted one. I had no fear on that score. For those who hear the call and have the flair, it is a wonderful profession. I knew it would mean only a very modest livelihood, and I was sensible enough to recognize that even relative poverty puts one at a disadvantage in our kind of society. I had no lack of respect for money. Luxury I can happily do without, but the authority and liberty a modest affluence assures are potent aids in every line of endeavor. Talent and achievement are better and sooner recognized when there is money back of them. It matters little whether the society is democratic or dictatorial. The man whose family holds some status within it possesses a bonus that enhances his personal merit, whereas sheer poverty is a heavy and often fatal bar to the evocation and the utilization of quality.

So I began what may seem a curious academic career. I have "professed" various subjects, political science, economics, sociology, in various seats of learning, but never a subject in which I myself had any serious instruction during my lengthy university training. Not long after I went to Aberdeen I was invited by the distinguished professor of Latin, Sir William Ramsay, to transfer to his department. I declined the invitation, being fully committed to the academically unesteemed and undeveloped field of the social sciences.

The modest niche they then occupied was typically illustrated by the situation I found in Aberdeen at King's College, the fine old edifice that housed the arts faculty. The seven venerable subjects of medieval lineage alone had professorships attached to them—one to each. The only social sciences with even a minimum foothold were economics and political science, the latter traditionally little more than an account of the doctrines of the well-known figures from Machiavelli to Hegel. Lecturers had no place on faculty councils, being represented by and wholly dependent upon the professors to whom they were respectively attached. I was under the authority of the professor of moral philosophy and had the further duty of assisting him in such matters as grading the essays of his students. My own class in political science was a small group of rather good students.

My work was pleasant, if not exciting. It was not heavy, and I welcomed the opportunity to explore my subject. I knew what I wanted to do and to be. In the course of my reading, I had become particularly interested in sociology, as the central study of society. It was regarded by the pundits as outside the pale, a bastard, quasi subject with a bastard name—the purists scorned its title derived half from a Greek and half from a Latin word. It was the kind of subject that caught on in the woolly American Midwest. The fact that the first stages in its development went back to the great treatises of Plato and Aristotle on the "city-community" (*polis*) was ignored. The study of the complicated relations of men and groups and of the institutions that had grown up to facilitate control of these relations or to stabilize them seemed to me a most worthwhile enterprise. I began, somewhat brashly, to plan the writing of a book, my first, along this line.

My associates were mostly instructors in the classical area. Many a discussion into the late hours we held in one another's rooms. I became intimately acquainted with several of them: Calder, with his quiet poise and shrewd observations, who became a professor at the University of Manchester; the sardonic John Fraser, who finally held a tutorship at Oxford; the reticent redheaded Alexander Petrie, who went to a professorship in Natal; and W. L. Michie, a big, bashful fellow who took a similar position in Brisbane, Australia.

There was a golf course up the Deeside valley on which I spent many an afternoon with one or another of my companions. I was a comfortable bachelor with modest needs and definite ambitions, but with no sense of urgency. I went to the university dances and got to know a few girls. They attracted me but did not excite me. I had no desire to get entangled with any one of them. I incline to think the history of my sexual development was in some respects peculiar. The deeper drive of sex and the commitment of the personality to an intimate and enduring relationship had at that time no appeal for me, nor did I have any desire for a liaison, which is so much easier to enter than to break off. It was no more a question of moral scruple but the shrinking from any invasion of my way of life, the fear of derailment from the track along which I was heading. I recall an episode that is curiously characteristic of my obsolete past. I made the acquaintance of a rather prosperous family and was invited to their house a number of times. We happened on one occasion to be talking about the pleasant spots along Deeside, and one of the two grown-up girls suggested we arrange a walk to what she said was a specially interesting part. On the agreed-upon date, the two of us set off and reached a secluded grove beside a narrow stream. We rested near the bank, chatting idly, stretched out with our heads against neighboring trees. It was a rather warm day in the late fall. Presently she cuddled up beside me and began to pull at my buttons. Taken unawares, I let this proceed for a few minutes and then on a sudden impulse sharply shooed her fingers away. The next thing I knew she had untied one of my shoes and flung it as far as she could among the trees. I hobbled to find the shoe, put it on, and said, "Let's go back." The return was a remarkably silent one, and I never saw the young lady again. It was by no means that I was immune but that I did not want to be hooked.

During the earlier years at Aberdeen I was not engrossed in any serious work of my own and readily took on a number of sideline activities. I spent a summer in Dresden, giving a course on modern English literature in a program for high-school teachers. In spite of my very poor German, it was quite enjoyable. The students were receptive, friendly, hospitable—and apparently unsophisticated. For several years I was an external examiner at the University of London, which meant some weeks of assiduous toil when the examination books of the far-flung candidates for a London degree arrived.

It gave me an opportunity to pay summer visits to London, visits that were brimming with interest. The people were so courteous, friendly, and responsive that my inquisitive explorations were delightful as well as informative, whether I was wandering among the docks or poking around Covent Garden listening and occasionally talking to costers and merchants and flower sellers, sampling little restaurants in Soho or chatting with acquaintances at the London School of Economics, visiting the great historic sites or riding to Hampton Court or Kew Gardens or Epping Forest. On one occasion I went on Derby day to Epsom Downs, my first visit to a racecourse and my first little gambling venture, and in my total ignorance of horses I was somehow able to return a few sovereigns richer. I fed my starved appetite for the theatre by frequent visits to playhouses and occasional ones to the opera.

I usually stayed at a cheap boarding house near the British Museum, and there I became acquainted with a less than likable characteristic of a section of the English people. I did meet there one or two distinctive persons, including an ardent, struggling young writer and a youngish lady who spent part of each year exploring all by herself, and with considerable aplomb, the remoter areas of Morocco and Algeria, but the majority of the residents were middle-aged ladies, widows or otherwise, who sat around and gossiped endlessly. What riled me was the stuffy snobbism they displayed, in the worst Kiplingesque style. The English were the natural rulers of the inferior "races" (which seemed a most inclusive category), and by the grace of God *they* were English, members of the Chosen People.

My London visits led me into one rather curious episode. The *Daily Mail* ran a series of letters to the editor on a controversy over the role and limits of government, and I joined in the correspondence. My participation had an unexpected result. I received an invitation to give a lecture on the subject at a conference on science and philosophy, to be held in Torquay. Some distinguished persons were to participate including Patrick Geddes, the great pioneer in the planning of cities, a man for whom I had high regard. The invitation included a two-week holiday at Torquay. It came at a very good time, after my London engagement, and I readily consented. I was asked to take a special train from Paddington on a certain afternoon. My first inkling of the kind of conference it would be came as I sat in the train and watched the party file in. It comprised in all between two and three hundred women and about a dozen men. I was struck by the esoteric, Rossettian garb a number of the women favored—a flap hanging free over one shoulder, or a Grecian ephebus hairdo, or a loose colorful robe to the ankles, and not infrequently sandalled, stockingless feet—I am not good at describing ladies' wear and can give only an impression. I noticed that one of the men wore a shaggy suit of heavy Harris tweed and another looked like an Oriental sage. I learned pretty soon that the great majority of them were theosophists. The conference itself was planned as a series of afternoon sessions on subjects not related to theosophy and a series of evening sessions for the initiated. My own lecture was of course in the afternoon. When I appeared to give my address, I was impressed by the style of the occasion. The platform was surrounded by a magnificent display of flowers, and the lecture was preceded by a musical program from a very good symphony orchestra. My talk itself seemed to evoke no response, until the dead silence with which it was greeted was broken by a violent attack on it from a wild-eyed Irishman. I failed completely to make out the ground of his onslaught. I was not invited to any association with the theosophical cohort and spent my time very pleasantly with other visitors at the hotel, on the golf course or the beach. I was, however, curious to learn something about theosophy and attended the evening lecture given by the leader of the party, an American named Dunlap. To me it seemed a curious performance. He drew triangles and circles on a blackboard, and the forms were given a high symbolic significance, betokening virtues and goals, temporal and eternal, with love triumphant over all. It seemed to me a sort of disjointed mysticism with an erotic undertone. The group represented various modulations of the faith. Some were Rosicrucians, with the symbol of the Rosy Cross; some were followers of the line of Mrs. Annie Besant or Madame Blavatsky; some were faith healers. One evening a timid, distressed gentleman accosted me, asking for counsel. His wife, who was a theosophist, had gone to a professional faith healer attending the conference and had come away thoroughly scared because he portended imminent, grave health hazards for her. I explained to my visitor how completely unscientific and misleading such practitioners were and that he should urge his wife to consult a genuine physician. But he left me sadly, doubting whether she would listen to any such advice. Most of the women were not only dedicated to the cause but also seemed to find through it much peace of mind. I learned that most of them were well-to-do and some of them quite wealthy. I had my doubts about the motives of some of the men. One of them was a Canadian, and I discovered afterward that he had married one of the wealthiest of them, a member of the family of a great Scottish industrialist.

These were the years when I was ready for almost any new experience. An associate of mine, a lecturer in English, persuaded me to join the "territorials," the volunteer auxiliary of the regular army. So I was inducted as a first lieutenant, spent a few weeks in camp, and went on marches with my Gordon Highlander kilt proudly swinging. As an officer I had quite an outfit of uniforms: working uniforms, parade uniforms, and a resplendent—and expensive— evening dress, with a red tunic, from one shoulder of which hung a fine tartan plaid fastened with a large cairngorm, a silken kilt with silver tassels on the sporran, a sword in its gleaming sheath, checkered stockings with a cairngorm-topped dirk attached to the right foot, and a blazoned Glengarry cap to crown it all. I remained with the territorials only a year or two. A feeling of revulsion gradually came over me. I particularly disliked bayonet practice and the instructions they gave you on how to plunge the weapon in most effectively. I disliked the gusto with which some of the men went

at it. I disliked the attitude of most of the professional soldiers we
met, including our own adjutant. It was supercilious, condescend-
ing, arrogant, reactionary. I disliked the depersonalization of human
beings, mechanically performing like motions in numbered lines,
expendable for causes they knew nothing about. I came to hate the
stupidity and the bestiality of war. Or perhaps I should not call it
bestiality, for the "beasts" kill in order to eat and rarely destroy
their own kind. I disliked the way our military men spoke of "the
service," with the suggestion that it was a higher and nobler career
than the activities that satisfy our daily needs or promote our culture. We were intended to be defenders of our country, but the
conception of "our country" entertained by most army men I met
was wholly different from mine.

One summer I roamed over parts of western Europe, mainly
France, Belgium, and Italy, and although I found much to engross
me I had not then learned the art of travel. I did not realize the
importance of letters of introduction, and so my observations were
more superficial than on some later visits. I spent occasional periods
at home and found the atmosphere less restrictive but more subdued. My young sister had fallen a victim to tuberculosis, then
rather prevalent on the island, and was fighting a losing battle. My
mother, valorous as ever, was striving to hold up against the weight
of her cares, but the burden was telling on her. My father was always
busy. His belief that "everything worked together for good" in
the end screened him somewhat from the stresses of home troubles,
but concern did break through. As his trim beard was greying, he
was becoming more tolerant, which is the antithesis of what often
happens. He had acquired one of the first automobiles on the island,
a Model T Ford, and we practiced driving together. Later on he
added a car-hiring establishment to his business.

My life at Aberdeen was diversified by occasional weeks on a
country estate, thanks to the good relations I established with my
sponsor and superior, the professor of moral philosophy. He was a
man of striking appearance, with a high brow and large, lustrous,
dark eyes in a broad well-proportioned face. Needless to say, he
caused the heart of many a girl student to flutter. He lectured in a

dignified manner, sometimes with a faraway look in his eyes, as though he were communing with the Absolute. He had married the niece of a peer of the realm, on whose estate his father had been the head gardener. They had no children, and his wife would from time to time be away from the lovely mansion they possessed on Deeside, being engaged in social affairs elsewhere. The professor did not care to live alone in the big house and would invite me to stay with him for weeks on end. So I shared his luxury and his butler. Sometimes we played golf in the afternoon and occasionally chess at nighttime. He was a better golfer than I was, but I improved enough to be a near match for him. I usually won at chess, but he gave that up after a short time. Our professor possessed a goodly share of vanity. On one occasion, when his lady was at home and I lunched with them both, she explained to me that the professor gave such deep thought to problems that it brought so much blood to his head he had to calm down during the late evening. That was why he stopped playing chess. "I don't suppose," she added, "that you take matters quite so seriously." I had no comeback.

Anyhow I had a pleasant time during these visits. We each went about our own business, always meeting around the dinner table, where we shared a good bottle of wine along with an excellent meal while we chatted about college affairs or the news of the day. He was engaged on a translation of the portentous *Phenomenology* of Hegel, and I would occasionally make suggestions on his rendering of a passage. Little did I guess then that our good relations would come to an abrupt ending.

10

Two Endings and a Beginning

I have never felt like settling down in any groove, however comfortable. It is good to belong, to feel at home in one's situation, but much as I enjoy the associations I make, the regret at parting from them has for me been several times outweighed by the prospect of new experience. I never reflected on these matters until I came to write this book, but now in retrospect I perceive a certain process that has always followed my changes of residence or of program. First, there comes a fairly long period of adjustment before I can habituate myself to the new conditions. During this period I am quite unproductive. That does not irk me. The ambition to make some kind of distinctive contribution is in abeyance. The itch to write subsides.

It was so during my first three years in Aberdeen. The city itself did not have for me the attraction of Edinburgh or of Oxford. It was clean, glistening, neither friendly nor unfriendly but remote. I found no associates working in the same subject area as myself. I lived alone, in a small lodging house. It was only rarely there was any entertainment that appealed to me. It took me some time before I became really intimate with my colleagues in the classics already referred to. When at length, however, I felt thoroughly at home, fresh impulses took strong possession. I wanted to secure the introduction of the demeaned subject of sociology into the curriculum and, being now on very good terms with my professor, succeeded in inducing him to propose that I become lecturer in political science *and* sociology. With his support the proposal carried. It was the first inclusion of the subject into the curriculum of any Scottish university, and when I left the university, it disappeared with me, and half a century passed before it was reinaugurated. I engaged in the writing of my first book, a broad and rather unqualified perspective on the lines of social evolution. A major thesis it developed was that man, being a social animal, became more individualized in the process of becoming socialized. In due course I submitted the typescript in a competition for a special Carnegie award open that year to all the Scottish universities, and it won. So my course was set and I felt in control of the situation.

I thought of myself as a social scientist—not as a sociologist or a political scientist or an economist. I had come to the conclusion that the demarcation of the social sciences into separate departmental boxes was artificial, mainly a device for the convenience of administration. You cannot, for example, pursue the study of economic phenomena and relationships any distance without getting involved in political issues, and vice versa. All the social sciences are aspects of the seamless fabric of society.

Another urge of a very different kind was ripening in me. Not until I was twenty-eight years old did I give serious consideration to the question of marriage. My financial uncertainty and Scottish caution no doubt had had something to do with it. But finally I found myself looking at girls with a new kind of speculative assessment. I was in no hurry to make so binding a commitment. I met a few rather attractive girls, but what lay behind the external attractiveness? What enduring qualities did it rest upon? There were always doubts. It was not like choosing something in a marketplace, nor had I the assurance that the chosen one would also choose me. I remained in this state of mind while a year slipped by. And then I met her. Ethel Peterkin was then taking some extra courses at the university after having spent a year tutoring in Paris. Among these subjects was moral philosophy, an old-time subject that allowed its Professor to expatiate on the order of the cosmos or the sound mind in a sound body or anything in between. Since she was one of the really good students, it fell to my lot to discuss her class papers with her. But her intellectual capacity was soon a minor consideration. I sensed the warmth of congeniality, the sympathetic outgoing understanding, and the ready responsiveness that time so well confirmed. She was sunny and sunny-haired. I asked no more. We were married in Aberdeen, where she had her home, and she has been my true helpmate through all the length of years.

We found a pleasant house of granite on a pleasant, quiet street, where we moved after honeymooning in the Lake District. I took lightly enough my new responsibilities as householder. I have no pretensions to being a handy man. I believe I save time and money by calling the mechanic, but I found pleasure in setting up my library and cultivating roses in our garden. There were great advantages to having a place of one's own. There was my own study, where I could work without disturbance. There was my own garden, where I could potter and plant. So things went happily for us for some two years. Our first son, Ian, was born. And then the time of troubles began.

One morning I entered the office or "retiring room" I shared with the professor, greeted him as usual, and received no response. He was seated at his desk and did not raise his head or give me a single glance. I made a second tentative effort—with the same result. Which of my sins had found me out? What gross violation of academic decency had I committed? Utterly at a loss, I presently left the office and waited around till the time of my class. Never again did I enter into meaningful conversation with him. If he required my services, a curt note would usually be left for me.

He never informed me how I had transgressed. I found it out indirectly, from others. I had published an article highly critical of a book entitled *The Philosophical Theory of the State,* by Bernard Bosanquet, a book I had studied at Oxford and that had considerable repute. It was based on the doctrine of Hegel, and my professor was also a follower of his. It seems he had taken my article as a slightly veiled attack upon himself. Nothing was further from my thoughts. My professor had no distinction in philosophy. I did not dream he would take my article personally. Only his vanity interpreted it that way. It throws an interesting sidelight on the situation that the gentleman whose views I was attacking wrote me a very kindly response, defending his position but recognizing fully the grounds of my argument. This led to a very interesting and pleasant correspondence. I treasure to this day the bundle of letters that passed between us.

I was in a very awkward situation. My first job was obviously ending with me in the black books of my employer. In his then frame of mind I had no hope of securing a helpful recommendation. I had given hostages to fortune and must find a new position. So I wrote to some of my former professors, since the market for scholarship is run through personal communications between professors or deans. One of them, Professor James Seth of Edinburgh, knew of an opening in the department of political science at the University of Toronto. The idea of emigrating had not been in my mind, but I was now a family man and under the circumstances could not afford to neglect any likely chance. With the support of my professor friend, I applied and in due course was appointed associate professor of political science at the University of Toronto, to take effect the following academic year.

Before that time a most ominous change had come over Europe and presently engulfed the whole world. The assassination of the Archduke Ferdinand seemed to us at first merely a drastic example of the violence that from time to time characterized the turbulent Balkan states. It was unthinkable that the act of a Serbian zealot could trigger the explosion of a whole civilization. The nightmare loomed nearer and nearer through the mists of diplomacy, as we waited and watched and recoiled before the short-sighted intrigues and the purblind nationalisms that had free scope in the alarming absence of statesmanship. Along with a historian friend I studied the various manifestoes and proclamations, followed by blue books and white papers and red books and all the rest, in which the various countries explained their innocence and their efforts to preserve the peace. We found inconsistencies and omissions in them and concluded that none of them gave an accurate account of the policies that led to the fateful end. To this day, with all the mountainous volumes of archives, historians are divided as to the responsibility for the war, especially concerning the respective roles of Germany and Russia. Certainly the leaders bungled; certainly none of them foresaw the dire consequences of their pride of power and the secret ambitions that dictated their policies. As for Great Britain, we thought her great misfortune was the lack of a strong leadership that would have pledged her balance of power and her command of the seas against whichever side dared to make a declaration of war.

On the fourth of August the lights went out over Europe. I had a troubled time of decision-making. If I were drafted, I would despairingly obey, giving up all my hopes for the future. But I would not voluntarily enlist again. My wife became pregnant for the second time and was in a state of high nervous apprehension. So that miserable winter dragged on, and the war situation worsened, confounding the expectations that it would last only a year or so. There was a darkening of the spirit as well as of the lights. I wondered whether I would be able to migrate to a new land, far from the embroilments of Europe. But the way remained open for me. I had to leave my wife, soon to be a mother again, and my son until conditions permitted the increased family to join me overseas.

11

Canadian Sojourn—Part 1

I had no expectation of ever remigrating to my native land. It was a total renunciation of the associations I held dear, of the treasured home of all my memories. My life could be diverted on to very different lines. I tried to keep these thoughts in the background as I journeyed to my new assignment. My natural optimism rebounded to thoughts of the new experience, the adventures, the "fresh woods and pastures new" Canada would hold for me.

Disembarking early in the morning at New York, I was to spend the day there prior to taking the night train to Toronto. It was an exceedingly hot and humid September day, and I was ill prepared for ninety degrees in the shade. Canada was our lady of the snows, and in my precautionary woollens, my baggage being all bonded through, I sweltered and stewed. I did not know winter came much later on this side of the Atlantic and that the fall season was long and mostly benign. My cabin companion, a Wall Street broker, had offered to show me round the financial district. This outgoing American hospitality was another of my first surprises. I could not imagine an English business man, the morning of his return from a trip abroad, spending it in the entertainment of a chance fellow traveler. I was taken through the canyons of the city, had lunch with my host, feeling excited in spite of the grilling heat. The rest of the day was a vain search for coolness—air conditioning was not then widely developed. But the oppressive air was freshened for me by the thought of being in a great land where the lights still shone, where the newspapers did not contain daily lists of casualties, and where men were concerned with other matters than war.

The next morning rose bright and fair in Toronto, and I went first to pay my respects to the head of our department, James Mavor. I was eagerly waiting a cablegram and asked, as he was conducting me around the campus, to be taken first to the University Post Office. The expected cablegram was handed to me. I stared at it and couldn't utter a word. "Anything wrong?" Mavor asked. "No," I said, and showed him the message. It contained one word, "bargain." I had to explain. Since we had expected our second child to arrive any day, my wife and I had had fun concocting code words ostensibly pertaining to business transactions. We had a word for boy and one for girl, with an addition to signify that all was well. "We're not through," I had said, half jesting. "We need three more words." Neither of our families had any record of twins, but we went ahead, and the word for "boy and girl, all well," was "bargain." I really thought that in the flurry of the situation I might have received the wrong code word, until the ensuing letter confirmed it.

I experienced very little difficulty in the transition to life in Canada. A Scot is not unlikely to feel more at ease migrating to Canada than living in England. But the ready acceptance I enjoyed did not develop into a genuine belongingness. I came gradually to recognize I was not only in a new land but among a different people, a conjuncture of heterogeneous migrations, unwelded by common traditions and dependent for their sense of unity on sentiments pertaining to the Canadian situation. Scottish and Northern Irish groups were dominant in Ontario.

The most pervading sentiment was a defensive feeling of difference from their big, encroaching neighbor, their only neighbor, stretching along two thousand miles of frontier. Canadians looked across the ocean for their spiritual home. They asserted a moral and spiritual superiority over their neighbor. They had a better form of government, less corruption and lawlessness, were not so eternally concerned with the "almighty dollar," were less "materialistic." In later years I initiated under the auspices of the Carnegie Endowment a program for the study of Canadian-American relationships, resulting in a work entitled *Canada and Her Great Neighbor* (edited by Angus). It contained a survey of Canadian attitudes toward the United States. The characteristics cited above were almost universally mentioned by the respondents, although on the other side, they also spoke of Americans as generous, hospitable, enterprising, ingenious, and friendly.

Another nearly universal sentiment was a conviction of the invincible future greatness of Canada, a land of boundless resources, of vast mineral wealth awaiting exploitation, the future granary of the world, where a prosperous population would multiply again and again.

But sentiments don't penetrate so deep or cement so well as do traditions. Although I enjoyed my life in Canada and made good friends, I never attained the warmth of a permanent attachment.

I spent twelve years in Toronto, and for eleven of them we lived as a family. Toronto was then a flat, sprawling, formless urban stretch along a harbor front of Lake Ontario. I had quarters at the first in Victoria College, one of the five constituent colleges of the university. Four of these colleges have different religious associations or loose affiliations, Victoria having a Methodist lineage. The respective colleges had their own curriculums in a variety of subjects, including philosophy and some languages. Other subjects were taught directly under university auspices, including those within the department of political science.

My chief, Mavor, was a remarkable character. He had a yellowing spade beard and piercing blue eyes. He rather resembled the portraits of Kropotkin—some asserted it was a cultivated resemblance. Among other exploits, Mavor had arranged for the settlement in western Canada of a bizarre Russian religious sect, the Doukhobors, who were oppressed by the Russian government because they refused to be drafted into the army. They appealed to the Canadian government for admission, and Mavor was sent to Russia to investigate. There he met Kropotkin, who himself had pacifist inclinations and had written a widely circulated book called *Mutual Aid*. Mavor cherished the friendship thus established and had a portrait of Kropotkin over his mantelpiece. He was a man with various tangential interests and among his other exploits had written a two-volume *History of Russia*. He was very much of a clubman, spending most of his evenings in one or another of the leading clubs of the city. A kindly man, he could on occasion be abrupt and peppery, letting loose a flood of highly colored language. I recall one occasion where at a meeting of the Royal Society of Canada he made a sudden furious attack on the economist and humorist, Stephen Leacock. He stigmatized the discourse Leacock had just delivered as a piece of "contemptible rhodomontade." He had a reputation for being absentminded. One morning, so it was told, his wife was seen wandering over the campus, anxiously inquiring of everyone whether they had seen James. She was carrying with her a pair of his pants. It appeared that she had laid out a suit for him for the day and had later discovered that he had taken only the coat of it. So this meek long-suffering lady had come to a wrong conclusion.

After I went to Toronto he was still having problems as a go-between for the Doukhobors. They refused to allow their children to attend the public schools, and they refused to pay the share of taxes that were allotted for the modest Canadian military establishment. They were in most respects very puritanical, but they had the curious custom of celebrating one great holy day by a ceremonial parade all in the nude. They were good farmers, but the soil they improved was encroached on and its boundaries disputed by outside land-grabbers. All these troubles they brought to Mavor. He once showed me a letter he had just received asking for his good services to save them. It was from their wily leader, Peter Veregin, who had a tight grip on this close-knit co-operative colony. In its fulsome appreciation of his services it contained a sentence that ran somewhat as follows: "There have been five great men in the history of the world, Socrates, Plato, Moses, Jesus Christ, and yourself, my dear Professor Mavor."

With all these preoccupations of his, it fell to my lot to look after the needs of the department. When I had to consult him on an important decision he would always reply, "Let's talk about it this evening." There was no use looking for him before 11:00 P.M. Then I would visit his house, the only one on the campus, and be shown into his immense library, divided into parallel close-set stacks so that there was only one corner where we could sit. I would raise the question to be resolved. "First," he would say, "a game of chess." We were pretty well matched. Very likely a second game would follow, and it would be between 1:00 and 2:00 A.M. before I was finally allowed to get down to business. "What do you propose?" he would say, and after my statement, nearly always with no further discussion, "Very well, do it."

We made a relatively small department then, and as so often in university departments, each member was engrossed in his own affairs and knew practically nothing about what the others were doing. In economics, the more distinctive members were a bright young statistician and a buoyant society-minded Englishman whose main field was money and banking. Mavor's own subjects straddled economics and government, as did mine. Since the war had not yet gripped Canada, we had quite large classes.

Teaching was always stimulating to me. It was a delight to establish rapport with younger minds, to provoke them into lively discussion. I am allergic to dependence on techniques or any formality in instruction. I dislike to follow any textbook, even my own. These props become a barrier to direct communication. Teaching I regard as the most socially important of all the arts. The effective teacher must be thoroughly at ease in his subject and keen to convey its significance. The commonest crime is to feed out separate gobbets of mere information and expect the student victim to memorize them. The one who memorizes the best goes to the head of the class.

The winter was long and icebound, and the late spring sent torrents down the streets. It was then I had the joy of welcoming the arrival of the family and for the first time viewing my "bargain." I had arranged for our occupation through the summer of the house of one of my colleagues, where we settled very comfortably. But the summer became hot and oppressive, and our boy twin was taken with meningitis and under the best medical care fought a life-and-death battle that went on for weeks. Happily he made a full recovery.

We spent eleven more years in Canada, long enough to acquire a satisfactory accommodation. Toronto itself seemed less a city than a sprawling conurbation that kept growing planlessly as real estate interests determined. (More recent developments have considerably improved its character in that respect.) But I gained an increasing interest in Canada itself, in its long-run potentialities and in its immediate problems. It was strangely configured, a narrow continental belt of inhabited territory beyond which vast wilderness and wastelands stretch to the North Pole. Here was a country where clean political separation scarcely interfered with travel and free communication and a vast amount of business dealings across the unarmed frontier. Canada is a loosely conjoined chain of five dissimilar aggregations, the Maritimes, Quebec, Ontario, the prairie provinces, and British Columbia. It boasts of enormous resources, but it exploits only a small fraction of them. Canada is a geographical anomaly, defying the natural lines of communication and trade, which run north and south, not east and west. The bond of union is thinnest between Quebec and the rest, but Quebec repudiates alike its "godless" homeland France and its "materialistic" southern neighbor rather more than it does its sister provinces. So the loose bond of union holds, and sentiment combines with some entrenched interests to support the notion of a common land and a common destiny.

Canada strives hard to achieve a distinctive culture, but it is a precarious endeavor, especially in the field of literature, where the pull of the United States is powerful on its successful authors. French Canada can probably be counted out, since it takes refuge in its own traditions, strengthened by its separatist Catholicism. In the pictorial and plastic arts, some special achievements have been registered. I had an opportunity to appreciate some aspects of this endeavor, having had good relationships with the then dominant group of painters and sculptors, at the time centered in Toronto. Under the leadership of men like Fred Varley, A. Y. Jackson, and Lauren Harris, who were associated in the "Group of Seven," these artists evoked a style suited to a landscape of lake and island, muskeg and floe, under windy northern skies. Writers, however, were less successful in achieving a characteristic style. They might depict Canadian scenes and portray Canadian folk, but they had their eye on American circulation, and numbers of them wrote for American periodicals or migrated to the United States.

I had never before lived among people who were so pleasantly receptive or among whom I made so many friends. Within a few years I was made a member of the Arts and Letters Club, the Canadian P.E.N., and the Royal Society of Canada. One little group to which I belonged was composed of leading business men, who participated in a series of discussions of major issues of the times. The organizer of the group, a distinguished and highly cultivated industrialist, J. Stanley McLean, became a cherished friend.

In every respect I lived a very different life from ever before. I was in closer association with the currents of affairs and in some contact with a number of the political leaders as well as with men in business and the professions. In the summer months I was free, and this time was also spent in a new way. After the first unhappy summer, we passed almost every long vacation far away from the city of Toronto, at first in a little cottage at a small resort village on Lake Huron, afterward in the great holiday area of the Muskoka Lakes. These summers were marvellous, we found, for young children, since they were close to nature and could learn the lore of the wild.

In my third year in Canada a new task disrupted the share of leisure I was enjoying. The war, which at first had seemed from the Canadian standpoint an Old World embroilment, to which out of loyalty to the great Commonwealth Canada would contribute a quota of volunteers, had spread its grisly tentacles over the greater part of the earth, and Canada became fully committed. I was appointed vice-chairman of the Dominion of Canada War Labor Board. The task was one I found particularly congenial, since it included planning for the reinstatement of the soldiers returning from the war. Any activity that enabled one to cast his thoughts ahead to a time of sanity and peace was indeed welcome. I had a good deal of responsibility in the direction of the program, since the chairman was a senator who was fully engaged otherwise. But the amount of actual accomplishment was small.

12

Canadian Sojourn—Part 2

Peace returned to the world, and most of us returned to our old ways. The compulsions of wartime ceased. I could concentrate on my own work. The future became real again, something you could plan for. I could visit my old home and homeland, as I did in the summer of 1921.

But peace had returned to a vastly changed world, and most of us failed to realize the difference. The old myths still prevailed. The militarists made plans for defense against a facsimile of the First World War. The politicians dictated a peace modeled on the ancient principle that the goal of victory is spoliation. It was determined by the competing land-grabs of the victors, and it imposed intolerable burdens on the vanquished, thus sowing the dragon's teeth of even greater evils to be harvested by the next generation. I was seriously disturbed as the terms of the evil peace gradually became clear. Individuals sometimes learn a lesson from painful experiences. Why can't peoples learn any lesson from even the most hideous collective experience? We failed to read the signs of the times, and we grossly misread the portent of the Soviet state.

The Soviet Revolution, even more than the French Revolution, was an epochal event in the history of the world. It demanded the cool assessment of every thinking man, of our statesmen first of all. But we saw it only in the flickering light of our immediate interests.

True, it was a menace to us. Its leaders were ruthless men, utterly without scruple if it served their cause or their power. But they could win, as Marx himself had postulated, only by fostering strong communist movements in the capitalist world. There was mighty little chance of any such development in Canada or in the United States. If capitalist countries could stave off severe and continued economic crises and depressions, they had at their command resources that could provide the working classes with a prosperity as well as a freedom unknown to Soviet workers. But our leaders and our people gave little thought to these considerations. Some believed the Russian people would rise against their masters, given some encouragement and aid. Some believed the system was bound to collapse. I had many an argument with my good industrial friend on that topic. He maintained that, lacking the incentive of profit, bureaucratic controls would result in total inefficiency, lowering productivity and increasing prices to such an extent that the system could no longer be tolerated.

Canada was intrinsically less affected by these mighty changes than most other lands. It had no territories that had changed hands, no direct touch of wartime ravage, no insurgent groups aroused to seek independence, no great alteration of status, no vast wartime debts, no significant communist underground. On the surface it was, in most respects, again "business as usual."

For myself, the earlier post-war years were affected by the disillusionment I experienced over the gross stupidity and pettiness of the men of power. It was not enough to have blundered into a world-embracing war. The victors of the holocaust, cheered on by the huzzas of their peoples, insisted on a settlement that showed an invincible capacity for unreason. The nineteenth-century belief in progress I had imbibed in my youth was a utopian dream. Humanity was not ready to march forward. It was doomed to suffer retreats after every advance, throwbacks to the near barbarism that marked the endlessly recurring wars of the ages, consuming the youth that were the never-fulfilled promise of a better future.

I began to question the value I had set on scholarship. The amassing of knowledge, the advancement of science, the triumph of technology, brought little benefit. More knowledge did not convey more wisdom, and without social wisdom the destroyers are stronger than the builders.

Such musings bred in me a restlessness, a loss of conviction. My ambition was dulled and even the itch to write became directionless. I did what I had to do, took whatever enjoyments each passing day offered. Part of several summers in our Muskoka abode I composed several playlets in a dilettante fashion, making no effort to study the requirements of the stage. Some years afterward I read them with a critical eye and consigned them to the flames. One of them had meantime been purloined by a friend, and the following winter, at a birthday party that was given for me, much to my surprise my playlet was performed. The scene was a studio that had been a church, where two good sculptress friends of ours, Frances Loring and Florence Wyle, lived and worked. They were members of an artistic circle, including most of the then dominant school of painting called the Group of Seven. I thought there was some good dialogue in the skit but that it lacked the bite of life.

When you have lost confidence in the future you live for the day. You take what pleasures it offers, while they are yours to take. The experience you miss today is never the experience you may gain tomorrow. I would not call myself a hedonist, but in this period I came nearer to being one than in any other. I was still bound by some fundamental loyalties but permitted myself a more elastic interpretation of them. The experience of wartime unlocks tendencies in human nature that usually are curbed or at least not given overt expression. For some the resort to violence becomes less restrained, as the rising statistics of crime indicate. Scruples of every kind are eroded by the inculcated unscrupulousness of waging war. One natural tendency of mankind that has freer vent in the aftermath of war is the erotic one. I believe the majority of men are in effect monogamic—many conditions conspire to promote the enduring husband-wife relationship. But that does not preclude an occasional straying from the fold, since there is frequently a stage in which the longing for new erotic experience is powerful. According to the temperament on both sides, the gratification of this longing may lead to the breakup of a marriage or may instead actually safeguard it. For my own part I never wavered in the assurance of the complete tie between Ethel and myself, but at this time I confess I was not above yielding to temptation.

During the war years my first book, *Community*, was at length published. It was a broad survey of the principles and interrelationships that bound men together in a common life. It had a mixed reception. The English reviews were most gratifyingly favorable. The *Athenaeum* called it "a masterly book," and the *Times Literary Supplement* characterized it as a work of "unmistakable originality." A number of English authorities gave it warm praise. Lord Bryce wrote that he was reading it "with great interest and profit," George Unwin of Manchester University said "it ought to make an epoch in English sociology and political science." There were one or two favorable American reviews. The *American Economic Review* named it "easily the most notable book of the year in sociology," and the *American Sociological Review* spoke of its "comprehensiveness of knowledge, depth of insight, clarity of vision, cogency of argument, simplicity of language." But the leading American sociologist of the day, Robert E. Park, damned it as being thin, vague, insubstantial, and "jejune." I pondered that last adjective. I had an inkling of what was troubling him and I attributed his animadversions as much to his limitations as to mine. But the book had no circulation among American sociologists. It is curious that Park's damning review alone after many years lingered in my memory, and it was only while I was looking over some old records during the preparation of this work that I rediscovered to my agreeable surprise the encomia received so long ago.

I have by no means always felt grateful to my publishers, but I came to have a warm feeling for the English Macmillan Company, which kept the book in circulation on very modest returns through many decades and even recently, when I thought it was extinct, arranged for a new paperback edition. I was little discouraged by the lack of American acceptance and continued my interest in sociology, although there was then no opportunity to teach it at Toronto. My activities on the War Labor Board had brought me into fairly close touch with the labor movement in Canada and its affiliation with United States trade unionism. I was active also in the development of the Workers' Education Association along the English model. So I took time off to write a cursory book on *Labor in the Changing World*, published soon after the war ended. Its conclusions would seem trite enough today, but at that time, in Canada, they came as a bit of a jolt to many readers. I followed this with a more popular little book in the same vein as *Community*, intended for W.E.A. classes in England, *Elements of Social Science*. It has lived on ever since 1921, the kind of modest, thin, back-street longevity so many of my books have enjoyed.

These were sideline affairs, requiring relatively little effort. It was only in the last years of my Canadian sojourn that I broke from routine activity. I gave long and careful thought to a book entitled *The Modern State*. Its focus was a fundamental principle of government which viewed the state as not the inclusive and all-encompassing organization of a society but as itself one mode of association, one which, though of prime importance, still leaves room for many others that perform functions the state cannot properly fulfill and should not attempt to. All through the ages state and community, state and society, have been falsely identified, with unhappy practical consequences. One of the worst results of this identification was that it put religion within the sphere of the state. To be a citizen you had to profess the established faith. It meant centuries of internal strife and ravaging wars. Only when the church was recognized as autonomous, independent of the state in matters of faith but without coercive power, did this gross and spendthrift confusion come to an end. The identification has been emphasized by the most distinguished political philosophers, from Plato to Hegel and down to the present day. It has received the self-interested support of kings and dictators and the magnates of power and their followers. Some of the confusion that remains is due to the double sense in which we use the names of countries. We say, for example, "the United States made a treaty with Japan," and we say, "the United States grows quantities of corn and tobacco," or "the United States has a multitude of religious sects." Only the first of these three sentences refers to the state, acting as always through its agency of government. The others express characteristics of the society of the United States. They refer to the country or community, *not* to the state. But I have said enough to indicate the motif of the book. It has had an encouraging history since its publication in 1926.

Meanwhile our Department of Political Science continued to grow at a rather rapid rate. Mavor had resigned and I had become its chairman. We introduced a number of new staff members, one of whom, a very distinctive and enterprising scholar, Harold Innes, succeeded me when I left. Another of a group of really good men was the Englishman Vincent Bladen, and from the History Department we acquired our professor of constitutional law, the somewhat erratic but distinguished W.P.M. Kennedy. I became quite proud of our department.

In addition to heading the department I found myself saddled for a time with the direction of a struggling School of Social Work annexed to the university. Its director had proved quite unsatisfactory, and on his induced departure no successor could be immediately found to repair the damage and raise the reputation of the school. Our president, Sir Robert Falconer, begged me to undertake the task, and with the aid of a very competent assistant I was able to accomplish what was needed.

One episode occurred during this period that caused me considerable vexation. As a device for calling attention to recent advances in the social work field, I arranged a short series of public lectures under the auspices of the school. I invited as the first speaker the famous lady of Hull House in Chicago, Jane Addams, who graciously consented to come. After motions were sent out for the lectures, protests began to reach me from people who objected to Miss Addams as a wartime "pacifist." The aftermath of war, the hardening of intolerances, the noisy retrospective "patriotism" of reaction, was showing itself. A local newspaper began to print indignant letters. The president called me in and advised me to call off the meeting—since the university was a provincial institution dependent on annual grants, he was concerned about political repercussions. He didn't order me to cancel the engagement, and he understood my reasons when I told him I would not willingly yield. But a week later, shortly before the date of the lecture, he called me again and said he had received a definite message from a veteran's group that they would break up the meeting if it were held. This could not be brooked and might even be unsafe for our guest. Thus I had no alternative except to make abject apology to her. It was a forerunner of situations that developed later in the United States under the infamous stimulation of Senator Joseph McCarthy. This was my first direct acquaintance with the vicious vehemence and persecuting mob spirit of self-righteous, ignorant groups. It reaches down to the hatred of difference that we are all in some degree susceptible to, especially in times of stress, and that has always been the enemy of every advance in the civilization of man.

Outside of my work at the university, my life in Canada was distinctive in the amount of vigorous recreation I found the opportunity to enjoy. My summers were free, mostly spent in our cottage on Lake Muskoka. We had a peninsula largely to ourselves, except, happily, for the cottage across the way of a university colleague, Sidney Brett, philosopher and historian of psychology, with his wife Marion, whose children were the co-agers of our own. Our children learned many things about the world of nature—and their parents learned as well, in the endeavor to teach—about trees and flowers, butterflies and moths, bugs and other crawling creatures, the local fauna, stars and constellations. Only one kind of obvious natural phenomenon proved beyond the range of available information. When troops of rather large white "toadstools" appeared in August among the pine needles and the usual question came, I was stumped. I bought a popular book on mushrooms, but three out of four we found did not seem to be included in it. I invited a biologist from the university, but funguses were not his field. I determined not to be beaten and began acquiring scientific books on the subject, beginning with the excellent volume of Kauffman on the Agaricaceae of Michigan. I found it an exciting quest. There were so many problems of diagnosis, so many fine points for investigation, always some unknown one I couldn't find in the books, and then there was the pleasure of bringing strange esculents to the table. In short, to answer the children's questions I made mycology my hobby and have pursued it every summer since those far-off days.

We became quite devoted to our Muskoka cottage. It was right at the edge of a strait of the lake, with a landing stage from which I would often plunge in for a pre-breakfast swim. Below the bunga-low was a grove of pines with a path leading to a rather large boathouse, where we kept canoes, a launch with an outboard motor, and later on a sailboat. In those early years it was a peaceful scene, before the popularity of our lakes filled the air with the noise of speedboats. Our summering there was the most leisurely period of all our lives. Ethel usually had a good maid imported from Scot-land, and I had rarely any need to attend to any departmental busi-ness. It was, however, the *dolce far niente* that made my own devo-tion to our pleasant retreat less wholehearted than that of the others. I fretted at times for the stimulus of company, for more entertain-ment, for some incentive to fresh activity.

My mornings I usually spent in the secluded study I had equipped in our boathouse, except on occasions when we went on excursions or canoe trips. It was a land of lakes and streams, and nothing was more enjoyable than our canoe voyaging when, with some colleague or with my prospector brother Keith, who was an expert camper, and later on with my elder son, we set forth for a week or ten days in the wilds. Our first expeditions took us down the dark Musquash river to Georgian Bay, where we coasted through the islands of the bay to the Moon River and then ascended to Lake Muskoka by an-other route. There were many portages on the way and also an occa-sional rapid we could shoot. It was a delight after paddling and portaging all day to come to a camping place, set up our little tent, strew the floor with balsam boughs, spread our blankets, and light a fire, often to cook the fish we caught with a troll en route, some-times to fish for our dinner after a swim in a deep pool. Later on we took more ambitious trips, higher up on the French and Pickerel rivers, sometimes losing our way, on one occasion losing our provi-sions. We loved roughing it. It was lonely country, and we would usually not see another human being for a week or more. We did see black bears occasionally and listened to the melancholy timber wolves at night. Once we picked up a baby bear cub, but it was too dangerous a possession and quickly dropped. Once we heard in the middle of the night a slow heavy tread approaching the tent. We went on the alert and I picked up my rifle. The creature began nuzzling our tent ropes. I cautiously raised a flap—it was a cow! We had camped near that very rare phenomenon, a farm in the wilderness.

In that flat, unpeopled northland of rocks and pines, of streams and marshes and lakes and islands, I gained a sense of intimacy with nature I never had known before. Echoes of it still reverberate in my memory—the wavering, lonely call of the loon, the white stripe of the skunk threading through the trees in the evening, unmoved and fearless as we passed, the savor of the shallow lily pond where we hunted for bull frogs, the ledge below the little waterfall where we camped at night, the sough of the fresh breeze at dawn, the sudden storm of a late afternoon, the fire round which we sat under the wakening stars and listened to the whispering scrabbles in the undergrowths, the insistent, raucous note of the nightly whippoorwill.

When speaking of our canoe trip I referred to my "prospector brother," and I should digress to explain how my youngest brother, Keith, came to be in Canada. During active war service in Palestine and Mesopotamia, he contracted recurrent malaria and, after a stay at home in Scotland to recuperate, he planned to go back to a position he had held on a Malaysian rubber plantation before the war. When I heard of this, it seemed too big a risk, and after obtaining an assurance from my good friend J. S. McLean, the industrialist, that he would take Keith into his business and could promise him a career, I was able to persuade him to join us in Canada. However, my brother was not the kind who took kindly to a big business establishment, and after a short time he quit, took a mining engineering course at the university, and became a free-lance prospector, cheerfully roughing it in the wilds and morasses of the Canadian north.

In the early years the Canadian winter seemed wearisomely long to me. The snow usually lay on the city streets from November through March, and I longed for the release when we could smell the earth again. But my attitude changed, thanks largely to the influence of an athletic colleague, S. H. Hooke, professor of Old

Testament studies, a man I greatly liked. He was an excellent golfer, who could always give me a substantial handicap, and he was a very good skier and figure skater. He gave me lessons in skiing but I never advanced very far. He also persuaded me to take up figure skating, and that was what made all the difference. I joined the Toronto Skating Club and took assiduous lessons from the pro. Soon I was able to participate in the Wednesday evening and Saturday afternoon dances at the club, waltzes and mazurkas and ten-steps on ice. It was great exercise and much fun, and I made good friends. Dancing was a delight to me, both at the skating rink and on the ordinary dance floor.

I am long past all that. I have not found growing old at all grievous. I still enjoy life to the full, both work and recreation. My moments of regret over the encroachments of time come when something recalls the days that were, not least the nights at the skating rink or the dance floor and the good partners I had then, the days when I could "sport with Amaryllis in the shade." To this day, when I happen to hear a waltz from *The Nutcracker Suite* or *The Merry Widow* or *The Blue Danube,* I throb again to the swinging rhythms of the skating rink. Those years in Canada stand out as my great age of sport.

These were good years for our family, too. My wife made many and enduring friends and with her artistic bent had happy associations with the painters whom I have already mentioned who were developing a distinctive style to depict the landscapes of the Canadian North. Our oldest child, Ian, was being educated at Upper Canada College, and our other son, Donald, and our daughter, Betty, were attending Brown School. Ian became greatly attracted by Canadian painting and in later years did some fine water colors of scenes from the northern wilds of Ontario. For every one of us there was more than a pang of regret at leaving behind our days and years in Canada.

*　　*　　*　　*　　*　　*　　*　　*

I mention in this chapter a visit I made abroad in the early summer of 1921, when after a week or two in my old home I did a bit of traveling over a sadly changed Europe. I recently unearthed some notes I had scribbled at that time on the paper of the Hotel de France in Vienna. They consisted of a series of reflections that throw some light on my moods and feelings at that stage. I append them here, with a little filling in of the jotted lines.

Patriotism. "Daddy, what did you do in the Great War?" "I lived to beget you, my son." That answer may serve for the days when the pathetic ghosts of glory wander cold and abhorrent over the disillusioned earth.

Chance and Circumstance. Take the chance when it comes, for we are the children of chance.

Chance of parentage, chance of ancestry, chance of conception, chance of birth, chance of survival—so it goes every step of the way, that we are, what we are, what we become.

How can we think of ourselves as of account except to ourselves and to those we serve? How can we think of ourselves as children of destiny? That is overweening. We have no claims on fortune.

Take then all the boons that are given. We have faculties to develop. We have good things to enjoy. We have friendships to cultivate.

Money and Love. You can tell pretty well what a women will do in love-making by what she does with money. If she is niggardly with money, most likely she will be niggardly with love. If she is spendthrift with money, she will be spendthrift also with love.

Love that is bought—don't sneer at it. If indeed you can buy it, it is the cheapest thing to buy, no matter what the price. But you buy substitutes instead, so easy and so worthless a purchase.

The Art of Living. I am watching the crowds in a city street at night. They drift along, wandering aimlessly up and down, unobservant of their crowding fellows, always returning where the throng is densest as though wanting to be lost in the contiguity of the multitude. It is the ancient call of the herd, the lowest form of association, without content, without aim, without cultivation—the nadir of the art of living.

First Realization. Dumbness and wonder, a vague unease, and the imperious vibrating call—and a power that breaks with firm pitiless hands the shell of experience till we stand free, bewildered, rapt, shelterless, before the overpowering warmth of this new sun. Fear breaks in, a sense of ourselves naked in the light, the swamping consciousness of another, tremors of our mortal flesh—and the surprising reality, a mystery at once and a revelation, so that we feel we were alone before, and now, now, we share the night, the universe. But then the retreat, the chastening return, and haply thereafter the lyric episode.

Second Migration

The call came in 1927. I was invited to become the head of the Department of Economics and Sociology at Barnard College, the women's college of Columbia University, and also to be attached to the Department of Public Law and Government, of the postgraduate Faculty of Political Science at Columbia University. My own teaching would be the introductory course in sociology at Barnard and the political theory courses in the Faculty of Political Science.

It was too tempting an offer. I had not been able to introduce sociology at Toronto. Now I would be able to participate in its development. I envisioned a few prospects at Toronto. Now new opportunities would be open. I would be in the center of the great movements of the times. I would be in a competitive area, associated with scholars interested in the subjects most dear to me. I could see the new plays and hear the great symphony orchestras and visit art galleries and museums.

On a September morning we all arrived in New York, to make, as it turned out, the United States our homeland ever thereafter. I had previously been there a number of times, to visit a student friend in Mansfield, Ohio, to undertake a study, one summer of the operations of the Russell Sage Foundation in New York, and once to be for a few months a free-lance lecturer at pleasant Reed College in Portland, Oregon. This last occasion was particularly stimulating, partly because the college was in an experimental stage under a devoted president Richard Scholz who was finding the struggle too much for his strength, but mainly because I had as a close associate Alexander Meiklejohn, who had very recently lost the presidency of Amherst, a man of verve, vitality, and vision with whom I had much good discourse and many a lively argument.

I had a cordial reception to the university from the erudite Professor E. R. A. Seligman, head of the Department of Economics, from Dean Virginia Gildersleeve of Barnard College and, among others, from the economic historian, Vladimir Simkhovitch, a remarkable man who became my very dear friend. An apartment was found for us in a building owned by the university on Claremont Avenue. Migration is always discommoding, the disruptive transfer of household goods and, not least vexatious for me, the painfully selective weeding out of my library to fit a narrower space. New conditions of life may have advantages, but they nearly always have disadvantages as well. We felt cribbed in an apartment after having had a bungalow from which one could step out-of-doors into a quiet little roadway or into one's own garden. The children could not run freely in the streets. Fortunately the university school, Horace Mann, was only a block or so away. But there were plenty of adjustments we had to make. I missed my skating rink. I missed my golf—it was a more arduous business to join a club and travel to it. I missed having a car in my own garage and driving freely whenever I was so minded. I missed all my old friends and colleagues. In short, it was altogether a quite different way of life.

I felt like a semi-foreigner at first among my new colleagues. With my different background and training, and not knowing the folk they gossiped about or the situations they discussed, I was a listener more than a participant in their company—a role I was not used to. I retained and have always kept a bit of a Scottish Highland accent that seemed more conspicuous against the characteristic American intonation of the majority of my colleagues. But the feeling of being an outsider was dissipated soon enough in a society where "standing on ceremony" is rare and hospitality is warm and pervasive.

The students in my classes were of different categories than those

I had previously taught. At Barnard I had a large introductory class of girls, well over a hundred, who dutifully listened to what I said but, with some exceptions, were not particularly interested. My class of graduates, potential candidates for a doctoral degree, was at first of very moderate size and nearly a third of the students were Oriental, largely Chinese. The latter were avid learners but poorly trained, and they frequently did not understand English well enough to grasp much of what I tried to teach. Some of the others were really able, but the majority lacked the capacity to express themselves effectively. I came to the conclusion that most schools gave a poor training in English. In later years these Chinese students vanished, and my Columbia class in political theory became very large, with some excellent students among them.

That first winter gave me a new stimulus. It was one of exploration in various directions. In the first place I had to read widely in the subjects I was teaching to acquire a decent control of them under the new conditions. Then we had to gain some acquaintance with the great metropolis. We went fairly often to the theater and subscribed to a series of Philharmonic concerts. It was all new and engrossing.

In the later part of the winter a number of developments of some moment occurred. Our renowned president, Nicholas Murray Butler, revived an ancient Columbia institution, the President's House Meeting. It betokened the need to canvass some issue affecting the university's academic policy. The issue on this occasion was whether the Department of Sociology, one of the divisions of the graduate Faculty of Political Science, should be abolished. Sociology was not then established at the other leading universities of the Northeast, and many regarded it as a dubious or spurious aspirant to academic recognition. But there were special reasons for head-shaking over the status of the Columbia department—as I discovered more fully afterward to my cost. So the various deans and the leading members of departments which might in any way be concerned in the matter were summoned to solemn conference. Though I had no connection with the department I was invited as an interested party. Most of the historians present and a few others argued for abolition. Most of the economists spoke for retention and development. The renowned John Dewey made an effective plea to the effect that the sociological approach was different from and as significant as the historic, economic, or political approach. There was a majority in favor of retention. The department was saved.

It was not long after that meeting that I had a visit from the newly appointed head of the sociology department, Samuel McCune Lindsay. He was head *faute de mieux,* his own interest being in social welfare legislation, a subject loosely annexed to the department. He was a pleasant, mild-mannered gentleman, and he had come to invite me to take over the headship. The department had been from its inception dominated by the formidable Franklin H. Giddings, now about to retire, a highly controversial figure. I was loathe to accept, being comfortably placed as I was. It would not only be an additional task but a troublesome and rather invidious one. However, I felt I could not decently refuse.

That winter was enlivened in another unexpected manner. I was asked to take one of the evening "extension" classes the second semester. At that time they were courses for the interested public, not specially designed for candidates for degrees. To my surprise it proved to be a very lively class as well as large. And this particular one contained a more diverse and distinctive group than did any other class I have taught. In the course of the session quite a number of the students came to my office to consult me on their private problems or to tell me about their interests and their lives. I had had considerable experience listening to the tales of students but nothing to compare with these occasions. There was, for example, the massive Negro of striking appearance, who was striving to galvanize a Negro organization into effective action and met obstacles at every turn. There was the physician, a man of later middle years, who planned to set up his own foundation and wanted me to be its director, but soon afterward he suffered a serious car accident and I saw him no more. There was the southern girl, neat looking and debonair, who visited my office one evening and told me her tale of woe. Her mother, a widow, had brought up her four older brothers and herself and had tirelessly spurred them to make a name for themselves. The brothers had succeeded brilliantly, but she was a failure. She had got nowhere and never would. "There is only one thing I could do well at—I could be a wonderful mother." "Why not then?" I said, "You have still plenty of time." "How old do you think I am?" I looked at her and said, honestly enough, "around twenty-four." She had a clear rose-and-milk complexion, without a line on her face. "I am thirty-nine. What's more, I'm *not* going to marry anyone." "That makes it rather difficult." "Well, you see, I have made excellent arrangements for bringing a child up. I have an uncle down South, who would be happy to take me in and adopt a child of mine." At this point I felt called on to sound a warning note, which rather abruptly brought the interview to an end. A month or so later she looked in on me for a minute, to tell me some gentleman from Yale would be her guest in summer. Then at the very end of the session she visited me once more. "I'm married," she said, but before I could respond, she added sharply: "Don't congratulate me! I married a convict. He's been condemned to a long prison term for embezzlement. Good-bye." I tried vainly afterward to learn what became of it all, but she had left the university with no forwarding address.

One more case must end my story of this incredible class. There was a tall, handsome, spruce middle-aged gentleman sitting in one of the front rows who attracted my attention from the first. Early in the session he came to see me. He told me in confidence that he was living under an assumed name, that his father had had a high place in the czarist ministry, had foreseen the revolution, had transferred the family fortune to the care of a banking institution in Amsterdam. Would I do him the honor of being his guest at the Metropolitan Opera—he had a grand tier box—would I come this week, next week, when? I stalled on the offer, wanting to make some inquiry regarding his status at the university. It turned out that he was attending classes by two of my colleagues as well, that he was not enrolled for any degree, but was taking these courses in order to gain as a stranger a better knowledge of American social and political affairs. So when next he called I accepted his offer for a date the following week. But two days later he returned and in a tone of anguish said: "I beg you to pardon my gaucherie. Excuse me if I ask if you are married," followed by, "Would Madam be gracious enough to join our company." Madam, however, did not feel like it on this occasion. On the evening in question he did more than provide our box seats. During the first entr'acte, he whispered to me, "Are your colleagues dry?" I assured him to the contrary. So we trooped into the foyer after the second act, sat down at a table reserved for us, all set with champagne glasses. And at a signal from our host to the majordomo, a waiter with a wrapped bottle filled the glasses. "My own Veuve Cliquot," he remarked. After the opera we went with him to the St. Regis Everglades, then the most fashionable night club, and the same type of ritual occurred. And this was during the great prohibition era!

Only once again did I accept his rather frequent invitations and this time Ethel accompanied me. We had the same full treatment, in every detail, as before. When on the former occasion he had apologized for not asking about my wife, he had murmured something mysterious about his hesitation to meet a lady in the dark! Though much intrigued, I did not feel I could pursue the subject. But he visited me once or twice afterward and told me some remarkable stories about his past experiences, including an explanation of that strange remark. I have never publicly told the story before. It was a harrowing tale that began with a childhood betrothal arranged between two great landowners of adjacent estates for the marriage of the son of one—my informant—to the daughter of the other. The pair never met until in their later teens the plans for a formal affiancement took the representatives of the two families to a winter festival party at Grindelwald in Switzerland. The gay young people, a group of four, were skating one day on a large rink, one end of which was out of bounds as dangerous. They disregarded the warning signs and spiraled beyond the limits, and all four were immersed. Three of them were none the worse for the ducking, but the fourth, the fiancée, became seriously ill. Her illness progressively worsened, until the doctor declared her case was beyond hope. My friend spent the time at her bedside, and one morning she whispered faintly to him. "I'm going to die. I have one wish before I die; I want to fulfill my dream and be married to you." The priest was at hand, and a truncated marriage ceremony was performed that evening. The young man sat through the night hours silently holding her hand. He must have fallen into a doze, for he suddenly came to himself with the thought that the hand he was holding was cold. The first dawn was showing through the narrow casement panes. In its dim light he saw the white face with a narrow red line below the mouth. It was the end.

The war came and he was wounded in the head. He made me put my fingers in the hole it left above his forehead. He lay for long months on his back on a hospital cot, looking up at the white-washed ceiling. His fevered imagination projected on to it the last scene at the Grindelwald Inn. It haunted him day and night. He had no power to banish it. And the impress still remained.

He also told me stories of his life in Russia, and I can say only that if they were "the stuff that dreams are made on "the world lost in him a remarkable novelist. Our relations came to a sudden and unexpected end. We happened to be talking about cars, and I mentioned that I was about to buy one. "You mustn't without consulting me. How about a Lincoln? I have a spare one, practically new, with some very special fittings. Would that do?" I laughed and said I wasn't in that class. "What would you want to pay?" Not more than a thousand dollars, I told him. "Take it then for a thousand dollars." I followed the line of least resistance and said I would have to consult madam. "She'll love it," he replied. I told her that evening, knowing what the answer would be. "Impossible," she said, giving several reasons, not least the figure we would cut with our neighbors when we went to our country cottage. Ethel was always modest and self-effacing, disliking display of any kind. She was less inclined than I was to take chances, to approve of anything speculative. On this occasion I agreed with her. When I told him he seemed taken aback. "At least come and ride in it, so you can see what a beauty it is." I couldn't refuse that and made a date for the following Saturday. He would phone me between nine and ten that morning. But during that hour I had an urgent summons to the dean's office— a serious problem had arisen that concerned one of my students. So I missed his call. I tried in vain to reach him and later wrote explaining and apologizing. No answer came. I never saw him again. He ceased attending my class. At the end of the session he disappeared altogether from the university scene.

I could add one or two more stories, but I have said enough in tribute to the most extraordinary class I have taught in forty-five years of teaching.

14

New Tests and Troubles

The average professor has less financial recompense than that of his colleagues in any of the other well-established professions, and even if he wins distinction in academe he does not approach the worldly reward of, say, a leading physician or lawyer. All through my length of years in three universities my salary left no margin for luxuries, and the miserable pension I received on retiring would not support the humblest artisan in comfort. Since then, however, there has been a marked improvement in salary standards in the leading endowed universities and in municipal and state institutions of learning.

On the other hand, the professorial life has substantial advantages. After his first year or two of teaching, the average professor has ample time at his disposal. The amount of work he puts in is at his own discretion. He can deliver his lectures, meet a few students, and leave for the day. Some days he need not appear at all. He has vacations running up to three or four months in the year. He acquires tenure and becomes reasonably secure. The studious ones and the ambitious ones work quite hard, keeping up with and con-tributing to their subjects, writing articles and learned books. Espe-cially in the endowed universities, this is the way to promotion and possibly to distinction. Others augment their salaries by engaging in extraprofessional or organizational activities. On the whole it is a comfortable free-lancing existence, and there is no occupational reason why a professor with tenure should ever develop ulcers.

My own earlier years at Columbia, however, were not so very comfortable. I had less opportunity than usual to enjoy the amenities of the scholarly life. In the first place I was in charge of two departments, and the second one was a bit of a headache. Soon after taking it on, the coming of the Great Depression thrust upon me in addition a most unexpected and problematic task.

The department of sociology was in a parlous state. From its initiation it had been presided over by Franklin H. Giddings, a forceful personality who had some insights but little scholarship, a bit of a preacher as well. In his later years he was a strong advocate of statistical methods but made very little use of them himself. His staff appointments were determined less by ability than by the virtue of discipleship, a quality in strong men that has not infrequently had deleterious effects. The reputation of the department had fallen. It did not attract many able students. Leadership had passed to other institutions, notably to the flourishing sociology department at the University of Chicago. To reform the department was inevitably a slow and vexatious process. In order not to be invidious, I confine myself to saying that the department lacked the quality and was wholly without the distinction one might expect in the graduate department of a great university. It took quite a number of years before we had again a really reputable department, and then incompatibilities and divisions developed within it. All through my time as executive officer of the department I had difficult problems of staffing.

I had been at Columbia some two years before the onset of the Great Depression. Somehow it is hard to recall the despair and distress caused by the ever deepening impact of what at first was regarded as merely a sharp market correction of gross speculative inflation, but when the placid optimism of President Hoover and the reassurances of some leading financiers were discredited by the persistent and drastic downward trend, the settled gloom was confirmed by the moving army of the unemployed, the bread lines outside the welfare agencies, the apple-sellers on the streets, the bankruptcies, the shutdown banks, and the suicides. The programs of the Roosevelt administration brought mitigations and new hopes, but the return to some degree of "normalcy" was agonizingly slow.

No occupational group was more immune from the direct effects of the depression than the staff of well-established colleges and universities. The student body needed as many teachers and as many administrators as before. The salary rates remained pretty much the same, and the greater the deflation the greater the purchasing power they provided. In fact, for many studious ones whose thoughts were remote from the arenas of profit and loss, the old notion of the denizen of the ivory tower seemed more applicable than before. As for the economists and other students of the business world, their services were now at a premium.

The last remark introduces the second of the serious problems I encountered in my early years at Columbia. One of the by-products of the depression was the public emergence of the purveyors of nostrums for its cure and for the eternal prevention of its return. There were the "share the wealth" slogans of "the Kingfish" of Louisiana and the zealous proclamations of Father Charles Coughlin and the "social credit" heresy imported from the Canadian West. Any confident trumpeter of a panacea attracted the anxious wishful-thinking crowds. There were, on the other hand, the standpat conservatives who insisted on the pre-established harmony of the economic system, asserting that "the depression was its own cure." But the most respectable of the new prescriptions, sponsored by people of some standing and winning many advocates in the Far West, was technocracy, the doctrine that the over-all regulation of the economic mechanism should be entrusted not to the politicians but to the industrial engineers. And it happened that two prominent technocrats were members of the Columbia faculty.

I do not know how far this last fact precipitated a decision taken by our president, Nicholas Murray Butler. At any rate I received a summons to his office. He was setting up a commission, he said, under Columbia auspices, with myself as chairman, for the study and solution of the problems of the depression. He bade me bring together the leading economists and financial experts for this purpose. "It is the qualified scholars, and not the sciolists, who can find the answers. Choose the best people available across the country. The university will provide the resources." That was all!

It was a command. It would not have served for me to have told our imperious head that others were much better qualified for this mission than I was. I was fortunate in being able to enlist the most distinguished economists of the country, drawn from Harvard, Yale, Chicago, Cornell, and the University of California, along with five from Columbia. I added the economist of the Chase National Bank, Benjamin Anderson, Adolf Berle from our Law School, the dean of our School of Engineering, Joseph W. Barker, Harlow G. Person of the Taylor Society, Alvin Johnson of the New School for Social Research, and George H. Soule, director-at-large of the National Bureau of Economic Research. Arrangements were made for the assignment of the various areas of investigation to appropriate scholars who after a period of several months were to present their respective findings to a full meeting of the commission.

We assembled for a three-day session at Asbury Park, at a season when there were more seagulls than people around. Various scholars read papers, followed by lengthy and animated discussions. When, for example, Alvin Hansen of Harvard presented his conclusions on the rescue of the railroads from their bankrupt conditions, there were those who insisted no such drastic plan was needed. When Jim Angell of Columbia presented a scheme for a stabilized banking policy much on the lines of the later-established Federal Reserve System, there was disagreement on specific points, while one member was violently opposed to the whole principle. So it went on, with objections raised to every plan submitted. On the last morning Adolf Berle, who with Gardiner Means had written a distinguished work on *The Modern Corporation and Private Property,* offered a perspective on the whole situation involving a sweeping program of reform, and the critics went into action again. On no issue did there seem to be any consensus. There is an old saying referring to the way doctors differ which I felt might be applied to economists— where there are two economists, there are three opinions.

Further discussions and interchanges of views brought us no nearer to an agreement. I strove hard to gain such modifications and concessions as would permit us to reach a modest approach to consensus or at least a clear-cut majority on some major issues. My efforts all seemed unavailing. I could not ask our able secretary, Arthur Gayer of Barnard College, to write a report on the basis of our discussions. That would have given little guidance to whatever public it was addressed to. I feared I would sadly have to admit failure to our president. He had written me such warm letters concerning "the most striking public service" we would be rendering. He had the highest expectation that Columbia would indeed lead the country out of the depression. In my perplexity I had a heart-to-heart talk with my good friend Wesley Mitchell, a member of our Columbia group on whose judgment I placed great reliance. "Don't give up," he counselled. "Write the report yourself, submit it to the members, and ask them for their reservations. Put the reservations in an appendix."

I followed his advice, taking a positive line wherever there was an important part of the group that more or less accepted it. To my surprise and delight the objections and reservations that had loomed so large in our discussions reduced themselves to relatively few and on the whole rather minor differences. The task was greatly aided by the prior resignation of our most obdurate out-and-out laissez faire member, Benjamin Anderson. He resigned in disgust because while the other members disagreed among themselves only on certain issues he disagreed with everyone on every issue. I liked him personally but was glad to see him go. Others who would probably have been willing to sign had been called into the service of the national administration, to join Roosevelt's famous "brain trust." These were Adolf Berle, James H. Rogers, and Leo Wolman. One member, Jacob Viner, was called abroad some time before the report was drafted.

All the remaining members signed the general report. There were a number of valuable supplementary reports on special topics. One was on productive capacity, contributed by our two members identified with engineering and industrial management, Joseph W. Barker and Harlow G. Person, together with Wesley Mitchell, which in effect dealt with the technocratic doctrine. Four others, contributed by Arthur Gayer, were on problems of monetary policy. Other reports were prepared by John M. Clark, Alvin Hansen, and Josef A. Schumpeter. Schumpeter had also an addendum suggesting a difference of emphasis on one or two issues.

The published report, issued in 1934 under the title of *Economic Reconstruction,* won headlines for a day or two but soon was forgotten. Actually, some of the programs for banking, monetary policy, and the railroads then being initiated by the federal government were much along the lines of the report, and the members who left us for government service had a considerable role in the enactment of these programs.

A great burden fell from my shoulders when that book saw the light. Most thankfully I returned to my own studies. The restoration of one's cherished way of living is balm to the spirit. I had been most toilsomely cultivating a garden that was not my own, and I felt I had no claim to its produce, whatever it might be. I turned to the writing of a book I had in mind when the alien summons came, a different kind of introduction to sociology, with a unity and focus I held to be lacking in those I had to use. The work, *Society—a Textbook of Sociology,* took some time to develop. It had a very moderate degree of success and never really competed with the prevailing style of textbook. Teachers complained it was too difficult, or too abstruse, for their students, but I was conceited enough to regard this attitude as a reflection on the proficiency of both teachers and students.

Sociology has always been for me a kind of beloved mistress with whom I seemed unable to get on really comfortable terms. I regarded, and still regard, it as a great and challenging subject. I fought lone battles to get it accepted in Scotland and in Canada. Yet I was never happy with my accomplishment in that field. My own books in sociology did not give me anything like the degree of satisfaction I got from my books in political science, *The Modern State, The Web of Government,* and *Power Transformed.* The popular texts of the time I regarded as diffuse, lacking definition, sprawling over into genetics and anthropology and ethics, whereas I wanted to offer a systematic account of the structure of society.

I was generally out of line with the prevailing notions and doctrines of American sociology. In earlier years I carried on controversies with the leading exponents of these doctrines. Even before I left Canada I took a strong position, on a committee of the Social Science Research Council, against the fuss sociologists made over the proper methods of sociological study, against their attempt to sound like physical scientists, against the vogue of the cramping formulas they called "behaviorism" and "positivism." It was many years before I learned the futility of engaging in controversy with the champions of the current vogues. Vogues come and vogues pass. They all get decent burial without anyone's being able to do much to hasten their demise.

In presenting the tale of my troubles during these early Columbia years, I have been giving only one side of the picture. At Columbia I found good company and a new intellectual challenge. I made fewer close friends than I did in Toronto, but I had a larger number of stimulating and evocative acquaintances. The university was then at the height of its success under the headship of President Butler. It had distinguished departments in the arts, the sciences, and the humanities. Butler had been a strong administrator and a successful fund-raiser. In later years, however, he became much more engrossed in world affairs than in the business of the university, and a longish period began in which Columbia was in effect without leadership. In consequence it lost some ground and its rank as the recipient of contributions from alumni and other donors fell considerably.

The Graduate Faculty of Political Science, to which I was attached, had some very interesting features. The chairmen of its departments of History, Public Law and Government, and Economics, were all forthright and independent men, and there were at times acute differences between one and another of them. Nevertheless the faculty itself had a coherence I had not found in other institutions. One reason was that the affairs of the faculty as a whole were conducted mainly through a committee, the Committee on Instruction, composed of one representative elected for each department together with a fifth as chairman. All questions of promotion, new appointments, scholarship awards, and changes in faculty regulations came before it for approval or rejection. Members of different departments thus had frequent opportunities to meet and discuss their common and particular interests.

Moreover, in the last two hectic months of the spring session, when the daily roster contained one, two, or more oral doctoral examinations, representatives of the various departments were present at each of them and the decision whether or not to pass the candidate was argued out between them.

Some of these examinations for Ph.D. candidates were unhappy occasions. High standards were generally maintained, and the percentage of failures was considerable. It was a fateful two hours for the candidate, and one felt a pang of regret when some plodding but not too bright candidate was told that his labor had all been in vain. Sometimes, too, a bright student became so nervous over the ordeal that he was either tongue-tied, confused, or unresponsive, and his showing was so poor that the examiners could not feel justified in passing him. Such mishaps confirmed my opinion that oral examinations should not be the major or final determinant of scholarly capacity. There were other aspects of these occasions I found unpleasant. Some examiners, for example, bombarded the candidate with a rapid fire of purely factual questions, perhaps on a subject the examiner was himself studying. "Who was the postmaster-general under Coolidge?" "What were the principal works of Nicholas of Cusa?"—that sort of memory test, which a retentive semimoron might answer at least as well as an able scholar.

One of the examinations I witnessed was a comedy of frustrations: the subject, international law; the candidate, a youth with a tendency to stutter, which is always aggravated by the tension of an oral; the examiner, a rather deaf gentleman who kept asking highly involved questions regarding specific applications of the international "laws of war." The candidate would struggle long and painfully to deliver an answer, and when he was through the examiner, with his hand cupping an ear, would say, "I beg your pardon?'

My very first examination at Columbia, before I took over the department of sociology, was the most unhappy one I ever attended.

The candidate was an aggressive lady in her middle years, with marked psychopathic symptoms. She was up to "defend" her dissertation. In any properly run department, she would never have been allowed to proceed so far, incurring such needless cost and toil. At that time dissertations had to be presented in galley form, since Columbia refused to confer the Ph.D. degree unless the dissertation was printed. The practice was to refuse permission to proceed to the dissertation examination unless there was a strong possibility of a successful "defense." There was no such likelihood in this case. The lady had threatened dire results if she were balked, and the responsible member of the department had supinely taken the line of least resistance.

It was a pathetic occasion. The examiners were all assembled, but the candidate had not arrived. They waited some ten minutes, and in strode the lady. The chairman, mild-mannered Samuel McCune Lindsay, greeted her as she stood akimbo facing us all. "Won't you sit down, Miss X?" he said ingratiatingly, pointing to her assigned seat. "I will not sit down. You knew Monday was my worst day. You knew ten o'clock in the morning was my worst hour. I won't have it." "Now, Miss X, we must make the best of it. Perhaps if you walked about the campus for a little, you'll change your mind. We'll wait for you." She left the room, returned after five minutes, and took her seat.

But the examination was a fiasco. It should have been a foregone conclusion, since the work was badly organized and had little coherence. There were one or two members who advocated acceptance, subject to revision. It was, they argued, the way out of an impossible situation; the lady was never going to use the degree; rejection would lead to new troubles—a lawsuit, perhaps, and if not, some violent outbreak. But the majority were adamant, standards must be maintained no matter what the cost.

So when I took over the department in the fall of that year, I inherited Miss X, and many a time she thrust her way into my office and berated me, uttering dark threats. She wrote lengthy screeds to our president—which he never saw. But after two years more she disappeared.

This case was of course very exceptional, but I have dwelt on my experiences with doctoral examinations—giving only a sample of the many evidences I could offer—in order to give some substance to my claim that our whole system of testing the proficiency of doctoral candidates is antiquated, ill adapted, and vexatious.

15

Travel Time

Now that my dreams were no longer haunted by nightmare visions of economists endlessly rebutting one another, I could turn my thoughts to the troubles of my own department of sociology. To give full time to my graduate faculty responsibilities, I had given up my Barnard College position. I felt a bit sorry to say farewell to the congenial Barnard group. It was a tidy, smooth-running department. In addition to scoiology it had a good economic sector, with its very competent senior member, Elizabeth Baker, and an able young English economist, Arthur R. Burns, who came to us at the same time that his wife, Eveline, joined the graduate economics department at Columbia. Young women were less exciting to teach than young men—I am speaking purely in pedagogical terms. They seemed to have fewer academic worries than young men. If they came to consult you, it was more likely to be about personal matters than intellectual ones. My Columbia work was much more demanding. Besides, at its one hundred seventy-fifth anniversary celebration in 1929 I had been appointed to a newly named chair, Lieber Professor of Political Philosophy and Sociology, at the same time receiving an honorary degree.

I was trying hard to get good new sociologists for the department, and after some years obtained the first important accession, Robert Lynd, whose work, *Middletown,* in conjunction with his wife, Helen, had won wide acclaim. I hoped he would initiate a program on the sociology of the metropolis, but he turned his interest in other directions. I had already introduced the subject at Barnard with a study of Greenwich Village, which proved quite successful. It was under a good leader, and it gave valuable practical experience to a whole cohort of Barnard girls. On later occasions I made efforts to introduce the subject, but again the staff member whom I hoped would undertake it shifted to other areas of study. It was difficult enough to hold that department together without trying to impose on reluctant professors a program that failed to elicit their interest. Curiously enough, I was finally able to inaugurate a thoroughgoing program for the study of metropolitan affairs, but that was long after I had retired from Columbia.

In the late twenties and during the decade of the thirties, some of the ominous consequences of the First World War and the unhappy peace "settlement" came to light. One was the reversal of the forward march of democracy, spurred by movements toward a new kind of dictatorship, totally unlike the Roman type and much more "totalitarian" than the Latin-American variety. As a political scientist I was anxious to explore these movements at first hand and paid several visits to Italy and to Germany. My second visit to Italy I found particularly enlightening. In Rome I visited Senator Einaudi, who because of his high standing had not been molested by Mussolini, though he was anti-Fascist. He gave me much information on economic and social conditions and took me to visit the only remnant of parliamentary government that survived, a senate limited to a convenient range of administrative detail. It was a very dull session concerned with the planning of highways. In Milan, by a happy accident, I learned another side of the story. I had an introduction to the head of the Università Bocconi, Signor Fraza, who was most considerate, explained the work of the institution, and loaded me with its publications. So far I managed to get along with my bad Italian. Then he turned and asked me to tell him about my own work. Whereupon I became tongue-tied, vainly groping for the right words. Seeing my plight, he pushed a button and asked that a professor of English come to act as intermediary. A pleasant-faced, tubby little man appeared and enabled me to carry on. When at length the president asked to be excused, he added, "My colleague here will take you out to afternoon tea." "I have a class at this hour, Mr. President," said the professor of English. "Dismiss your class," said the president as we parted. The English professor—I've forgotten his name—asked me if I would like to see him dismiss the class. It seemed a curious remark, but I went along with him through various corridors until we reached the classroom door. He made an about-turn, clicked his heels, and shouted down the corridor, "Avanti!" Then he went to the far end of the room, diagonally across from the entrance. Each student, as he entered, stood at attention, threw his head up, gave the Fascist salute, which the professor punctiliously returned, and took his place. When the thirty-odd students had gone through the ritual, the professor cursorily announced the class would not be held. Thereupon, as they filed to the exit, the salutation process was repeated, beginning with an about-turn. I calculated it took ten or eleven minutes to dismiss the class, Fascist style.

We went to a pleasant tea house, where my companion cheerfully chatted, telling me among other things that he had learned his English when the members of a touring operatic troupe to which he belonged were stranded in Australia for lack of funds and had to work there on odd jobs for a good part of a year before they were able to return to Italy. I did notice his English had a touch of Cockney. As we said good-bye, he wanted to know if I was engaged that evening. Being free, I arranged to meet him—he said he would "show me the town." The expression meant for him a round of visits to a variety of dives, where there was weird erotic dancing or folksy singing or minstrels with strange instruments and outlandish costume. As we entered each dim hole-in-the-wall, my conductor would say, "Have you ever tried such-and-such a drink?" mentioning names wholly unknown to me. I went on the principle that I was willing to try any drink once. The process was repeated until we arrived at the fourth dive. Evidently the libations had loosened my partner's tongue, for he suddenly said: "What did you think of the way I dismissed the class?" "I never saw anything like that before," I

answered noncommittally. "I hate the goddam thing!" he burst out."
"If it weren't I have a wife and two kids I'd leave the goddam
country." We stayed there until late into the night, while he told
in unsparing detail how the majority of the staff were anti-Fascist
but dominated by a Fascist minority and afraid to speak, lest one
of Mussolini's sycophants reported it, and how tense the situation
was for both professors and students. Some months after I returned
home, I learned that the president had been dismissed.

I shall mention only one other item from my study travels. I was
in Munich a little before the Reichstag elections in 1930, the first
at which the Nazis made considerable gains. The economic situation
was deteriorating, partly because of the adverse policies of the allies,
not least, those of the United States. There were disturbances, angry
shouting and violent interruption while candidates were speaking,
but I observed that a seeming majority of the people still thought
of Hitler as a mountebank whose party had no chance of gaining
control. What at that time I feared more was an outbreak of civil
war, because of the fierce clashes (though not so much in Munich)
between Communists and Nazis. Sometime thereafter I wrote, for
The Office of War Information, a critical commentary on *Mein
Kampf*.

The big finale of this period of foreign travel came with my first
sabbatical, in 1935. We had looked forward to it with eager expectation. My work on *Economic Reconstruction* had been published.
I had no other engrossment, no serious work on hand, to interfere
with a whole spring and summer of European experience. For the
first time, I would be taking the family along for an extensive tour
abroad. My wife and I were leaving early in February to wander
through various countries at leisure. The twins were to join us for
the summer, most of which we arranged to spend in a villa we had
rented at Étretat for the season. For the first time we could afford to
indulge ourselves without counting the pennies. We had a happy
time planning what we would see and where we would stay, studying maps for itineraries and reading up on places of interest. I had
a new car for the occasion. But the actuality proved sadly different
from the prospect.

My wife and I set out on an Italian liner, and our series of misfortunes began during the passage. After being out for a few days, I developed an eye trouble I had suffered for the first time a year or two before, just when I had arrived at our summer cottage in Canada after the winter session. The eyeball became inflamed and a little painful, and I could not endure any light. I used a makeshift bandage and moped for the rest of the voyage. We disembarked at Palermo, where no eye specialist seemed available and spent two miserable weeks in our hotel until the trouble subsided. We then set out in our car around the coast on our way to Messina. We stopped at the usual places of interest, looking at Greek temples and Roman remains. Leaving Agrigento, where we passed the night, we were nearing the town of Gela when a cyclist suddenly swerved right in front of the car. He fell off his bicycle, landing on his head. We carried him stretched out on the back seat to the hospital at Gela and informed the police, who let us at length proceed on our way. We went on to Syracuse, where we spent a few days. An official emissary came to see us, informed us the injury had been mortal. He was very particular about the kind of insurance I carried. Fortunately it was adequate, and he let us go. I did not have any trust in the local officialdom. They accused me of driving at an excessively high speed, when I had actually been driving very slowly, not above twenty-five miles an hour, since my new car had run less than two hundred miles and I was following instructions not to exceed twenty-five for the first five hundred miles. From Syracuse we drove to Taormina, where we stayed more than a week, took the ferry to Reggio, and had an interesting time meandering through Calabria, with its marvellous scenery and incredibly bad hotels. We had no further troubles during our Italian tour, crossed the border into the French Riviera, and stopped at Èze-les-Roses, where we were entertained by American friends who had a lovely estate there.

Then came the third stroke of misfortune, one that darkened all the rest of our sabbatical. With our friends we climbed a hill at Èze, and on the descent Ethel complained her knee was hurting. It swelled somewhat but did not become particularly troublesome as we traveled through Provence, up the Rhône Valley to Lyons and then northwest, visiting among other places Chartres and Versailles, avoiding Paris and passing through Rouen, till finally we reached our destination in Étretat. Now the knee became more and more swollen. We had a doctor who seemed to think it not very serious and came regularly with his bedside manner and his *piqûres*. Alas, the *piqûres* were of no avail. Doctors did not appear to understand the trouble.

Presently Ethel became quite crippled, rarely leaving the house. It was small consolation that we had a beautiful villa belonging to an artist, with a great studio, several steps below the rest of the house, where massive paintings adorned the walls. Our one special problem at first was that we couldn't find the bathroom, although it was mentioned in the deed. After some days of exploration we discovered it. It was entirely hidden by a picture about seven feet high. Only when you turned the picture round was the door disclosed. Behind the door was a large gaunt room with a bath on one side, an array of six taps, and a coil that had to be lit to heat the water. I struggled with the system in vain—the hot water came in slow drops so that before you had three or four inches of water the bottom layers were already cold. We gave up the unequal struggle and resorted to a five-franc bath in the village bathhouse.

In due course the twins arrived to cheer us up. They enjoyed the beach and the cliffs, did the marketing, and learned a bit of French in the process. We took occasional rides to countryside places, where the inn always provided good fare before we returned home. It would have been very enticing but for the shadow over it all.

Of those days in Étretat a characteristic memory takes me walking moodily and alone from the gates of our villa, downhill to the village clustered between the opposing cliffs, while an afternoon breeze brings the freshening sound and smell of the sea. I walk over cobbled stones to the edge of a dock where two or three fishermen are standing. I hear one say, *la mer monte,* as he scans the darkening horizon. I cross over to the beach, where children are noisily playing, nurses shouting to their charges to get out of the water. An inertia possesses me. I drift into the casino; a group is standing round the boule tables, and I waste a dollar or two playing that rather feeble game where the odds are heavily against the players.

Ethel's trouble remained stationary, and she was resting comfortably enough. She was very patient and remained remarkably cheerful. Our French maid looked after things—more or less—and the children were helpful. I took ten days off, with a brief uninformative stopover in Berlin, to visit a distinguished Polish sociologist, Florian Znaniecki, the author with W. I. Thomas of one of the few sociological classics of our time, *The Polish Peasant*. He was a good friend, and my visit was full of interesting meetings and discussions. At the beginning he begged me to sit for my portrait by a reputed painter, explaining that in the impoverished condition of Poland the artists were in effect starving. I couldn't resist the appeal. The artist's method was to limit each sitting to an hour and a half each morning, and I had always to be engaged in conversation with someone. When after six sittings I had to leave, the portrait was complete except for the hands. I resisted appeals to remain another day, took the rolled-up canvas and said good-bye.

The train from Warsaw to Berlin was very late, and as I was waiting at the station, my long-time Columbia colleague, Theodore Abel, himself Polish, having just arrived in Poznan, came to the station hoping to greet me. As we were chatting he wanted to see the kind of visa they had given me, purely from curiosity. When I showed him my passport, he said, "Where is the red strip?" It appeared that under the new regime every visitor to Poland had to exhibit his passport for an authoritative check and if there was nothing against the visitor a red slip was affixed to it. There was a heavy fine for every day after the first for the omission of this requirement. It was impossible to leave the country without it. Had I been staying at a hotel the matter would have been attended to at the office, but my good professor had completely forgotten about it. So I carried my baggage back, and my host was greatly agitated. Fortunately he was a man of high standing and good family, but he had to go right up to the mayor of Poznan before I got clearance. The next morning, before I took the train, we had the artist come and paint in the hands. It is a distinctive portrait. In a letter I received on my return from my host, Znaniecki, he informed me the painter,

Mannytkiewicz, had remarked that he found my face "uncommonly interesting but correspondingly difficult to paint."

As a sequel to this story, I should tell how I invited Florian to spend the summer of 1939 with us as a lecturer at our Columbia summer session. He did so, but I became concerned about him during the course of the summer. He lacked his usual vigor. In late July the war cloud over Europe was growing darker. Nothing seemed to stop the fanatical Hitler. I pleaded with Florian not to return to Poland. He was the gentlest of spirits, but he was obdurate. He had promised the Polish government, he said, that if war broke out he would write a sociological study of the Polish resistance. I could not convince him how futile, how tragi-comic even, his expectations were. After the summer session was over, he spent two weeks with us at our Lake Muskoka cottage. He was now quite ill and passed the whole day in a hammock, looking like the ghost of himself. I found a good professorial position for him at a midwestern university, but he was determined to leave on a Polish liner near the end of August.

He never reached Poland. A British submarine intercepted the liner and took it to Inverness. Florian was taken down to Leeds and put in a hospital, where the good British medical service found the cause of his trouble and brought him back to health. I was able to unearth a temporary lectureship for him at Columbia, so that he could get immediate readmission, and thereafter he had a happy career at the University of Illinois. His wife was American and was able to join him from Poland after the war.

We cut a little short our time at Étretat, since I was anxious to get Ethel the services of a London specialist on arthritis, if that indeed was the ailment. He took a very serious view of the case and recommended as the best hope the treatment offered at a sanitarium in Derbyshire. We left her there, and I went with the others to Scotland to visit some relatives. This treatment, however, brought no improvement either, and the medical authorities shook their heads over the likelihood of a cure. So at length our wretched sabbatical came to an end. Arriving in New York, we left Ethel at St. Luke's Hospital, where we found the first note of encouragement in the more cheerful attitude of the doctor. But it still seemed a kind of miracle when within a few weeks, and not because of any special treatment but thanks to what in the old days was called in Latin "the remedial power of nature," the whole trouble disappeared—and never returned. So our bleak sabbatical ended on a happy note.

I find nothing more zestful than returning to work I love after a protracted interval. The hunger of ingrained habits enhances the call of new activities. It was good to have again the challenge of superior students, and the itch to write became urgent. In retrospect, that sabbatical seemed a waste and I had to redeem the time. A period of high activity lay ahead. I would not, I resolved, be tempted to use any part of the long, free professorial summer for travel.

Always, indeed, I have felt myself between the counter pulls of habit and novelty, the persistent desire to follow through and advance the work I have on hand and the urge for new experience, especially through travel. The latter has been like one of those organic wants that are stilled by being gratified but after a while begin to prick again. There is truth in what Horace said: "It is their sky they change and not their mind when people hasten across the sea." Scenery can stimulate for a few days, but you soon take it for granted. You may meet interesting people, but you are as likely to meet them if you stay at home—in the great center where I live, rather more likely. I had little inclination to visit my old home after my mother died—too young. I particularly enjoyed visits to London, the most courteous and accommodating of cities, where no one tried to cheat you, where it was so easy to get theatre tickets, and where I had access to a good club. I spent part of a summer at the school for international studies in Geneva directed by Alfred Zimmern, the distinguished author of *The Greek Commonwealth,* whom I met while living in Canada. I went twice to Vienna where I spent a delightful time, having an introduction to its literary circle through my membership in the Canadian P.E.N. club. Once I visited Budapest at a time when an abortive revolution was taking place. But always on my return I realized how superficial such passing contacts are and how little the transient outsider can feel the pulse of life that beats beneath the commonplace of casual acquaintance.

As a coda to these travel episodes I return to the first of our sabbatical troubles. The eye infection I developed on shipboard recurred for the third time two winters later. I was then in New York and at last able to consult an oculist of high standing. He said it was due to an infection and sent me to the Opthalmic Institute for a series of tests. When my period at the hospital ended, he announced that all the tests were negative. No trace of infection could be found. And I had no history of any previous ailments. He concluded that the epithelial tissue of the eye needed the winter sunlight my mode of life failed to supply and made me solemnly promise I would spend two weeks in some warm, sunny clime in the course of the winter. The prescription was more pleasant than most, and I observed it rather faithfully, taking advantage of the intersemester period and making acquaintance with many delectable Caribbean resorts. Certainly, the trouble did not occur again for nearly two decades, and then only once, after an unusually arduous period in which I had delayed taking my winter break.

16

Reflections en Route

I was now in my fifties—to my surprise I had joined the category of the middle-aged. If the designation referred only to the calendar of years it could not be gainsaid, but "middle-aged" carries the connotation of staidness, suggests one who has found his level and is set in his ways—a suggestion I vigorously rejected. I had no feeling that youthfulness and the joys of youth belonged to the past, nor did I act as though they had. I did not worry about growing older. It was only in my early youth that this thought weighed on me. I remember when I was fourteen feeling sorry for the sixteener. Occasionally a birthday would bring a pang at the thought I would never be, say, thirty or, say, under forty, again. The inexorable irremediability of the continuous flow of time for mortals, of the sand sinking with insistent monotony of motion in the glass, would evoke a mood of quiet brooding. What happened this day, this hour, would never happen that way again, was forever fixed—what happened to me, or in that far country where men were shooting their fellowmen, or anywhere up to the most distant galaxy, all that was on the record, passing and forever past. But this mood would be short-lived, itself on the record, while I busied myself with the call of every new day. One trouble I never suffered from was boredom.

I am reminded here of another disturbing youthful thought that did not survive my teens. It was the fear of what might happen

after death, the horrendous everlasting torment that lay await for
the unbeliever or the impious. Indoctrinated as I was, I wondered
sometimes how even the professing Christian could think of it with
so much complacency. Before I could read, I was taught a bedtime
prayer that ran somewhat as follows:

> Now I lay me down to sleep,
> I pray the Lord my soul to keep,
> If I should die before I wake,
> I pray the Lord my soul to take.

Only after a long and agonizing struggle had I liberated myself
altogether from the influence of these ancient myths, bred of the
union of Eastern mysticism and the ranker Calvinist superstition.

I am not a churchgoer. I can, even though I now rarely do, enjoy
the sonorous grandeur of the great organ, the atmosphere of solemnity and peace that pervades a noble church, the devotional call of
the chorales, but then the voice of the preacher breaks the spell,
when in the name of the holy truth he tediously embroiders some
outmoded myth. I maintain good relations with some religious
groups who are concerned with the values by which men live.
Human beings cannot live without values and aspirations. Religion
has been all through history the main embodiment and the buttress
of human values. But it has been imprisoned in ecclesiasticism and
skewed by being used as an instrument of domination. It has too
rarely been "pure and undefiled." It has too rarely lived in the
hearts of men. It is always in need of renewal, and the sanctification
of its forms has prevented it from being responsive to new insights,
from relating its enduring values to the new and always growing
knowledge we possess concerning the nature of things. The cosmos
we live in is inconceivably more magnificent than the groping narrow conceptions of it that are perpetuated in ancient lores. We
need a new formulation of religion that abolishes the notion of a
heaven up above us, that can contemplate a universe stretching
into infinite space and containing coutless billions of suns ranged in
their vast galaxies. Whatever thoughts we entertain of Godhead
must be accommodated, in whatever degree we can achieve it, to
this stupendous reality. Religion always needs renewal. It will be

the unfinished work of devout minds, through the ages to come. In my little book, *The Pursuit of Happiness,* I have expressed some of my thoughts on this subject.

What I mean by the prison of ecclesiasticism is illustrated by the present controversy over birth control. I am not inclined to argue over theological doctrines as such but only against the reactionary social attitudes that are frequently derived from them. The Roman Catholic church has been rigorously opposed to contraception, with the exception of the "rhythm method." Other religious sects have taken a similar line. The controversy is therefore one of method. I cannot see how it has much relation to religion or any but the most dubious relation to Christian teaching. Nor is the argument against contraception based on the social consequences, except in a most biased way that does not face the grave danger of excessive populations condemned to live in abject, reliefless penury with all its perils alike to the people themselves and to the peace of the world. Instead, the appeal is to the interpretation of ancient dicta and the tradition of the church.

I am an agnostic, which is very different from being an atheist. If you think about it you will realize that most believers are agnostics, without being conscious of it. They have no conception of the God they worship. They cannot have. The name of God conveys only the dim sense of the effulgence of almighty power. St. Paul spoke of the Athenians who had erected an altar To THE UNKNOWN GOD, declaring he would reveal the true God to them. The ignorance he thought he could dispel remains, but the modern attitude no longer invests the name with the anthropomorphic attributes of ancient beliefs.

To sense the mysterious throb of the universe, to contemplate its wonder and its terror and its beauty and its majesty, to realize its supreme unboundedness, such that the most infinitesimal particle that exists as such for the millionth of a millionth of a second still far exceeds the infinitely small in the space-time scale, such that the furthest reach of man's telescope to the edge of galaxies moving from us at nearly the speed of light still cannot approach the infinitely beyond—this is to participate in the spirit of religion. Everything is immeasurably more complex than our finest imagining. The human body is a marvel of adaptations that we are only beginning to comprehend, and all our doctrines of evolution tell us only the stages of its development, not how it came to possess its intricate quality of being. Even the tiniest germ that floats in the air has a structure that no human artificer can emulate. Man is not at the center of the universe but crawls on the surface of the minor planet of a minor star, and there must be millions of other planets on which life has evolved, perhaps to much higher levels than the brash, young, fumbling race of man has attained. The human being and the human earth are insignificant in the scale of creation, but man possesses a power, a gift, that puts him in a category above all the immensity of millions of galaxies, the gift to perceive and to explore, the power to think, in an increasing measure to direct and to control. Man is the knower. Herein is the ground for his faith, for his aspiration, and for his humility in the contemplation of the cosmos. What he knows is but a spot on the surface of the vast unknown. What he knows is also a revelation of the wonder of it all. Herein is the ground for religion.

Man lives in the presence of immortal power. All he achieves comes from the harnessing of a mite of the power that sustains the universe. He lives in the presence of inexorable law, of an order that keeps the stars in their courses, the atoms in their eternal whirl, his own body in the ceaseless process from life to death while it prodigally generates his kind through countless generations. And there are also more intimate revelations in the creations of his own mind, the messages that are hauntingly adumbrated in great music, in poetry and myth, in all the expressions of our cultural heritage. They suggest the further heights and the profounder deeps of being that are experienced and communicated in the radiance of mind alone. Science discovers the external forms and forces of the cosmos, but art explores another dimension altogether.

Science—or perhaps we should say, the scientist—is sometimes regarded as hostile to religion, and certainly the churches have been very slow to bring their theology into accord with scientific knowledge. Once you tamper with the sacred canon, you are opening the gates to questionings and doubts. You have to interpret many statements in the sacred writ as symbolical or metaphorical, not as literally true. But symbols and metaphors are susceptible to different interpretations, and we have lost the firmament of revealed truth that theology asserts and craves. There are theologians who break away from the establishment, and there are scientists who devoutly accept some form of theology, but they are exceptions to the prevailing tendency in either camp. Scientists are typically eternal questioners of all doctrines, including their own.

In a genuinely intelligent society, science and religion would no longer be aloof or alien, since its God would no longer be anthropomorphic or prescribe precise ordinances for mortals. There would be not only a new orientation to religion but also the development of a relevant function science performs. For science is not only the explorer of the nature of things but also its interpreter. Science is more than a measurer, discovering the dimensions, the distances, the directions, the velocities, the rates, the proportions, the processes of things—it is also the synthesizer, the formulator of embracing laws and great principles that are a revelation of the majestic order and level-abidingness of the cosmos. It reaches out to new inclusive principles, relativity, parity, the bonds that bind atoms or galaxies, the relations of waves and particles in the outflow of energies. The objective of all science is the discovery not of the size and scale of things but of the relations and interrelations that can be inferred, deduced, or hypothesized from such measurements. The vision thus attainable and the conception of the infinite power that holds atoms and galaxies and everything between in their appointed ways are the preconditions of any religion worthy of modern man.

Measurement is never the end or the goal of science, but only a way of approach to it. I have been accused of being "anti-quantitative," which means that I have depreciated statistical studies. I do not plead guilty to that charge. Statistics are essential for the assessment of every form of change, for the evaluation of all differentials, in a world full of diversity and subject to incessant movement. We could get nowhere without them. Most research of any kind and practically all social research require the amassment and application of statistics. My first public address of any significance was based on an analysis of statistics in the reports of the British census and of the registrar general on the differential birthrates of the various professions and grades of workers in Britain. It was delivered at a meeting of the British Association for the Advancement of Science in Toronto while I was teaching there. But I have sharply attacked those sociologists who thought their task was done when they had offered us figures and eschewed conclusions as being "subjective" and therefore unscientific—who told us, for example, the percentages of Roman Catholics who voted for the Republican party in an election, or, say, of Methodists, and stopped there. The really interesting part of an investigation often begins where the statistics end. I found that my own graduate students were lamentably deficient, from lack of training, in the ability to draw inferences, deductions, and meaningful hypotheses from statistical tables. I have tested a class of graduates numbering over a hundred, by presenting them with, for example, a set of tables giving the respective rates of illegitimacy for first-generation immigrants, second-generation immigrants, and longer-established Americans, according to residence in the South, North, East, Middle West, and Pacific States, and in large cities, middle-sized cities, and rural areas. The respective rates varied very considerably. Some explanatory hypotheses were rather obvious and some deductions could readily be drawn, but these students for the most part failed to reach them.

Social scientists are presumably students of society, but society itself is a subjective reality, not something you can measure with a tape. Society is belongingness, community, interdependence, intragroup and intergroup relations, schisms, combinations, dominances. Where there is a group, there is a purpose, and where there is a society, there is an invisible unity. The individual, the unit, is an individual only because society creates and shapes and informs his unit being. Society is a dynamic of invisible forces, urgings and needs and passions and values, swaying in the tides of change.

Subject to the milling of these uniting and dividing forces, society is endlessly changeful. A single generation, even a few years of crisis, can transform the social landscape in nearly all its aspects, political, economic, demographic, attitudinal, cultural. Even while you study it, the phase you are studying is passing. Each generation is a different "mix" of hereditary characters and exposed to different situations and different problems from those of their fathers.

The fact that human beings belong together in groups, classes, nations, and brotherhoods of all kinds means more than that they feel alike, believe alike, and think alike in many respects. They have, as unities, a *common* feeling evoked by their togetherness. They are social animals. Every group has its particular ethos, its characteristic way of looking at things and responding to them. Every nation has its particular modes of expression. Community, not likeness, is the primary social fact, but it is a fact that does not exist in the purely physical world. You cannot see or touch or photograph a community. All the essential features of a society are of this kind. An institution is not an edifice. It exists only because men recognize its existence. A state does not stand in outer nature: it is not a country but a system of government within a country. It makes laws that the majority of the people obey. They obey because they accept its authority. If its people rejected its authority, it would no longer exist. In other words, it exists only in the acceptance of its reality by those who make it real. States are made in the minds of men. The pseudorealists who deal only with hard "objective" facts confuse themselves and their followers when they profess to be studying society.

Community has always been the central theme of my work, and thus the title of my first book (*Community*) was prophetic of a life interest. I have been particularly concerned to emphasize the distinction between the state and the community, as the necessary basis for any theory of democracy. I have been consistently a believer in democracy and continued to be so after I came in closer contact with its many defects. Democracy is a very aggravating arrangement. The majority of the electorate are inert, ignorant of the issues, moved by petty personal likes or dislikes or by mean calculations of private advantage, responsive to the crude appeals of the demagogue and the exploiter, preferring the cheap politicians to the able statesmen, lavishing their votes on the local boss who doles out a few crumbs from his spoils. But what is the alternative? Aristocracy? But what elite has ever chosen the best to rule? Benevolent dictatorship? But only the power-hungry can trample down opposition, and for other ends than benevolence.

Good government, it has been said many times, is the choice of the second best. Democracy is the second best, as near as you can get it. For democracy is never what it claims to be. The equal right to vote is negated by poverty and dependence and ignorance. There are insiders who pick the candidates you can vote for and there are people of wealth and position and prestige who control the press and the purse strings and bring their influence to bear on the elections when they do not actually corrupt voters or manipulate the returns. Democracy is the most messy form of government.

Why then do I call it the second best, the best available in the multitudinous complexity of our society? Because it is the only expedient we have to limit the rank abuse of power by rulers and by the men of property and position who always support a ruling class. Democracy arose through the revolt of the oppressed, the poorer classes, the powerless classes, composed of the yeomen, the servants, the agricultural laborers, the serfs, and the slaves of the power-holders. They manned the armies with which the powerful controlled the people and fought their endless wars of spoliation and annexation. They were kept ignorant, illiterate, propertyless, most of them living on the verge of destitution.

Uncontrolled political power is the curse of society. Uncontrolled power becomes insolent, ruthless, contemptuous of humanity. It is always greedy for more, no matter what the cost to the exploited. To increase its strength it makes the weak weaker. To increase its possessions it makes others poor and makes the poor poorer. To increase its luxuries it deprives others of necessities. It degrades those it uses, destroying their self-respect. It robs them of the primary freedom, the freedom to think one's own thoughts and to express one's own opinions. Nothing is sacred to uncontrolled power —it has perverted religion and turned it into a subservient ally. And it has made the whole earth the graveyard of the fallen in its wars.

The day must come when men will no more be forced to fight bloody wars at the will of their masters.

The virtue of democracy is that it has placed limits on the absoluteness of power. The value of this service to mankind is beyond estimation. It has made citizens out of subjects, free men out of bondmen. It has opened doors of opportunity to those who were formerly condemned before their birth to live lives of abject poverty. It has spread the benefits of education to include all the people. It has given the common man a degree of dignity previously denied him. He has a voice and a potential share in the widened distribution of power. It has created the great community where before there was only the class society. However imperfectly democracy has rendered these signal services, it took long and bitter struggles to achieve this much, and the promise of the future depends alike on the expansion to new areas of democratic liberties and the advancement beyond what has been thus far attained. The thrust of power is unceasing, no matter where the power lies, no matter what class dominates, but the counter demand for liberty lives on and its partial possession gives men some impetus for future goals.

Mid-Career

The years that followed my ill-starred sabbatical were not particularly eventful or productive, nor was I disturbed by the sense of the unattained, the falling short of the mark, with the concomitant urge toward creative activity, that at other times would not let me alone. I had become established as of some account in the profession. I seemed to be moving more or less contentedly on a kind of plateau. I had received my second honorary degree, and the one I held in the higher esteem, when I was included in the roster of scholars, drawn from countries across the world, who were recipients of this recognition during the tercentenary celebrations of Harvard University in 1936. The final ceremonies were on the grand scale, with notables headed by the President of the United States in attendance, with week-end parties, a concert by the Boston Symphony Orchestra, and various other events. A series of special lectures was included, one of which I was privileged to give.

I had much enjoyment from my teaching, having classes of considerable size, both in political science and in sociology. I took special delight in a course entitled "Modern Ideas of the State," not least in the give-and-take of argument with keen students, including a small coterie of Marxists who always lay in wait for an occasion to convict me of error. In later years the Marxists became almost mute, being afraid of the consequences to their careers in the hostile climate of opinion. It was a pity, not merely because it took a bit of relish out of that class, but because the subversion-hunters took a stupid, ineffectual way to achieve their end. I could have told them how two of my students who had been active participants in the communist infiltration had asked me for guidance in preparing for new careers, since they had come to reject their communist affiliation as a result of class discussions—but these F.B.I.-minded patriots would in their simplicity have labelled me a "pinko" for my pains, as indeed some of their kidney did.

I was still far from happy over our sociology department. It was certainly better than when I took it over, but it was understaffed, without coherence, respectable enough on the social-theory side but somewhat ragged in its coverage of other important areas. The only senior sociologist I had been able to acquire for the department was Robert Lynd, and his interest had switched from the subject in which he had won distinction, the study of the small and the medium-sized city, to courses on the consumer and on the distribution of power in society. This is not a criticism of his preferences, but I had hoped that he would develop the sociological study of the metropolis. I felt that the major fields of sociological interest were still largely uncultivated by us, and I was unable, with the tight budgets of those years, to obtain additional staff members.

This was the period in which, more than ever before or after, I let myself be enlisted in those sideline activities that, unless kept to a modicum, divert faculty members from the concentration of effort that alone can yield work of scholarly significance. I wrote reviews for learned journals, gave occasional public addresses, served on a plethora of committees, and took a fairly active part in various "learned societies" and other organizations that appeal to the social scientist. I was a member of the American Sociological Society (A.S.S., later to become A.S.A.), of a political science organization, of the Social Science Research Council, and thereafter of the American Council of Learned Societies. I was elected to membership in the American Academy of Arts and Sciences and later in the most distinguished of our learned societites, the American Philosophical Society, which went back to Benjamin Franklin. I became a member of the boards of the American Civil Liberties Union, the most demanding committee on which I ever served, the Russell Sage Foundation, with which I had kept in touch since conducting an investigation of its organization many years before, the New York School of Social Work, and the New School for Social Research. The last-mentioned institution was presided over by Alvin Johnson, a very remarkable gentleman with whom I had most happy relations. Alvin was at once a brooding scholar learned in classical lore, a countryman who enjoyed the feel and the folksiness of the farm, a free-souled adventurer for causes dear to him, a felicitous phrase-maker, warm-hearted and a bit wayward. We had many interests in common, and after he valorously established the "University in Exile" in 1934, to rescue distinguished professors from European dictatorships, mostly from Hitler's Germany, depending entirely on his own persuasive power to meet the costs, my connection with the New School became closer. Alvin would from time to time send me one of his characteristically generous tributes. I permit myself to quote from one of them, however little I may have deserved it. It was when he was urging me to undertake a mission intended to raise the standard of the teaching of civics in the public schools.

The last person in this world I'd really want to load excessive labor on is Robert MacIver. For yours is the purest voice of true liberalism in America.

I read your last book [*The More Perfect Union*]. I felt that if MacIver had never done anything else in life but write this book his place in the Heaven of the intellectual and moral elite would be sufficiently established.

Little did I dream that at the end of my career I would be occupying the place he then so notably filled.

I attended the annual conventions of one, sometimes of two, associations. These conferences are usually a three- or four-day affair, held at some hotel, where members of the society flock from all over the country. Papers are read all day long, in a great spread of sectional meetings, usually by aspiring younger scholars who are out for recognition and an article in their particular journal. The conference serves as a mart where those still on the lower academic levels are the sellers and the older professors and heads of departments are the potential buyers. Most of the members stay away from the rooms where papers are being read and instead chat with acquaintances and get introductions in the corridors or make their way to the lounges and bars. Very few attend in order to learn more about their respective subjects.

As I look back on this period I wonder how I could have been so ready to crowd the days with such an assortment of affairs. I did not neglect my students. I spent a considerable amount of time discussing their essays and dissertations. I particularly enjoyed a Sunday evening symposium held at our apartment on Riverside Drive to which I invited a group of advanced students and department members. I arranged for someone, not infrequently a visiting professor, a behaviorist or positivist or, say, a classical authoritarian such as Mortimer Adler, to introduce a controversial subject. And then the discussion would become fast and furious, and at times rather heated, into the midnight hours.

There were good friends who took agreeable toll on my time. There were evening get-togethers with colleagues, where we talked about the state of the world. After lunch at the Faculty Club I would often spend an hour or two over the chessboard. I went to an occasional concert or movie, party, or dance. But it became an uneasy time, with the ominous shadow that darkened over Europe creating a sense of the futility of serious endeavor. That at least was the way it took me. I had developed a total hatred of war.

The variety of vocational and avocational activities that filled these days is not untypical of one way of being a professor. Although I found it agreeable enough at the time, I was conscious something was lacking. I was not giving what I conceived to be my best. I was not fully utilizing the opportunities a university position offers. I had no feeling of achievement. Now and then the impulse to ponder over significant questions, to write something that might be a contribution, would catch me, but it did not bite deep. I wrote an article or two and began to plan a study of social causation. But it was only in the fateful year 1939 that I produced anything that pleased me. It was a little book entitled *Leviathan and the People*, a study of the implications of Marxism. It was the result of a few lectures I gave at the University of Louisiana, and I allowed it to be published by the press of that university. Perhaps it wasn't their kind of book.

In that same year of doom I was facing new problems, so petty in perspective, in that troublesome department of sociology. There were times when I wished I had accepted an overture to abandon it and become a full-time member of the Department of Public Law and Government, which was well organized and had a very competent staff. On this occasion the trouble was a sharp cleavage within the department. I had been its chairman for more than a decade, and now there was an active revolt. The leader of the opposition was my major colleague, Robert Lynd. From the beginning we had differences of viewpoint on the focus of sociology and on the function of university instruction. He wanted to professionalize the teaching, to make it primarily utilitarian, preparing students for professional service. I laid stress on the significance of sociology for the understanding of society and the development of a coherent science of society, claiming that our students were provided—and would be more so if we had an adequate staff—with a broad training that would enable them to play their parts in responsible positions. I had always welcomed difference of viewpoint within the department and was aware of Professor Lynd's position before inviting him to join us.

The division was fostered by our junior statistical associates, who claimed that their contribution was not given due weight. One of them was disgruntled because he had not been promoted—I had tried him out and he had shown no capacity whatever for teaching. What brought the issue to a head was a rather injudicious action of my own. Professor Lynd had published a book entitled *Knowledge for What,* in which he emphasized the utilitarian conception of education. I was invited to write a review of it—and did so, trenchantly enough. This was the breaking point.

It was unwise to write a highly critical review of a book by a colleague. Several times in my university career I have run into trouble by writing critiques. Without ever wanting to be offensive, I have unhappily succeeded in being so. The first time, as I have already recounted, was when I lost my first job at Aberdeen through offending a gentleman whose connection with the book I was reviewing had never entered my mind. Again, I seriously offended a scholar for whom I had high regard, Pitirim Sorokin, by a review of a rather apocalyptic work of his. Happily he has forgiven me since the days when I penned my too inconsiderate review.

The department was in a state of tension. Each side put forward statements expressing its ideas of what the future of the department should be. Professor Lynd issued a lengthy memorandum on the subject, and I wrote one of similar dimensions. I had on my side, besides the aid of my earliest colleague, Theodore Abel, the support of my sociological colleagues in the other sectors of the university, who were at the same time teaching members in our department. One was Pete Waller of Barnard, a fine, sensitive, if somewhat troubled, spirit whose promise was cut off by an untimely death. Another was William Casey of Columbia College, a man of extraordinary originality, who taught with great éclat but had a curious inhibition against writing, now a retired colleague whom I cherish as a friend. The third was Edmund Brunner of Teacher's College, a quietly thoughtful sociologist who did his best to play a mediating role. But the division was too sharp to be mitigated, and it remained a very unsatisfactory situation for several years.

A happier note will end this page of my story. The year 1939 was our last in the great city. Ethel yearned for a home of her own in the country. I was willing, but to find a countryside location that did not require long commuting was a problem. My colleague Theodore Abel and I had been scouting for around a year for so desirable a spot, and we had found the answer across the Hudson, about thirteen miles north of the George Washington Bridge. It was on a heavily wooded plateau beyond the river palisades. The snag was that the lot in question was a parcel of twenty-six acres and had to be purchased as a whole. It was much larger than we could contemplate, but we took the chance of finding four friends with whom we could divide it and plunged into the purchase with the aid of a mortgage. The plan worked out. The two of us had a common architect and built modern houses of British Columbia redwood that fitted into the landscape. On an old map we found a name for our address, Heyhoe Woods, a Dutch name in a region originally settled by Dutchmen from New Amsterdam.

The change made a considerable difference in the feel of living, and the distance from the city at that period was not a serious drawback. I could drive to the city and park my car within thirty-five minutes of leaving my new home. Only in icy or snowy weather did I find any disadvantage in the change, and that didn't count against the amenities of our location. We had our own earth, our own little circle, and we lived in a pleasant neighborhood. I was near to the soil and could watch the coming of the snowdrops and the opening of the winter-long buds of the dogwoods and see them again when the leaves turned russet and pinky-red and darkened for the fall. The seasons took on new meaning. The air was purer, and the noise of the klaxons and rattling trucks was heard no more. In my secluded study I could ponder and write in peace. In a moment I could be in the woods, among the tall tulip trees, the sweet gums, the maples, the oaks, and the beech trees, and many a bush and tree besides. I could go hunting for the wild mushrooms until the frost came, and every year there were surprises and often new trophies for the larder. In the good seasons there would be months on end when the kitchen had an almost continuous supply of delicious edibles misnamed "toadstools." We had studied them long enough never to make a mistake!

For a scholar it was a doubly rewarding peace, although at the time it was clouded by thoughts of what was happening in the peace-forsaken land I had come from and in those other lands that were already stricken by the ravage let loose by the brutish pride of a near maniac. How witless is the government of man that such things could be! Against my feelings of empathic dismay, another thought obtruded that had come to me many times before. Sometimes this thought would strike when I read about the eternally impoverished and hungry millions of China or India or when I walked through the stinking, lightless native quarter of Algiers or a near-barren, emaciated village on some Latin-American upland. But sometimes it would emerge when I felt that I had not received some recognition I felt I deserved or had been excluded from a list of significant contributors to the subject I was devoted to—petty considerations that were vexing at the moment. I would turn to what was for me a kind of statistical reckoning. Was not I favored beyond ninety and nine per cent of the human race? Was I not born where the advantages of civilization were bestowed on me, of a family that was free from cramping poverty? Was I not spared the sufferings and mutilations of millions exposed to the fury of war? Was I not blessed with the marvellous gift of a healthy body and a mind that had every opportunity to reveal its potentiality? Incalculable statistical odds were against the possession of these boons by any member of the human race. So rare and fair a lot had fallen to me. Was not that a cause for profound thankfulness, for a decent humility, for an outgoing heart toward the woes of a suffering humanity? And how could I repine if in the midst of such bounty some little favor was denied me?

18

During the Stricken Years

We seemed to walk in the shadow of reality as we carried on much as usual while the older civilizations of our time were flaming in a monstrous war and no one knew where next the flame would spread. In my own department we argued strenuously and at times bitterly over objectives and directions, and each side kept on presenting memoranda and rejoinders. Fortunately, the faculty made an end to it by appointing a faculty committee to examine the whole situation. The immediate reason alleged was that the sudden death of our elder statistician, a kindly, retreating gentleman who had had his fill of trouble, called for some co-ordination of the statistical services offered in various departments and schools, but this was preliminary to the more urgent issue. One thing both sides agreed on was that the department of sociology was seriously undermanned, but each side had different ideas about the choice of new members. My first choice was Robert Merton, a Harvard graduate whom I regarded as the most promising of our younger sociologists. Professor Lynd and some others particularly favored Paul Lazarsfeld, a Vienna graduate who had transferred from mathematics to research in social psychology and sociology and was a forceful proponent of quantitative methods in the social sciences. The upshot was that both of these scholars were elected. I had meantime resigned as the chairman of the department, by no means with regret.

The worsening war in the great world outside had a steadily depressing effect on me at that time. The stakes were so great, and the menace was growing deeper. Instead of forearming against so deadly a peril, some governments had temporized, some had connived, and some, counting the spoils of victory, now made common cause with Hitler. I found a little relief in giving addresses and writing articles on such subjects as "The Price of Peace," "The Nature of the Challenge," "The Roots of Totalitarianism," "Wrong Steps toward World Security," and "The Devil and the Peace." And I wrote a little book entitled *Towards an Abiding Peace*. These and related activities blocked any progress in my more professional studies. I was under no illusion that such teachings would have any influence on public opinion or on the trend of affairs, but I was so deeply moved by the incalculable misery created by the blind passions of men and governments that I had to hug the satisfaction of being one of the "voices crying in the wilderness."

During this period I did, however, assume one or two unusual roles that, while directly or indirectly related to the war, were more in line with my professional interest. The first of these proved to be a trying experience. I was asked to be the director of a summer school for potential leaders. It happened this way. There was an active student organization that was associated with a high-level committee whose most prominent member was Mrs. Eleanor Roosevelt. There was a feeling that the great emergency had revealed the need for more effective leaders, and it was essential to discover and train young persons who had the potential of leadership. As the result of a scouting program throughout the country, some thirty students were chosen as members of a summer camp on the Roosevelt properties at Campobello. The experiment was conducted throughout two summers. President Nielsen of Smith College directed the camp for the first summer, and I was in charge for the second, that of 1942.

It proved to be more than I had bargained for, and very different from what I had conceived it would be. In the first place I quite failed to understand what the criteria of selection were that brought together this particular group of students as potential leaders. A small number were really able, but the rest had no manifest claim to distinction, present or future. And why should three of the thirty-odd students have been chosen from a certain New York City educational system? The obvious disproportion suggested that the basis of selection was biased in some way. The suspicion increased when early in the session I had a deputation of five students, in which the New York City contingent was prominent, to complain they weren't getting what they needed. The courses they were offered were not "practical" enough, by which I soon found they meant not radical enough. I asked them if they came as representatives of the group as a whole. They replied they represented themselves alone. But they were abetted by my associate director, who proved throughout to be a thorn in my flesh. This group formed a kind of underground and tried their best to foment discontent. They wanted me to invite leftist speakers for propaganda purposes. I told them I would have no propagandist lecturers, whether rightist or leftist. We would have leading scholars without considerations of their affiliations, and we would have free discussions in which all sides could participate equally.

Actually the program seemed to me well adapted to the purpose of the camp. We had morning addresses given by authorities in governmental, economic, and social problems, with some new lecturers from week to week. The afternoons were free for student affairs, excursions, discussions, and so forth. In the evenings we had a succession of distinguished speakers who gave well-illustrated talks on such subjects as modern music, astronomy, literature, the changing times. One evening a professor who had a special gift for reading and interpreting poetry spoke for us. So we combined cultural diversion with training courses.

My own task was arduous enough. I had to be alert to attempts to undermine my authority and bring in some speaker I had not approved. There were occasionally minor disturbances in some class when a member of the little gang was not content with raising objections to what the lecturer said but insisted on holding the floor. I could never be sure that my instructions were being carried out.

There was another feature of the situation that increased my load.

The students were housed in the big Franklin D. Roosevelt Cottage, while the staff, including my wife and myself and the visiting lecturers, found accommodation in the neighboring cottage of Mrs. James Roosevelt. Campobello, being within the province of New Brunswick, was then dry territory. We had, however, a good cache of liquor in the staff cottage. Since we had visiting lecturers and other guests arriving almost every day, the demands of hospitality required me to spend the evening with them and see that they were provided with adequate refreshment. Every night, in consequence, we carried on animated conversation into the midnight hours. Nevertheless, for the reason mentioned above, I had to be up betimes so as to be around for the nine o'clock lecture.

Toward the end of the third week there was an outbreak of influenza among the students. I was one of the last to catch the infection and had a rather severe attack. I was still suffering from it when we had a visit from Eleanor Roosevelt, and I could not do the honors as director. However, before she left, I was able to accompany her part of the way on one of those hikes she led with her buoyant stride. But I missed the opportunity to chat with her about camp affairs.

Actually, the situation began to show considerable improvement. I had gradually won the confidence and the co-operation of nearly all the students. One of the New York City group, a young man of sharp intelligence and one of the original five troublemakers, kept in touch with me throughout his career as a Harvard student and then as an academician who has made distinctive contributions in the sociology of religion. Another student, whom I adjudged as one of the very few with special promise and who became a university administrator, Jay Stein, not only has kept contact but has dedicated to me a fine memorial gift he contributed to Southwestern (Memphis).

We ended that toilsome camp period with a most cordial get-together. But I felt rather like going to a rest home to recuperate from it.

The following summer, 1943, I was engaged on a much less exciting mission. Under the auspices of the State Department I spent two months in Mexico City as a kind of cultural envoy, helping to promote relations with Mexican scholars and writers. Whatever other purpose it may have served, I at least made some pleasant acquaintanceships. I taught an occasional class in the social sciences at the Colegio de Mexico—in English, but with my smattering of Spanish I tried to answer students' questions in their own language. Altogether it was one of those unexciting tasks that are more pleasure than toil. On week ends I would take off for an excursion somewhere or visit an English friend and his family who had a delightful villa in Cuernavaca.

The Campobello affair had a lucky sequel for us. My good sociologist friend, Florian Znaniecki, wrote while I was there asking if we would care to occupy his cottage on Martha's Vineyard, which would be vacant for the period between the closing of the camp and the opening of the university fall session, around five weeks later. We were glad to accept. My friend's cottage was a welcome retreat and we fell in love with the island. We decided we would find a place of our own on it. The timing was right. Throughout our years in New York we had kept our cottage on Lake Muskoka. The distance was occasionally a drawback, but we had grown so attached to it that this disadvantage was of little account. After 1939, however, new obligations prevented us from further visits to it, and since the winter and the spring thaws on northern lakes are often damaging, especially to docks and boathouses, and the guardianship of our property was unreliable, we felt it was necessary to sell it.

It was a reluctant decision. For twenty summers Muskoka had been our home. We were abandoning, forever, those northland scenes, where we had our fill of new experiences. We had nostalgic visions of that cropless, unpeopled expanse of creeks and pine-topped islands and rock-strewn rivulets, dark river pools fringed with cardinal flowers, lily ponds where bullfrogs croaked, gorges with swirling rapids, thickets to which the black bear came to feast on blueberries.

I would miss the pre-breakfast plunge from the cottage jetty, the struggle to reel in a smallmouthed black bass as we paddled across some small lake, the savor of frying fish at sunset after we had pitched our tent, the stars reflected in the still midnight water when our boat seemed suspended between earth and sky, the scrubby woods that were remarkably prolific in the funguses I sought, the sudden, sharp thunderstorms advancing over us from Georgian Bay —these and many other memories would not again be renewed.

But now we had by chance discovered a delectable new summer opportunity, one I particularly was attracted to, since I longed to get back from the neutrality of lake water to the ancestral breath and the abounding life of the sea. The next year we rented a cottage at Menemsha, and after another year or two we bought our own land at Chilmark, with a very old Cape Cod cottage, which became an increasing delight as the years went by. There was another advantage here over our northern cottage, in that the island provided very good companionship. Indeed, I know no summer place where one can find so goodly a company of congenial spirits. The feeling of grateful familiarity with a neighborhood, of widened belongingness over the countryside, provides a sustaining background for everyday living.

But it was only after the war years ended that I could properly enjoy the serenity of our new summer abode, aside from the fact that in the meantime other tasks and preoccupations took me away from it during part of the summers.

It was not that the end of the war brought peace on earth or even a "peace settlement." Instead, it furnished the most extraordinary exhibit of the greatness and the weakness of civilized man. On the one hand, with penetrating, persistent skill and no reckoning of costs, he devised a new weapon of incredible destructive power, itself based on the genius of the scientific mind that discovered how to harness atomic energy. On the other hand, his leaders showed only a fumbling and inconsistent approach when they constructed a United Nations to settle disputes between the powers by pacific means. And as the war in the East was nearing its end, no better way to hasten it was contrived than to destroy two Japanese cities with the terrible new bomb. Thereafter the making of an established peace was frustrated by the bitter tension between the two mightiest victors, each denouncing the ideology of the other as a devil's brew, each fearful of the power of the other, each totally discounting the new agency for peace to which both had pledged devotion by a feverish and inordinately expensive expenditure on terror. The amazing new energy resource was almost wholly devoted to engines of destruction; its vast potentiality for the increase of productivity and the abolition of age-old poverty was most grudgingly and slowly explored. Can anyone deny that civilized man is still indeed sophomoric, wise in science and in technological achievement but sadly lacking wisdom in the arts of government and in the understanding of his relations with his fellow men?

I had thoughts of writing a work that would show how the same antithesis runs through the whole age of modern science. Since the eighteenth century, man has overcome most of the atavistic resistances to the liberation of the scientific mind. But the richest benefits to society that might have accrued from this liberation have been limited and perverted by the resistances that have blocked the development of social wisdom. Power is esteemed, not for the service it can render to human well-being, but as an instrument of dominion and a means of aggrandizing the interests of the powerful.

The contrast leaps to the eyes. But hidden conjunctures are always at work to overthrow the balance of power. The tide of affairs has its own slow efficacy to change the stubborn ways of men. Perhaps that is why I never wrote that book. Certainly it is why I reluctantly placed more trust in the terror of the bomb than in the councils of the United Nations.

19

Retrospect
on a Scholar's Way of Life

There are scholars who are not teachers and teachers who are not scholars, but the better way to be a teacher is to be a scholar, too. That way his studying enriches his teaching and his teaching freshens his studying, suggesting new viewpoints. So must Chaucer's "clerk of Oxenford" have felt, for "gladly would he learn and gladly teach." There is the recluse scholar who thinks teaching a bore and a waste of his precious time. He has an opus that makes insatiable demands on him. He is a specialist who writes only for specialists. Frequently he is a nibbler at the far end of his particular lore. His ambition is to be the monopolist of a special corner of his specialism, adding new data to the boundless store of "facts."

The more significant kind of scholar is an interpreter more than a fact-digger. He is searching for the relationships between his data and is concerned with the yet-to-be-known because of the light it may throw on the already-known. He realizes that all phenomena are evidence of the links that bind all things together in unswerving obedience to eternal laws. Our best knowledge is a very partial revelation of an incredibly intricate nexus. The army of scholars is always adding new links with that nexus, mostly minute patches of the cosmic web. Some seek to piece together the outlook on life of a thinker or a poet or the ethos of a group as shaped by the buffetings of its times. Some strive to understand an aspect of the impact of institutions on group behavior in a historic setting. Some seek to trace the derivations of the mating habits of a genus of birds. But there are myriads of diverse pursuits all directed to the same goal. A small number reach magistral conclusions on some major nexus of the cosmic order, as in our own day men like Bohr and Planck and Heisenberg and Einstein have done.

There remains a large and very important group whose members may be included in the ranks of scholars—but with a qualification. They are most frequently found in the area of the social sciences but are by no means unknown in biology and occasionally appear even in the physical sciences. They have played a very significant role in the history of ideas and have had a powerful impact on public opinion. A few of them may perhaps be described as great thinkers—but not as great scholars. They diverge from the scholarly type in two respects. First, they are so enamored of some thesis, discovery, or conclusion of their own that they disregard, discount, or explain away any evidences that might be in conflict with it. They may be men of keen insight; they may be fertile in new ideas. Usually they have a new approach to an old subject. But they turn a partial truth into a sweeping generalization. They take one aspect to be the whole picture. Partial truths make whole gospels—then they become so much more impressive than the limited conclusions of the scholar. Second, the members of this group make direct appeal to a wider public, with relatively little concern for the opinion of the scholar fraternity. They are men with a mission, to enlighten mankind or to reform society, as well as, no doubt, to win renown.

The great exemplar of this type is Karl Marx, who delivered from his mountain top the fundamental law of social evolution, which enabled him infallibly to predict the future course of social history. By the strange workings of the schemes and counterschemes of warring nations, his doctrine found its opportunity and had a profound effect on the course of history, though in a way he himself could never have anticipated. Another representative of the type was Sigmund Freud. He was rather more of a scholar, an explorer of areas of human behavior that had been ignored or hidden under the veil of morality, but he was too obsessed by his findings to be concerned about their limitations and was not infrequently content with dubious interpretations, especially when he sought to explain the genesis of folkways, as in his *Totem and Taboo*. The erudite Oswald Spengler, with his neat doctrine of the great cycle of organic society, in which every civilization passed successively through its spring, summer, autumn, and winter, provides another example of the plausible but uncritical imposition of a preconceived order on the course of human affairs. In our own day the tribe has many members, most of all in the area of social psychology and psychoanalysis. Many of the more popular writers in this area can be assigned to the category —the reader can easily supply some names.

Even the accredited scholar is not immune from the temptation to overemphasize some doctrine, some conclusion, for which he finds warrant in his evidences. The scholar is a social animal as well as a reasoning one. He wants to have a role, a standing among his fellows—above them, if he can. He will abandon a conclusion if he is convinced the evidence does not sustain it, but he readily gives himself the benefit of every doubt. The scales in which he weighs his favorable evidences are biased, without his being aware of it. The authority of an established doctrine, established more by consensus in its favor than by indubitable proof, may lead him to assume its consistency with new evidences that are hard to reconcile with it. The Darwinian theory reigned for a century as the sole explanation of the process of organic evolution, and only recently has its adequacy been seriously questioned. Its major proposition, the primary role of the superior fitness of chance variations in the emergence of new species, contains an assumption that might well have been questioned earlier, had it not been for the weight of authority.

When a few leaders unite in favor of a particular approach, a technique for research, say, or a mode of interpretation, it tends to create a vogue. Ambitious followers proclaim the same approach. A school of thought is created. Vogues of this sort have followed one another throughout the history of the social sciences, especially in sociology and social psychology. Most of my time I have been opposed to these vogues, and in earlier days I enjoyed arguing against their proponents—until I learned it was a waste of time and energy. The social sciences have been and still are obsessed with methodology. They would be further advanced had they forgotten about it altogether.

No scholar, except perhaps the very greatest, is a "pure" scholar. Every scholar bears the stamp of his time and environment, with its thought-forms, traditions, and predilections. The pure scholar would be a reasoning animal who never rationalizes, unswerved by his social animality.

Some, however, seek to preserve their scholarly purity in misguided ways. They shy away from the contagion of the social arena. They are publicly mute on the problems and controversies of their time. In private they may sneer at the trickeries of politicians and the stupidities of the masses. They eschew the forum and the press. They do nothing to inform a larger public of the new viewpoints and perspectives that science opens up. They turn up their noses at popularizers, as though they demeaned the profession.

Scholars have a reputation for social timidity, for being unassertive even of their own rights and their own special interests. They have not been vocal in the defense of causes dear to them. They have been loath to give public expression to the results of their inquiries when these were contrary to prevailing opinions. There have always been notable exceptions, forthright advocates of unpalatable truths. But these exceptions showed up the supineness of the majority. When a young scholar in Tennessee insisted on his right to teach what scientific research had established concerning the evolution of man and was prosecuted in a famous trial, there was no great uprising of scholars in the South to give him support. When McCarthy and his cohorts made foul accusations against teachers who believed in social welfare legislation or governmental regulation of industry or who held Keynesian views about deficit financing, there were too many scholars who held their peace, and too often, when one institution came under attack, sister institutions gave no cooperation to the defenders. The American Association of University

Professors took up cases where academic freedom was violated but at that time lacked the spirit of leadership.

There has, however, been a distinct advance in quite recent years. With the ever increasing numbers seeking admission to universities and colleges and the corresponding increase in the number and size of institutions of learning, the scholar as teacher has been in great demand, and as it has been put, when demand outruns supply, supply ceases to be suppliant. His salary level is higher, and that makes for independence and outspokenness. Moreover, a lead was taken by the atomic scientists in a journal that is devoted mainly to the public responsibilities of scientists in the light of the menace and the promise of nuclear energy. Since social scientists like to ape the practices of the more prestigious physical scientists, the lead taken by the latter probably stimulated the growing tendency of the former to express themselves on social, economic, and political issues that came within their various fields of study and research.

Every occupation has a service to render to society beyond the mere fulfillment of its specific function. Every profession has its special contribution to make for the advancement of social well-being. To make that contribution, it must transcend its own economic or specialist interest. This is obviously true for the medical, legal, architectural, and other professions. The academic profession is unique in one respect. It pursues knowledge, not primarily for the advantage of the profession, as does the engineer or the doctor, but for its intrinsic value, for the light it throws on the human heritage, for its service in training the mind, for its role in the exploration of nature and of the vast cosmos itself. The first principle of scholarship is the rejection of bias. The scholar must follow the quest for knowledge unskewed by self-interest or the advantage of any group or any doctrine, including his own. The politician seeks to win votes, to justify the positions taken by his party. The business man is out to present the most favorable case for his own products. The lawyer is out to win a verdict. Propagandism is rife everywhere. The scholar has an almost unique aloofness from special interests, from partisanship, from influences that deflect the faithful rendering of the evidence. He has, therefore, a peculiar obligation to express his conclusions on matters of serious public concern that come within the range of his studies, on economic issues if he is an economist, on the consequences of political decisions if they come within his field as a political scientist, and so forth. The scholar has no monopoly on the truth. His conclusions are never gospel. He has his limitations and his temperamental preferences. Scholars are themselves divided on controversial issues. But at least the scholar is better informed on many matters that concern the public, and he seldom has the temptation of the man of affairs to purvey one-sided statements in order to enhance his reputation or advance his interests.

The real scholar is no lover of the arena. He steps into it only because he is a citizen as well as a scholar. Public controversy is not only a distraction; it tends, if frequently engaged in, to promote attitudes antagonistic to the scholar's way of life and thought. I have known younger men of scholarly capacity whose fondness for public disputation at length undermined their studious quality. The scholar needs frequent intervals in the seclusion of his study, for sessions of silent thoughtfulness.

The institution of learning itself is no cloistered retreat. There are grievances and jealousies, frustrated ambitions, dominating cliques, contentions for status, backbitings; yes men toady for unearned recognition; rivals compete for promotion or for administrative appointments. Some departments are relatively free from troubles, while others are rife with feuds. I have known the rather extreme case of a department whose members were all devotees of their distinguished chairman; when he left and a new head was appointed who belonged to a different school of thought, the staff—they were mostly women, too—made his life so miserable that he had to resign for the sake of his health as well as his peace of mind. I have been in several departments where concord prevailed. I have been in one where dissension was never-ending until finally one clever manipulator made everyone toe the line—his line.

But these rifts and disputes seldom bite as deep as do the conflicts in the arena of politics or generally in the world of affairs. The real scholar can nearly always follow his own way and cultivate his own garden. He usually teaches what he wants to teach, and as he wants to teach. After some years of experience, he receives tenure and is safely ensconced in an assured position, with salary increments as the years go by. The real scholar finds incentive and reward in the work itself. He has satisfaction in imparting knowledge and is an active member of a great fraternity engaged in the advancement of knowledge.

I have never regretted my choice of a vocation. I can conceive no other that has greater potential for enriching the mind and stimulating the imagination. I loved the constant communication with eager young minds. I loved to argue and plead for causes endangered by narrow interests, prejudices, and ignorance. The effort may be wholly unavailing, but one is still moved to take a stand. The occasional frictions and disturbances of academic life never seriously discomfited me, although I've been in the thick of many an academic battle, many more than I have recounted in this work. I fortunately have a temperament that saves me from lying awake thinking of my sins —or of the cussedness of my fellow men. I have been cramped at times by the inadequacy of an academic salary, have had to forego the amplitude of living I coveted; but that limitation I regarded as overcompensated for by the advantages and privileges of my calling. The work of a scholar demands for full efficiency long hours of patient research, and the writing end of it is a constant struggle for apt expression. I gladly accepted the travail. I have lived laborious days but without scorning delights.

20

Preoccupations
of the Late Professorial Years

When the killing ceased and men could go their ways again, it was in a world where the power system had been wholly transformed, and nowhere was the change more manifest than in the new role and status of the United States. Unwittingly, we were at that moment the dominant power of the earth, with one potential rival eager to become our challenger. The prevailing attitude in this country had no resemblance to that after the First World War. Now there was no retreat into revulsive isolation, no complacent resort to "business as usual" as of a nation apart, but instead a robust if unreflective mood of commitment to world affairs. There were visions of new horizons, far-reaching negotiations, new alignments, lavish programs of foreign aid, though the performance was marred by a short-sighted crusading spirit. There was a heightening of the simple-minded viewpoint that ideologies contrary to our own are spawned of the devil while we, as the God-fearing champions of righteousness, must never be content to live and let live but must do everything possible to discomfit them. The same viewpoint, from the opposite side of the fence, was taken under Lenin more cautiously and under Stalin more brutally. The war was scarcely over before the wartime allies made rickety the state of peace.

In spite of consequent forebodings, life became again enjoyable for me. My ambitions revived. I began steady work on a book to which I had been giving only casual attention, "The Web of Government." It was an analysis, against a background of theory, of the forms, functions, limits, and goals of government. I felt more satisfied with the finished product than was usually the case when my typescript became a book. It had a wider reception than was accorded any previous work of mine. Later on it was revised and expanded for a paperback edition. The idea of it came to me in a leisurely hour during my wartime visit to Mexico. I had been giving alternately two courses in political science at Columbia during that period, one on modern political theory, the other on the structure of government. It occurred to me that a free amalgam of the two, setting a review of the various forms, functions, limits, and objectives of governments against a background of political doctrines or ideologies, would give the student a better perspective on the nature and problems of politics than he might otherwise attain. The idea excited me, and I began planning it there and then.

I contemplated a companion work, a large-scale volume on the political doctrines or ideologies of the modern age. It was the one subject I had taught continuously, from the days of my first little lectureship at Aberdeen University. It was the subject I felt most at home with, the subject of my favorite and largest class. But I kept on postponing the task, and now it will be postponed for always. Some other literary endeavor always had right of way. At this particular time my growing concern over the increasingly dangerous rifts and cleavages among the American people spurred me to write somewhat less academic books for the occasion. In the first of these, *The More Perfect Union*, I dwelt on the character and consequences of the gross racial and ethnic prejudices that festered in our peculiarly multigroup society. The complacent, spurious idea of the melting pot had long been obsolete. With the successive waves of immigration that had swelled the population and thereafter the in-migration of southern Negores and Puerto Ricans into our deteriorating urban centers, the social and economic consequences of discrimination had become a mounting national peril. The book laid stress on the vicious

circle of which discrimination is the precipitant—discrimination →
educational retardation → deprivation of opportunity → seething
revolt → reinforced discrimination. The book was published in
1949, some years before the uprisings of the Negroes in the South
and in our great northern cities assumed massive proportions. It was
followed by a companion volume, *The Ramparts We Guard*—the
term of our national anthem, "watch," was not appropriate here. The
theme was our repudiation of what we laud as our national heritage,
the rejection of the substance of democracy by the abridgment of
the liberty of speech, by the tendency, fanned by unscrupulous politicians, of the crowd to regard leftward differences of opinion as
"subversive," by the confusion of individualism with laissez-faire,
and by the grossly unequal treatment meted out to our "second-class
citizens." The second book was based on a special lecture series given
at the University of North Carolina. It cut no ice. The first book
had a moderately good reception.

During this period, being free from administrative duties, I took
more pains (which in this case meant more pleasure) in developing
new lectures for my students, especially in my two favorite subjects,
political theory and social causation. I became involved also in some
extra-academic activities, two of which may be worth recording.
One was a bitter and protracted controversy over a requirement for
the Ph.D. degree. The requirement was one no other institution at
that time demanded, with the exception of Catholic University. It
called for the printing of the dissertation before the candidate could
append the beneficial letters to his name. I had always regarded
this as an unfair and gratuitous imposition. The preparation for the
Ph.D. meant years of postgraduate study, usually followed by several
more years before the candidate, who had now to earn his living,
could complete a dissertation satisfactory to the examining committee. After his long and expensive training, he then had to find somehow a sum ranging from several hundred to one or two thousand
dollars to finance publication. It was a rare enough dissertation that
any publisher would accept as a commercial proposition, and only
a chosen few came under a special arrangement with our university
press, which absorbed much of the cost. The consequence was that

quite a number who had successfully passed all the examination requirements were unable to call themselves "doctor" until a much later date and others never received the degree they had rightfully earned. I recall, for example, the case of one lady student of mine who had ingeniously cultivated friendship with the matriarch of an isolated Ozark community and had gotten her to recount day after day, week after week, the story of her folk, the happenings of every kind that made up the distinctive life of the area over which she had exercised considerable authority. It was an admirable contribution, but to tell the tale in its full flavor required a document running to many hundred pages, which would have been quite costly to publish. My student couldn't meet the expense or find a publisher willing to undertake it. So she never obtained the Ph.D. she had so well earned.

A colleague, Jim Angell of the Economics Department, and I started a campaign for the abolition of the publishing requirement. We had the members of our two departments nearly all on our side, but there was some resistance from members of the government department and a nearly unanimous opposition from the largest department in our faculty, history. Our faculty was the only one of the three graduate faculties that blocked reform. On our first faculty accounting we failed to get a majority. There was then a strenuous canvassing by both sides to enlist the inactive and absentee faculty members. At an ensuing faculty meeting we won by a narrow margin.

After the result was announced, a senior member of the history department delivered a dirge over the decease of the printing requirement. Presently he waxed rhetorical. The good ship Columbia had weathered many a storm and survived many a battle. But now it was hit below the waterline, and its days of greatness were ended. He concluded with the famous expression from Virgil—*facilis descensus Averni* ("easy is the descent to Hell"). I could not resist the temptation to jump up and remark, "Would my learned colleague check on the accuracy of his quotation?" He should, incidentally, have said *Averno* instead of *Averni*. But I confess I felt a bit mean to have crowed over my defeated opponent.

This affair was a striking exhibit of academic conservatism. The arguments adduced on the other side seemed to me to have very little substance. And I do not believe that even a handful of faculty members would, after the change was well established, have voted for a return to the old system.

The second activity was one rarely assigned to university teachers. After the long reign of Nicholas Murray Butler, often dubbed Nicholas Miraculous by admirers and others, the trustees appeared at a loss in the search for his successor. The years passed and an "acting president," the secretary of the university, was appointed as a stopgap, a resort which is often disadvantageous. At length the board took the unwonted step of inviting the teaching staff to aid it in the search. I have on several occasions commented adversely on the fact that of the older well-established professions in the United States ours is the only one that is almost wholly bereft of any final authority over its own affairs. Instead the direction is assigned to lawyers and bankers and clergymen and others. Columbia itself has a charter that expressly precludes any teaching staff member from being appointed to its board. This new move seemed to us a significant recognition of a proper function of the teaching staff.

The proposal was that each of the fourteen faculties or "schools" of the university should select one of its members to represent it on an advisory committee. The committee, presided over by the senior dean, was asked to assess the qualifications of persons suggested by its members or by others. I was elected the representative of the Faculty of Political Science. Several months were spent in the preparation of a dossier containing over a hundred names, and the committee after considerable deliberation chose eight from the list, as all highly eligible to be our president. We rated these eight in order of our priorities, though the margin of preference was in some instances very narrow. We submitted the lists with our comments to the board. They thanked us and invited us to a dinner at the University Club. Nothing further happened, except that once or twice we received a request to consider the qualifications of some person not in our dossier. We did so, but without adding him to our select list. We heard nothing more until at a considerably later date it was announced that the new president would be General Dwight D. Eisenhower. It appeared that a top-rated industrial leader had informed our board chairman that "Ike" might be available—and that was the end of the search. Our high respect for the five-star general had not tempted us to include his name in our dossier. It is another indication of the status of the scholar in America that men of prestige in other fields, with perhaps few or no academic qualifications, are thought to be appropriate heads of great universities. But who would be so crazy as to propose that a distinguished scholar, whose knowledge of military strategy was confined to squad drill in his teens, be made one of the chiefs of staff?

We had been enjoined to destroy our dossiers and keep our selection secret. But a secret shared by so many could not be kept inviolate. My own indiscretion will be limited to saying that the gentleman who headed our list has become a statesman after being president of a university, and the high service he has since been rendering to the nation, not least by the independence of his fine critical judgment, makes me feel it was well this recommendation went unheeded, lest he should have yielded to our call.

Having these matters off my hands, I accepted an invitation for the fall term of 1949 at the London School of Economics, where I already had good associations with the sociologists and political scientists. My lecturing program was light, less exacting than a similar one would have been at an American university. The reason is the different attitude of English students. I announced I would be in my office for a certain period each week. But most rarely did anyone come. The only inquiries I remember having during the whole term were from two American scholarship students and one flirtatious foreign lady student. Had I been a regular staff member I would no doubt have had more calls on my time, but all my experience confirms the opinion that American students are much readier to consult their teachers, sometimes to argue with them, than any others. So I had plenty of time to follow my own inclinations and to renew my acquaintance with London, to attend theatres and concerts, and to visit places of interest near and far, including a visit to my brother Donald and my cousins in Ayrshire.

The most clearly etched memory I have of a visit full of interesting occasions was of a lunch meeting near the end of my stay at which I sat with Carr-Saunders, the school's director, and Harold Laski. I knew Harold very well, had met and argued with him many times in the United States and corresponded with him in between. During the term we had been together a number of times, and I thought it pathetic that he lacked much of the buoyancy, the high-riding assurance, the prophetic deliverance that had been so characteristic of him. He was muffled and seemingly baffled, though at moments he recovered his former spirit. He had that year and the year before suffered setbacks that weighed heavily on him. He had lost his advisory role in the Labour party; he had been defeated in a lawsuit he brought for vindication against certain newspaper charges and was saddled with the heavy costs; and the book he regarded as his ripest product, *Democracy in America,* was severely criticized in our leading newspapers as containing many inaccuracies and erroneous generalizations. During our lunch the conversation turned to the conviction of Alger Hiss. None of us was happy about it. My own opinion was that the real story had not been revealed, that Hiss was somehow involved or was protecting someone but that there was no genuine proof of treason, especially as the evidence was circumstantial and curiously complicated while the chief witness against Hiss was on the record untrustworthy. Laski, however, went much further than Carr-Saunders and I were able to go. He asserted that Hiss was "framed" and was innocent in every particular. "I'll bet ten years of my life," he declared vehemently, "that Hiss is entirely innocent." It was a curious expression and I replied unguardedly, "Harold, you'd better stake something you can afford to lose." A few days later, when we were two days out on the liner returning to New York, I heard the news that Harold Laski had died.

I was then only a year from the time of my compulsory retirement. I did not feel the least bit like it. It was hard to believe that I was about to cease being a professor. I certainly had no intention of allowing myself to be put on the shelf. I would, of course, continue my writing, but I knew that would not be enough. Since I would receive only a featherweight pension and besides had considerable family obligations, I would need what is called "gainful employment." I felt confident enough it would be forthcoming, provided my health continued good.

Meanwhile I was enjoying life to the full. Among the many misleading notions instilled into me in my youth one was that in these later years, in one's sixties or even much earlier, the delights of living were inevitably, irretrievably, dimmed. It may happen so, from misfortune or ailment or grinding circumstances. But it is by no means inevitable. My own days were filled with welcome activities. There were always new challenges. I had work to do that demanded all I could give. I had good friends, and I had no prudish compunctions about limiting such friendships to my own sex. I belonged to a variety of significant organizations. And the out-of-doors, the summer beaches, the woods to roam in, called to me as strongly as ever.

Prominent among the organizations that during this period evoked my interest was the National Manpower Council. It owed its inception and leadership mainly to the resourcefulness of Professor Eli Ginzberg, a Columbia colleague who has been my warm and much-valued friend across the years. It was financed by the Ford Foundation and had strong official backing, headed by President Eisenhower, who had been impressed by the high proportion of unqualified, unhealthy, or miserably educated young men who appeared before the draft boards. Its mission was to explore the background of these deficiencies and to make recommendations for remedial services, for the evocation of undeveloped or neglected skills, for greater educational efficiency and realistic job-training, and for the utilization of unused capacities, not least those of "womanpower."

The membership of the council was of high caliber, with leading representatives from the fields of education, science, medicine, journalism, industry, trade unionism, and politics. Under its able executive director and editor, Henry David, it issued a series of pioneering and significant volumes, of which the most far-reaching was the work finally published under the title *Education and Manpower* (1960). Aside from the satisfaction of participating in a project of signal merit, not only in itself but for the call it sounded for a massive redirection of our welfare services, I enjoyed the opportunity, as a council member, to establish friendly relations with many of my colleagues, including Dr. Leo Bartemeier, Charles Taft, Lee DuBridge, Jacob Potofsky, Edwin D. Canham, and the late J. D. Zellerbach.

I shall mention particularly two of the associations that have held my interest over a very long period and right up to the present. One had its focus in the Jewish Theological Seminary of America, from which I received an honorary degree. (If I had been told in earlier years that I would receive a degree from a theological institution I would have wondered what strange transformation I had undergone—but no, the leopard had not changed his spots.) The chancellor of the seminary, Louis Finkelstein, is a man of far-sighted enterprise, who became my very good friend. He shared my conviction that those who worshipped at different shrines should regard one another not as aliens but as brethren who have the same common and universal concerns and should join together not only in order to advance them the better but also to learn, to understand, and to respect the diverse traditions, approaches, and experiences that make up the many-colored pattern of the human quest for the divine. To this end he obtained the resources to establish two closely related institutions. One was the Conference on Science, Philosophy, and Religion, which brought together for a series of meetings representatives of the sciences, of different philosophical schools, and of all faiths—and no specific faith—to illuminate the inclusive values, causes, and problems that overrode their differences. The other was the Institute for Religious and Social Studies, which was intended primarily to bring together clergymen of different faiths and denominations for talks and discussions on religious perspectives, "the basic issues confronting spiritually minded men," and the social problems that are of concern to clergymen and other citizens alike. Its main activity was a series of three successive sessions over a morning once a week for a period of thirteen weeks each year. The third session was a lunch meeting devoted to talks by authorities, followed by discussions, on major social problems.

In short, the whole plan was a scheme for the assertion of the broader and the universal interests that transcend our religious differences, our academic departmentalizations, our factitious demarcations of the sciences and the humanities and the arts. The response was most promising. In the discussions there was more agreement than disagreement and where there was disagreement there was very rarely discord, so that the difference itself stimulated the exchange of testimony. I noticed on various occasions that those who espoused divergent creeds disagreed naturally enough on major dogmas or a priori principles but in the actual discussions on practical social or ethical applications they were usually in full accord.

I had been a member of the initial planning group and continued to take an active role at the meetings. I became the organizer and moderator of the lunch sessions, and while I more than once felt it was time someone else took over, I have been persuaded to continue right up to the year of this writing. Over the twenty-odd years of the institute quite a number of volumes have been published containing the addresses delivered year by year. In our lunch series we developed some programs that anticipated the rise of public interest in particular issues, beginning in the forties with several series on the conditions, problems, and consequences of ethnic and racial discrimination and more recently with a series that focused on the need for massive antipoverty measures. In carrying out this program over so many years, I have been greatly aided by the remarkable efficiency of the lady in executive charge of the institute, Jessica Feingold.

Another organization that made special appeal to me was a small Columbia University group, an American-Hellenic society, which was devoted to selecting young students from Greece and providing for them college or university training in this country, on the express pledge that they go back to Greece to apply their new knowledge in the service of their country. The name "Greece" had always an endearing sound to the academic ear. Has not its little city-states accomplished the miracle of raising all the fine arts, as well as literature and scholarship and philosophy, to a level of distinction unprecedented in the world before, as an inspiration to men across the millenia? But it was now a land ravaged by war, poor and unorganized, without resources. Our group felt it could do something to serve it. We had practically no funds and made little headway in our efforts to obtain them. Operating on a shoestring, we have been able up to the present to take more than three hundred carefully selected students from all over Greece and educate them in such areas as agriculture, electronics, medicine, physics, education, home nursing, and social service. The colleges remitted their fees and the students did some work to earn their living. All this, however, would have been impossible had it not been for the devotion of a Greek student of mine, Chryst Loukas, and his wife, who lived on a pittance and devoted themselves throughout without stint to the cause. In recognition of the benefit to Greece, four of us were decorated by the king with the Royal Order of Phoenix.

The time officially set for retirement overtook me in 1950, but I had not yet to forsake Columbia. I said goodbye to the Department of Sociology, rather sadly recognizing that my long and troubled efforts to establish a leading, all-round department had not worked out as I had hoped. We did have at length some men of high standing. Lazarsfeld was a mainstay of quantitative methods and Merton was a versatile and incisive thinker, but the influence of the former was so dominant that in my judgment the operations of the department were one-sided and failed to do justice to very significant areas of sociological scholarship. Now I was to teach part time for a year or two by a special arrangement with the Department of Public Law and Government, and thus I would be able to carry on my favorite courses in political theory and the structure of government. It was two more years before my teaching career came to an end.

What I missed mostly thereafter was my contact with students. I had a great fondness for teaching. It was a two-way communication, and I enjoyed the give-and-take between teacher and student. It stimulated my desire to give clarity and clean expression to my topic. It made the subject more alive than it could become in the study. I liked to observe the different responses of different temperaments. I formed many friendships in that way, and the longer I taught the more former students kept in touch with me. I still have correspondence with students of as many as forty years back, with several students in India, with a few in Japan, including one devoted lady, now a professor in Tokyo, Ayako Kikuchi, who has kept regular and most friendly contact with me ever since, with a first-class

Nigerian student who has made his way to high position, with a few in England, and with many in this country. The end of teaching experience was for me much the most serious penalty of retirement.

It was my seventieth year. My students had already given a radiant party in my honor. Now my friends and associates organized a rather large-scale dinner to "celebrate" the birthday. (Somehow "celebrate" doesn't seem the most appropriate word to signify the end of a stage of the life span.) My friend Adolf Berle led off in high style, and I had some wonderful words of greeting from friends old and new. I had reached a certain disinterest in birthdays as such— a birthday is just the day after yesterday and the day before tomorrow. But it can be the occasion for the kind of get-together of one's good friends that generates a warm glow in the heart of the recipient of their greetings.

Of the many treasured letters I received for that occasion, I shall limit myself to quoting a passage from only one, that of my long-cherished friend Alvin Johnson, excessively generous though it be.

"There is one area in which he will always raise his voice—he will cry in the desert of cowardice when freedom is jeopardized. His valor is the manifestation of the lasting youthfulness of a wise man who has dedicated his life to the service of the living mind."

It is not easy to step down, when you still feel vigorous and eager to pursue further the long-traveled road—I had been a university teacher for one short of fifty years. It was the biggest break, the most deeply felt transition, in my whole life. But I knew that somehow I would be able to carry on, apart from the need I had to earn enough money to meet my obligations.

For the rest, my lines still fell in pleasant places. The family retained good health, with only quite minor troubles. My daughter was bringing up a young family, as the wife of a highly reputed sociologist, Robert Bierstedt; my older son, Ian, taught art at the University of Massachusetts, and my younger son, Donald, aside from other activities, was my aide for secretarial and various other services. Our Palisades home, snugly set in the woodland, had a quiet beauty of its own and the red cedarwood was weathering in a variety of hues. We had turned a jungle into a forest of tall tulip trees and sour gum and beech and maple, with enough undergrowth to keep it close to the state of nature. The village had its distinctive features. Behind our plateau it sloped down with many a curve to the Hudson, and on the slopes there lived, in homes delightfully set in niches, a colony of artists, writers, stage celebrities, and professional folk. This part of the Palisades is Sneden's Landing, but the name of the village as a whole was inadvisably changed to Palisades. On an extensive area looking down to the river there was then the estate of Thomas Lamont. My wife and I spent many a Sunday afternoon at his house, where nearly every week end he would have as his guest some distinguished visitor such as Arnold Toynbee or Julian Huxley. We got involved in many an argument there. Tom Lamont liked to talk about economic and political issues, while his wife Florence, who had studied philosophy at Columbia, was more interested in literature and in international relations. I carried on an occasional correspondence with Tom. On some matters we were in full agreement. I have, for example, one letter in which he said: "You have struck the nail on the head, or struck two nails on their respective heads. Price rigidity, and labor uncertainty, due to the fluctuations in business activity, are undoubtedly two grave problems." On other matters we were far apart. He was one of those who habitually referred to Franklin Roosevelt as "that man." Florence Lamont sometimes came round and we would sit in our garden or on the porch discussing the problem of peace or other topics. After Tom Lamont's death, when she wanted to give the beautiful estate on the Hudson to some tax-exempt institution, she talked about the problem with me and in the end decided to offer it to Columbia University.

There was a curious sequel to this gift. The Columbia department that could best utilize the estate and that had the funds to maintain the big property was the department of geology. The estate paid around a third of the local tax assessed on the village, and it so happened that the zoning ordinance Mr. Lamont had obtained to protect its amenity made no allowance for the introduction of a research laboratory. The property could therefore not be taken over by Columbia unless the village voted to change the zoning law. The inhabitants refused to do so unless the estate continued to pay a substantial portion of the tax. There was a village meeting at which two lawyers representing the university offered a compromise deal, threatening that it was a final offer and that if it were not accepted the village was likely to lose out altogether. The offer was rejected. Since I belonged to both camps, I tried to act as an intermediary. The university representatives came to a later meeting, and a deal was made on the basis of a superior offer. Now the Lamont Geological Laboratory has become a leader in oceanographic research, with its two far-ranging ships, and is an important new factor in the village life.

We found great satisfaction also in our new summer home on Martha's Vineyard. Our ancient Cape Cod cottage was constructed for the ages and gained new amenity as we worked to improve it. Our island retreat proved ideal for our purposes. The climate was temperate even in the dog days, and the sea breezes brought their cooling breath in the evening and through the night. On one side lay the sound, and only a mile or so across was the great ocean with its range of sandy beaches. There was golf for me down island and at my door were considerable stretches of unpeopled forest, where I could roam and hunt my fungus prey to my heart's content. And there was also a bountiful supply of berries to be picked in their seasons. Wild strawberries and raspberries and blackberries and high bush and low bush blueberries and in the fall the grapes from the myriad vines.

For a relatively small island it is remarkably diversified. There is the broad differentiation in the first place between down-island and up-island. Down-island has the only considerable towns, all within a few miles of each other, the business center of Vineyard Haven, the filigreed rococo of Oak Bluffs and the serene New England beauty of Edgartown. Up-island has a few villages but is mostly well-spaced cottages and estates, with the picturesque fishing village of Menemsha on the sound, a mile across from Chilmark and the ocean beaches, and the peninsula of Gay Head, with its colored cliffs and its Indian population, some members of which are dominant in the township's affairs. Scattered over the island there are also a number of enclaves each with a character of its own, among them the mansions of West Chop and Tashmoo Lake, Indian Hill, the Seven Gates Farm area, the many-inleted area of West Tisbury, and Chappaquiddick Island.

Our cottage is situated on an incline at the back of which a thicket of oak trees rises, the white oak predominating. In the summer pink-red climbing roses cover the front and invade the shingled roof. Below it, past cedars, a balsam, and a noble blue spruce, the lawn slopes toward the dry stone wall nearly hidden in the tangled growth, the rampant trumpet vine with reluctant orange-red tubes, the bittersweet everywhere insinuating its lush yellow-berried shoots, the tapering white and cream and pale-yellow petals of the honey-suckle emerging through the tangle. Here and there the vine of the Concord grape cloaks the surface with its flat drab-green leaves that rustle with every gust of wind. Below our gate an ever-full, ever-cold spring borders the edge of a marsh where a crescent of handsome poison sumac grows, happily just beyond easy reach.

Our own neighborhood contains many pleasant and cultured people, authors and artists and educators and men of affairs, among whom we have found many friends and acquaintances. One of my nearest neighbors, a man with a keen eye for whatever grows on the ground or flies through the air, is Roger Baldwin, whose family own the finest beach on the island, a great expanse of glistening sand, which we are privileged to use. One need never be at a loss to fill an evening. There is a plethora of cocktail parties, if one is so minded. What I enjoy much more are the quiet after-dinner sessions with a group of interesting folk, whether it leads to a casual exchange of ideas about people and things or to the discussion of some weighty issue. Occasional evenings my son and I play bridge with neighboring practitioners, our most frequent associate in later years being the many-talented Felicia Lamport (Kaplan). Nor should I omit from the list of virtues of this delectable isle its atmosphere conducive to quiet thought and to studious pursuits.

21

Testimony of a Writer

Writing was the occupation I found most engrossing. It pre-empted most of the time I could spare from other tasks. Hence this excursus on what the business of writing meant to me and the attitudes and habits it developed in me.

My boyhood dream was to be an author. I never became one in the full sense of my dream. Authorship as such did not become my profession. When people introduce me, they describe me as a sociologist or as a political scientist or perchance as a social philosopher —the last occasionally from a brother scientist with a slight tone of condescension—rather than as an author. But if the writing of books qualifies one for the title of author, I can claim to have earned it abundantly.

I have written twenty-one books, edited quite a few more, produced a number of reports of considerable size, contributed chapters to composite works, and published an uncounted number of articles and reviews. I had occasion recently to do a bit of calculation, and I found that for my twenty-one books I had seventeen different publishers. This was a surprising discovery. I am by no means a demanding author; I like to stay with whatever publisher I have. Sometimes I have grouched because he did not take much interest in my book or did not give it proper publicity. But I did not leave him on that account. How then did it happen?

There were two main reasons. One was that several of my books were delivered first as lectures at some university that had a special fund for the purpose, and so they were published in a series under its auspices. The other was that the editor of some library of books invited me to contribute a volume to it or, in one instance, several volumes. Aside from these reasons, some particular incident once or twice seduced me from the firm I had come to regard as my "regular" publisher. Once there was the split-up of a publishing house, and from my point of view I was in the wrong half of the split; and once my publisher was merged in a large combine, and somehow my pleasant relation with the firm came to an end.

I have always been a scribbler. I have played around with almost every form of literary composition, including short stories, plays, and poems. These last belonged to the days of yore and have been consigned to happy oblivion. There is a solitary exception—I confess to the writing of one poem, if I may so name it, one short lyric per annum, every year since 1911, for an audience of one, a New Year's Day greeting to my wife.

My exposed writings fall into three categories, more or less corresponding to three stages of my craving for expression. The first set had a professional complexion, textbooks, scholarly studies, and various research reports. My favorites in this class are *Social Causation,* an attempt to explore a much neglected but fundamental procedure for the interpretation of the trends of social change, and *The Web of Government.* I regarded *Social Causation* as a pioneering contribution in its field. Courses on social change were frequently offered in departments of sociology, but they mostly recounted the before and the after, with at best rough-and-ready attributions of a connection between them. Why, for example, was there a considerable rise in the statistics of crime and delinquency? A whole array of divergent explanations were offered, economic, moralistic, political, psychological, psychoanalytic, but little or no attempt was made to relate these "factors" in a systematic derivation of the resultant phenomenon. This was the problem I sought to tackle. My book received only the most perfunctory notices. There were two extensive reviews of it, one by our philosopher of science, Ernst Nagel, and the other by the economist theorist, Frank Knight, and they both damned it on the basis of the first two purely introductory chapters, which claimed, contrary to their position, that social causation is controlled by human urges, needs, passions, and wills, and calls for methods of inquiry that are absent entirely from the field of physical causation. The book was a dud in sociological circles, and it has only been in recent years that it attracted attention when a new paperback edition was published.

The second category consists of somewhat shorter volumes written in a freer vein and hopefully for a wider audience, each devoted to some question besetting American society. The one I like best is *The More Perfect Union,* and certainly since it was written the situation of our second-class citizens which it exposed as dangerous has become a blazing issue. Finally, there came the series of modest-sized books of reflection on the business of living. I felt I had more or less done my duty to scholarship. I could give free vent to my thoughts, without consulting authorities, without academic apparatus, without the buttress of statistics, without footnotes. These were the books that gave me the most satisfaction in the writing. Among them my favorite is *The Pursuit of Happiness.* I felt free as a bird when I wrote it. The title was not my preference, but somehow, contrary to my wont, I allowed it to stand. This was a book that somehow did not receive the attention I fondly thought it deserved, though I received some specially enthusiastic letters about it.

Most of the time writing is for me a pleasurable hardship.

> There be some sports are painful, and their labor
> Delight in them sets off.

It is exacting toil, this endeavor to fit one's ideas into the apt frame of words, to make one's thought so true to itself that the quest for expression is no longer embarrassed. I am never more at home with myself than when engaged in his toil. But I am never fully satisfied with the product, though sometimes, when after many years I find occasion to read what once I wrote I am agreeably surprised—"Why, it's better than I knew"! The complacency over it fades, however, when the writer's attendant imp whispers: "You're not so good as you were then."

When I have merely to talk, my ideas flow directly into words with little effort and no hesitation, but writing is a wholly different affair. My thoughts remain opaque until I have wrestled for expression. They flicker and flit and dissolve until I have struggled to pin them down on paper. Only in complete relaxation, when I am away from my desk, do they seem to flow into literary expression. Sometimes, in the middle of the night I waken into a mood of reverie, and ideas stir freshly into consciousness, already decently clothed in words. I speak quickly, but I write slowly, ruminating over what I have written. In earlier years, after the first script was laboriously completed, I rarely rewrote.

Writing is communicating, to an invisible, often quite unpredictable, audience. (English, by the way, lacks a word to denote the reader group as distinct from the hearer group.) It is recorded communication, capable of endless multiplication, enduring as long as it wins response from a sufficiency of readers to be a source of profit to a publisher. I do not write to please a specific audience. I would certainly like it if my books were a commercial success, but I do not make that a primary goal.

My earlier books were in the field of scholarship, but I thought of them as having a potential interest for a broader, moderately well-educated public. Even my two works that might be labeled textbooks did not supply the pabulum that is deemed appropriate for college students. My first text, *Society,* met with complaints from teachers that it was too abstruse and not simple enough or cut into neat lessons to suit their classes—as though it was not the task of the teacher to interpret and expound, instead of handing out gobbets of predigested information. Anyhow, the book never had the vogue to which every textbook writer aspires.

I am a voracious reader as well as a persistent writer. I range all the way from whodunits to philosophical treatises. Some books I consume; others I nibble at and reject. The latter treatment I accord to many novels, if I feel the author is sentimentalizing or sensation-mongering, more concerned to impress or shock the reader than to convey a true picture of the life of real men and women. Some popular novels that meet my criterion are those of Steinbeck and Bellow.

I discard ruthlessly those numerous successors of Sherlock Holmes who invent all kinds of fake clues, often notching a few more murders in the process, and on the next to last page, pick out the most innocent-looking member of the cast as the murderer, with a highly contrived explanation of why and how he did it. In the category of detection my favorite authors are the Australian Arthur Upfield, Josephine Tey, Mary Stewart, Rex Stout some of the time, and occasionally Ngaio Marsh and Malcolm Innes.

I am fond of the more discerning travel books—my favorite author here is Patrick Leigh Fermor, beginning with *The Traveller's Tree*—and I enjoy those books of exploration that convey a vivid sense of man's slow possession of the reluctant earth, such as Moorehead's *The White Nile* and *The Blue Nile*. I am choosy about biographies, since so many of them fail to give you any intimate sense of the kind of human being who is being portrayed. Often you get a better feel for the biographee from the pictures than from the text.

In my youth I greatly enjoyed poetry. It was part of my education to read the mighty Homeric epics, the great Greek tragedies of the fifth century B.C., and then Virgil, Lucretius, Horace, Catullus, and Ovid. But I did so with delight. I revelled in the poetic drama of the Elizabethan age and had some enthusiasm for Milton—even *Paradise Lost*—and so through the lyric outburst of the late eighteenth and early nineteenth centuries, Shelley, Wordsworth, Keats, Coleridge, and then Scott and Tennyson. But that literary epoch is past and its flair is spent. Now we think of poetry as occasional stanzas following magazine articles. Particularly since the early poems of T. S. Eliot, verse has been mostly contrived, contorted, esoteric, unmusical, obscure. We don't really read poetry any more.

I nearly always go to bed with a book, my effective approach to sleep. My chief bedtime reading is a whodunit or a theoretical study concerned with astronomy or physics or social or political science. I can also get lost in those rare works of sheer imagination of which J. R. R. Tolkien's epic series *The Lord of the Rings* is the finest modern representative. I have a simple explanation why these so utterly disparate kinds of reading are congenial to my bedtime hour. None of them puts any strain on the memory, the mental function that, at least in an occupation like mine, is least resilient at the end of the day. Theory does not consist of "facts," it's a way of interpreting them. And as for the *roman policier*, it can entertain you while you read, but it is properly relegated to oblivion when the mystery is solved.

Reading helps with my writing. I am intrigued by specially apt modes of statement, salient phrases, the *mot juste*. Some books I read not so much for their intrinsic interest but because of their distinctive use of language, the richness of vocabulary, the neatness of organization. An example would be the writings of Nabokov. Such stylistic expression not only pleases me in the reading, but it also gives me leads in my own struggle to convey my thoughts.

Often enough I am blocked for a moment in the process of writing. The desired word or phrase is not obedient to my call. The pen drops from my hand, as I rummage about for the language I need. Then I resort to one device or other. I may step out-of-doors for a few minutes to the edge of our woods and contemplate some growing thing while the question simmers in the subconscious. But my chief resort is to pick up the deck of cards always ready on my desk and to play one or two hands of a kind of patience I invented. It is a continuous patience that may run to a hundred hands or more before it is won or lost. Every hand counts and is immediately recorded. The semimechanical exercise removes the strain of the search for the five or ten minutes required. Somehow it liberates my invention, and when I take up the pen again the writing nearly always moves freely on. Some readers might like to know about my patience game, and so I'm giving an account of it as an appendix (pp. 252–254).

Although I am a slow writer—at most two or three pages in a full day—it's remarkable how fast and imperceptibly the pages mount up. After a longish day at my office, I find it quite refreshing to turn to the business of composition for an hour or two. I used to snatch time for a few lines before I left for my office in the morning. I always look forward to week ends, not merely because I can laze in the morning, have a family reunion, do a bit of shopping in the neighborhood with my wife, and perhaps have a Saturday night game of bridge, but also because all of these activities still leave good intervals for the travail of the desk. In recent years I have stolen Fridays from "gainful employment," whenever it was feasible, making my week ends beautifully long for the piling of the pages. In order to write I must be at home and at peace, and I confess also that I have come to regard a pipe in my mouth as an almost invariant condition of my writing ease. The pipe is out half the time, and I use up almost as many matches as shreds of tobacco.

When I am writing anything that has a chance of being utilizable for publication, it is always done first in longhand. I have tried the typewriter, but the mechanical intervention impedes the flow. I want my hands on the paper. I want the lines to grow before my eyes. I look critically at them as I proceed, change a word or clause for another, perhaps score out a sentence and write another over the scoring. My script is consequently messy, with small, thin lettering, but my home secretary, Donald, can practically always decipher it for typing. I may take a whole day or longer preparing the outline for a chapter. I may take a half-hour perpending how the next paragraph should go. The first writing of a chapter is nowadays followed by a rewriting. I don't ask whether it's worth all the effort. That I like doing it is enough.

Which brings me to the final question: What drives me to this incessant self-imposed task? Might it be the urge to leave something behind me when I am no more, as some people leave material possessions? Perhaps, but I doubt that it is an important incentive. Posthumous enjoyment is meaningless, though the present anticipation of future reputation is agreeable. But present reputation is certainly of more direct concern. That boon is both pleasurable and serviceable, and I must admit it is a genuine incentive. Nevertheless I believe I would keep on with my writing even if it won no esteem. I would rule out financial reward as having any weight, since I could have earned more by accepting relatively profitable administrative positions I rejected because they would have grossly limited my leisure for writing.

The urge to write was strong in me from my early youth, but what I yearned for was to communicate, to convey some kind of a message. I have the strong impulse of the social animal, not the gregarious kind, but the deeply committed kind. My vision is of the greater solidarity of society. Human life is social life, the expression of a primal instinct. But the form it takes, the way it is organized, the way it is governed, the range of its inclusiveness, the relation between one society and another, the internal relationships of its diversity of members, are all human constructs, subject to the distortion of power interests, group prejudices, economic exploitation, bureaucracy, and antiquated doctrines. Consequently, practically every society has been throughout history an area of disruptive conflicts, feuds, spoliations, wars, wastage, mass poverty, and manifold disasters. The instinctive social bond has been rifted, twisted, torn, and broken by the excessive drive of short-run private interests against the claims of the greater and more enduring common interest. Throughout the ages and especially in more recent times, aided by the impact of advancing technology and industrial development, the revolts of the disprivileged and the oppressed have gradually expanded the distribution of power and the range of civil rights. These developments have made society an exceedingly complex structure, but it is still beset by rending divisions, and its wars have grown progressively more slaughterous until today the menace of another great war is the prospect of near-total annihilation.

My urge to write took its direction and its major incentive from these considerations. I was eager to explore the problems of the social condition. There is no such thing as a social engineer in the sense in which we speak of, say, a mechanical engineer. You can't take society and experiment on it as you can with a machine. Even those who have the power to regulate society cannot do that. Their power is limited by elites, and they are subject to many opposing pressures, embarrassments, and complexities that impede their efficacy and defeat their purposes even when the pride and ambition that are always the accompaniments of authority do not turn them into despoilers of the people. But the writer can look on his society with uncommitted eyes and under any decent form of government can explore its shortcomings, its needs, and its potentialities. That is what I aspired to do from the first, from my earliest book *Community* to my latest (with the exception of this book), *Power Transformed*. Virtue is knowledge, said Socrates. Social virtue is essentially the understanding of the conditions of social well-being. One seeks to contribute one's mite to the increase of understanding.

22

A New Way of Life

That fine testimonial dinner on my departure from Columbia was not a memorial for the end of a career. Nor was that the spirit of the occasion. Rather it was a happy and stimulating send-off. I had the additional gratification of letters and telegrams from old associates and young friends, from men of eminence, from students in India and Japan and England and Latin-America—letters that must remain in my private treasury, since the friendly response to such an occasion overindulges the reality.

It was certainly the end of a way of life—no more classes, no new students, no more learning by teaching, no theses to cavil at, no scholastic committees, no more wrangling with colleagues, no more the daily usages of so many years. My work would still be that of the scholar; I had no other trade, but it was enough. I could still be exploring, researching, and always, always writing.

The line that had the strongest appeal to me was institutional research. I had offers of fill-in teaching jobs, but that would be very sporadic employment, mostly away from my home base. Already, during my two final years of part-time service at Columbia, I had undertaken two short institutional studies that I found to be absorbing and challenging. In much earlier years I had a modest initiation into this field. The first was a survey I conducted for the Russell Sage Foundation. I was invited to review the activities that engaged

various members of the staff, each of whom had charge of a separate
department, and to make recommendations for the improvement
and delimitation of their services. I felt at the time that the efficiency of the foundation called for a much more thorough investigation than my assignment permitted. That happened later, after a
change of administration.

My next task in this area carried a higher reponsibility. After the
First World War, a group of Protestant Clergymen, painfully conscious that the churches everywhere had played no significant role
in preventing the war or in mitigating wartime passions or in assur-
ing a better peace, resolved to investigate why the spirit of Christianity was of so little effect in the conduct of the affairs of men. The
Committee of One Hundred was set up and with foundation support instituted "An Inquiry into the Christian Way of Life." The
team commissioned to conduct this "inquiry," consisting of psychologists, sociologists, social workers, and educationalists, had been
operating for a number of years when questions about its procedures and its competence to fulfill so searching an assignment began
to arise. I was asked to investigate and report on it, one main
issue being whether the Rockefeller Foundation should continue to
finance it.

The further I investigated, the more doubtful I became that it
could fulfill its function. Its director, E. C. Carter, was a rather
evasive gentleman who somehow achieved a succession of curiously
diverse positions of leadership, in religious organizations, public
affairs, journalism, research activities, and later in an academic
administration. He was always ready to talk to me, but I obtained
little specific information from him. My first surprise was in finding
that its original name had been quietly abbreviated into, simply,
"The Inquiry." Its staff members had become concerned mainly with
techniques for making conferences more harmonious and ethnic
groups less prejudiced toward one another, objectives no doubt
worthy in themselves but certainly not reaching down to the roots of
the problem or adequate to the expectations of those who had commissioned study. Organizations not infrequently take on a character
of their own that deviates fron the intentions of the initiators or the

donors. This, however, was an extreme example of such deviation. After a period of some four months, I was ready to prepare my report, recommending that the staff be given a year to conclude work in hand and that "The Inquiry" then close its doors. The director made angry protests, supported by some but by no means all of his staff, but without avail.

Such was my introduction to this many-angled area of institutional research. My next investigation, in a new series, was undertaken under the auspices of a Jewish organization, while I was still associated with Columbia. There is a group of agencies that call themselves Jewish Community Relations Agencies or sometimes Defense Agencies. Their common objective is to combat anti-Semitism, to defend Jewish folk against malicious attacks, to expose prejudice and promote measures against discrimination directed against any minority group, and broadly to advance the cultural interests of their people as a whole. No people, to my knowledge, go in for such a multiplicity of organizations as do the Jews. This particular system at that time consisted of six central, or national, agencies, three of them with a broad range of activities—the American Jewish Committee, the Anti-Defamation League, and the American Jewish Congress— and three of them serving particular groups—the Jewish Labor Committee, the Jewish War Veterans, and the Union of American Hebrew Organizations, a division of the Jewish religious structure. Several of the agencies had branches or affiliations in cities across the country and also regional offices. The Anti-Defamation League not only had its own regional offices and its professionals in various centers but was itself a creation of the fraternal society, B'nai B'rith, which had a network of lodges spread through every city of any size. While some of the agencies carried on various other activities, the "defense" service was a major interest of them all.

Since all six were thus engaged and since their total expenditure for this purpose ran into millions per annum, contributed mainly from the local centers, there was considerable questioning of the need for this plethora of separate activities, of its efficacy, and of its costliness. Every year several of the agencies sent their professionals to the same local centers to solicit funds, and none of them was inclined to underrate the signal service it claimed to have contributed to the common cause. The ensuing dissatisfaction led to the establishment of an over-all co-ordinating body, the National Community Relations Advisory Council, presumably for the achievement of a common policy and the prevention of needless duplication or competitive programs. But while the staff of the organization strove to fulfill its function, the voting power of the representatives of the national agencies rendered its efforts less than effective. Later proposals and protests were of no avail. And at length, as the demands for reform became more insistent, it was arranged through the N.C.R.A.C. that an outsider be called in to investigate and report. I was the outsider, though the choice was not unanimous. I surmised the pitfalls that lay in wait, but I undertook the commission.

First I spent some months with the central offices. I found many devoted and efficient members on the staff. From the leaders I heard much about the special and unique approach developed by the particular agency each represented, the special audience each appealed to, the particular philosophy it stood for, the need for autonomy to protect the integrity of its total operation, and so forth. These plausible claims to a kind of separatist sovereignty, even if sometimes well grounded, did not appear to me so convincing in the light of the fact that it was the prejudice and discrimination of Gentiles that was the main objective of the appeals of these Jewish agencies. And in any event there was little or no evidence available as to the efficacy of their appeals. One general conclusion I reached was that co-operation and effective liaison with non-Jewish associations would be more likely to achieve results.

After exploring the work of the national agencies I visited the local community centers across the country, from New York to Atlanta and Dallas, from Boston to Los Angeles and San Francisco. Although there were many differences of viewpoint, there was a fairly general agreement that they were flooded with repetitious memoranda and bulletins from the central agencies, that too many agency professionals came to give them advice, and that the national agencies were too competitive with one another, in the recruiting of members, in the setting up of regional offices, and in the scramble for funds.

My report was somewhat elaborate and made a considerable number of recommendations. After dealing with broad questions of policy and approach, I made proposals for ending the needless duplication of services. I saw no good reason why, for example, the two largest agencies should have separate offices, with very little communication between them, for fact-finding, clipping newspapers and periodicals, issuing bulletins to locals far and wide, and so forth. I saw no proper ground why two major agencies should both maintain law departments for drafting model antidiscrimination laws, preparing *amicus* briefs for the courts, and so forth. I proposed a thorough recasting and co-ordination of the "mass appeals" programs emanating from the agencies, based on the need for careful scrutiny and testing of the response to them and on the desirability of relating them to the efforts of non-Jewish organizations serving the same end. I pleaded that the N.C.R.A.C. be assured genuine initiative in the over-all direction of strategy. In short, I was critical, I believe constructively critical, of the prevalent procedures over a wide range, including the method of fund-raising.

Never did I write a report that stirred up such a storm of controversy as this one did. The battle raged all around me, and for many months all the Jewish publications across the country featured the issue and took sides pro and con. For some I was "a Daniel come to judgment," for others "an enemy of the people." Nor were the consequences inconsiderable. Four of the six agencies accepted the report, if with an occasional demur, and teamed up under the aegis of the N.C.R.A.C. But the two biggest ones, which were responsible for the chief amount of duplication, broke away altogether, having set up a shaky agreement for joint fund-raising. Echoes of the controversy reverberated through the following decade, and only a year or two before the time of this writing, one of the two, the Anti-Defamation League, made overtures for its return to the fold of the N.C.R.A.C.

Thereafter I engaged in what I found to be a quite exciting experiment in a New York City public school. It could not be called

Stornoway harbor and castle grounds as R. M. MacIver knew them in his boyhood.

The town of Stornoway, *ca.* 1900. The MacIver home was at the far left edge, Bayhead. Stornoway castle can be seen in the upper left, and the entrance to Broad Bay in the background.

The MacIver family. Front row: Father, Isabel, Keith, and Mother; back row: Donald, Jack, and Robert.

As a lieutenant in the Territorials (Gordon Highlanders), Aberdeen, Scotland, *ca.* 1907.

After migration to New York City, 1927.

The MacIver children at the Muskoka boathouse, *ca.* 1932: Betty, Ian, and Donald.

The cottage at Lake Muskoka, *ca.* 1937.

At my favorite occupation, *ca.* 1942. (Photo by Manny Warman, Columbia University)

With my predecessor, Alvin Johnson, as president of the New School for Social
Research.

Ethel and Robert MacIver, 1967.

research, rather a kind of demonstration. I thought I had abandoned teaching altogether, but now for the first time I ventured into a bit of school teaching and did it, moreover, without possessing that vexatious permit that is unhappily the monopoly of teacher-training institutions. It happened this way.

I shared with some of my good friends the opinion that the teaching of civics in the schools was generally superficial and unrealistic, largely because the current textbooks were mostly concerned with the institutions of government, the formalities of lawmaking and administration, or with picturesque accounts of great moments and great men and rhetorical laudations of "the land of the free." They shied away from the rough-and-tumble of politics, from the party strife for place and power, from the real issues and the unending challenge of democracy, from the problems and responsibilities of the ordinary citizen. Spurred on by Alvin Johnson and with the aid of the noble lady Margaret Lewisohn, I was given the opportunity to teach a class or two in civics once a week through a semester in a public school of our choice. The school selected was Bronx Public School No. 7. I began by testing out all three grades in the junior high and decided to take the first or lowest grade, the seventh, with children around thirteen and under. There were many sections, and I chose one with a high I.Q. and one around median, each having up to fifty pupils. It worked better than my expectation. The students were most receptive and thoroughly interested. There were a few of the teachers who thought I should not speak of such live issues as the difference, where discernible, between Republicans and Democrats, but the school principal stood by me. The pupils readily undertook all kinds of after-hour activities for me. For example, when election time came around, they attended local meetings and reported to me what they thought of the candidates. Later on, they conducted an election campaign among themselves, with party divisions, leaders, speeches, canvassing, election posters and manifestoes. They debated questions that were actual issues of the time, having been provided with newspaper clippings and reports on both sides of the question. Toward the end of the term, they got down to local problems by organizing a tidy-up campaign for the neighborhood.

Never did I have a more enthusiastic class than the youngsters in that public school. I worked out the sketch of a new kind of civic textbook along the lines of the program I followed, but we did not find enough support from the school system or the publishers for so drastic a breakthrough.

I embarked next on the first longer-term research project of my new career. These researches were alike concerned with the policies and programs of organizations dedicated to the service of the public interest, and they were alike evaluative studies. This type of research tended to be looked on askance by the centers of sociological research, because it was concerned with "value judgments," contrary to the assumed principles of scientific inquiry. The professional vogue was for "quantitative" research, for such topics as the distribution of attitudes or opinions or modes of behavior as statistically established for selected samples. I maintained on the contrary that the kind of evaluative research which is occupied with the question how far and in what respects an organization fulfills or fails to fulfill its objective was no less scholarly, while it also called for discriminating judgment and not merely the manipulation of techniques. Some of my quantitatively oriented friends used to accuse me of being an "armchair theorist," but now my work had more bearing on the world where decisions are made than most of the researches of the sociological fraternity.

The first of these larger projects was an investigation of the precarious state of academic freedom at a time when that precious safeguard of the integrity of scholarship had been grossly assaulted by that spirit of evil, Senator Joseph McCarthy, and his cohorts. It was a grievous thing to watch this morbid senator not only stir into flame the latent intolerance and primitive fear of multitudes but also elicit willing or unwilling support from men in positions of trust and authority, including at least one high-placed churchman.

A remarkable gentleman, Louis Rabinowitz, who had come to this country from Russia in his early teens, with no resources and scanty schooling, and had acquired not only wealth but also a high level of culture, offered Columbia University the funds to conduct a study of the status of academic freedom. I was invited to direct it. It was planned as a double investigation, on the one hand, an analytic survey of the history of academic freedom in the United States and, on the other, a scrutiny of the existing situation. The former was assigned to two of our historians, Richard Hofstadter and Walter Metzger, whose researches resulted in an admirable review of earlier conditions. I took personal charge of the contemporary study. It was a many-sided story. At our best institutions the trustees generally resisted the attacks, and in this respect the major endowed universities and colleges were able to make a better showing than the state institutions. At other institutions the trustees frequently abetted or yielded to the enemy. I visited some institutions where the battle was still being waged, including Ohio State University and the University of California. The attacks themselves were of the most diverse character. Some, emanating usually from the well-to-do, were motivated by a genuine if quite disproportionate fear of the spread of communism. But communism frequently came to be identified with left-wing tendencies of any kind or degree or with unorthodox economic theories, including the advocacy of welfare legislation or of "Keynesianism." Other attacks were the expression of petty intolerance or malicious ignorance. The embattled zealots and bigots hunted in libraries for "subversive" books—in Los Angeles that category included a simple primer describing the United Nations, and elsewhere there was a band of women who wanted to save tender minds from exposure to the tale of Robin Hood.

The ensuing volume, entitled *Academic Freedom in Our Time,* contained, in addition to a commentary on the prevailing conditions and attitudes, an analysis of the social significance of academic freedom.

My next undertaking proved to be more laborious and less stimulating than the previous ones. The Carnegie Endowment, having in view the prospect that the United Nations Charter would be revised, invited representatives of the signatory countries to write reports severally on their country's experience with the United Nations, including comments on its structure, development, and value. I was invited by the president of the endowment, Joseph E.

Johnson, to review the resulting reports and write my comments on the significance and salient features of the series as a whole. A similar mission was assigned to a Swiss professor, Maurice Bourquin. I had to do the job piecemeal, since the reports dribbled in over a period of five years. Some of them had been assigned to individual authors, others to study groups associated with a relevant national organization. They were very uneven, many of them unimpressive, some perfunctory and rather formal, some of good quality, a few distinctive. I toiled through some twenty of them while planning my report. I was interrupted near the start by a period in the hospital for my one surgical operation. That went very well, but a few months elapsed before I felt fully myself again. However, the task was at length accomplished and I submitted my report, which contained some gratuitous and probably unwelcome comments of my own on United Nations problems. The endowment staff was by no means enthusiastic about it, but after several years of postponement it appeared as a volume entitled *The Nations and the United* nations. The subject at least was a worthy one.

My next research task took me into an entirely new area and was a very lengthy one. It had an important sequel for me and will be the subject of the next chapter.

My change of career had made some difference in my way of living. Lacking the carefree summers of my professional years, I could no longer take leisurely trips abroad. I was sorely tempted by an unusually generous offer of a visit of two or more months to Japan under very good auspices, and the only thing that prevented me from accepting it was what I called a recrudescence of my Scottish conscience. I have some devoted Japanese friends, and more of my books have been translated into Japanese than into any other language, a fact mainly to be attributed to the efforts of my dear longtime friend Ayako Kikuchi, now a professor of sociology in Tokyo. But the visit would have delayed the completion of my academic freedom study. Another difference from former times was the smaller amount of free time I had for my favorite occupation, independent writing. Aside from a little book published in my last Columbia years, *Democracy and the Economic Challenge,* the result of lectures delivered at the University of Michigan Law School, my sole publication other than research reports was *The Pursuit of Happiness* (1955). It was my first book of untrammelled reflection. Possibly the reason why it is my favorite brainchild is that it gave me so much satisfaction of an evening or over a week end to forget my studious researching and let my thoughts range free over our human lot and the vast beyond. The rare article I wrote during this time was equally free from the academic harness. There were two I put my heart into, "The Deep Beauty of the Golden Rule" and "The Art of Contemplation."

It remains for me to make acknowledgment of the fine tokens of scholarly recognition bestowed on me in this period. A follow-up of the testimonial dinner on my retirement from Columbia was the publication of a *Festschrift*. It was entitled *Freedom and Control in Modern Society,* edited by two of my former students, Morroe Berger and Charles H. Page, along with my sociological colleague of long standing and close neighbor, Theodore Abel. This volume contained a notable series of articles by distinguished associates and also included two generous assessments of my own work by old students, on the sociological side by the incisive thinker, Harry Alpert, and on the political side by a scholar who has done much to interpret the quality of democracy, David Spitz. A brochure of testimonies was issued at the same time, including a very touching one from my sociologist son-in-law, Robert Bierstedt. Through the generous contributions of special friends, there was also a lasting memorial in the form of an annual MacIver award, given for an outstanding work in the field of sociology, and I have taken pride in the roll of authors who have thus far been recipients. Besides, a number of honorary degrees were added to those I had earlier received, including Princeton, Yale, the Jewish Theological Seminary, the New School for Social Research, the University of Edinburgh, and the University of Toronto, as well as several awards, including the Woodrow Wilson Award for the best book of the year in political science and at a later time the Kurt Lewin Award from the Society for the Psychological Study of Social Issues.

Certain differences in the manner of presenting awards would make an interesting sociological study, but here I shall pause to note only a striking difference between the pomp and circumstance that attended the conferment of my one old-country honorary degree and the simple rituals observed by our own institutions. At Edinburgh one was expected to show up for the occasion in the cutaway coat and striped trousers of "morning dress" and don before the ceremony the magnificent scarlet robe of the doctorate. The conferment itself was conducted in an atmosphere of sonorous solemnity and followed by a stately service in St. Giles Cathedral. In the evening one sat on a dais at a full-dress banquet surrounded by university leaders and city dignitaries in official regalia. There was a series of toasts beginning with queen and country proposed in short stylish and witty speeches as the wine went round. Without being a devotee of ceremony, I felt it accented the significance of the occasion and made me sense more fully the honor that was being bestowed on me by a great historical institution.

I felt it proper to list these tributes, as part of the record. They tend to enhance a man's academic standing and give the comfortable feeling that he has the respect of his colleagues and that his endeavors are not wholly without influence. I am not, however, much elated by approbation or deflated by adverse criticism, though the latter may have something to teach me. I have my own standard and my own judgment as to how far I reach it and where I fall short. In the flush of writing I am not conscious of inadequacies, but as soon as the work is finished and even more when I see it in print, I am aware of its omissions, of things I ought to have said, and ways I ought to have said them, of apt illustrations I ought to have used. I have not been the adherent of any school, the follower of any vogue. This last remark has particular application to the sociology of the academies, where one dominating vogue is succeeded by another. In at least one respect I fail to live up to the image of the true scholar. I am not an assiduous delver for details. I don't have any particular interest in discovering whether it is 62 or 64 per cent of the well-to-do who subscribe to more than six periodicals or whether 46 or 51 per cent of urban dwellers think society would be better off if more people went regularly to church—and so with numerous other researches that engross our diligent sociologists. I am interested in the structure of organizations, the patterns and trends of social, economic, and political life, the moving forces that are forever changing the face of society, from the lonely homestead to the greatest conurbation, in the centers of world power and in the deeps of the most backward countries. Any details that can throw light on such processes I find well worth the search.

23

I Become
a Municipal Employee

This chapter is the chronicle of a large-scale evaluative research project commissioned by the greatest of municipalities. It is a story of frustrations and cross-purposes, of bureaucratic rigidities and pleas to deaf ears, but also of friends in need, of the devoted service of a grand team, and of very partial achievement.

I was a neophyte in the offices of government. Although as a student of political affairs I had an inkling of the special problems that lie in wait for the agent of a municipality or state, I now got a dose of experience that went far beyond my reckoning. I shall avoid naming names, wherever possible, though if I am to tell my story the anonymity must sometimes be thin.

While my United Nations study was drifting toward its close, new prospects were opening up. One that rather appealed to me was an invitation from the president of the Russell Sage Foundation, on the board of which I sat, to conduct a countrywide study of the training of social workers. I was still making up my mind about undertaking it when I was invited by Mayor Robert Wagner to become the director of an evaluative study of the agencies of the city that were active in programs and policies for the prevention or control of juvenile delinquency. I regarded the offer as a notable if unexpected challenge and accepted it forthwith. I had a modest acquaintance with the subject and had supervised several dissertations in this field by my Columbia graduates—which is a good enough way of advancing a teacher's education.

It was a somewhat unusual commission I was given. What led to it were the flagrant cases of juvenile slayings and gang "rumbles" that had been featured in the press and the statistical evidences of an increasing volume of delinquency almost every year since the Second World War. There was a consequent public outcry that "something be done about it." A preliminary survey, known as the Epstein Report, had just been issued, recommending a thorough five-year investigation.

So, as of January 1, 1956, I embarked on my new task. I was given quarters on a floor of the tower of City College—which bore no resemblance to the ivory tower I have been occasionally accused of occupying. There was a good reason why I was not housed in the Municipal Building or any other city office. A regulation was then in force, the Lyons law, one of those narrowly parochial ordinances that diminish alike the dignity and the civic efficiency of a great city, which required city employees to be residents within its borders. This regulation exempted teachers—even a nitwit could see the need for that—which explains why, after being appointed by the mayor, I was reappointed by the Board of Higher Education.

I began operations in a few bare offices with two staff members recruited in advance. My budget called for eight associate researchers, an assistant to the director, and some part-time consultants (for the last-mentioned provision I was able presently to substitute an assistant director). The business ahead of us was one of considerable magnitude. We were expected to investigate and evaluate the functioning of three houses of detention, for boys, girls, and adolescents, respectively; three city courts and their probation and parole systems; over twenty custodial centers for young delinquents, including state "training schools" and private religious or undenominational institutions, all city-supported; several city departments having relevant programs, including the Departments of Health, Welfare, and Correction; the programs for behavioral and vocational guidance in the public school system and also some special schools of particular interest to us; and finally the major city agency for delinquency control, the Youth Board.

As our research staff gradually increased, I developed a plan for the accomplishment of our many-sided tasks. It involved what in the jargon of the academy was called a multidisciplinary team, political scientists, psychologists, sociologists, a social worker, and a lawyer. Each was assigned a particular institution, agency branch, or program for intensive investigation over a period varying from six months to a year or longer; a second member would be asked to make an occasional visit to check on the findings of the primary researcher. I prepared the way by preliminary visits to the head officials in the various areas of our research. Each researcher reported to me at intervals, and in due course submitted his draft report. This was read by the whole staff and thereafter given a critical scrutiny in a full-scale session.

This review session was quite an ordeal for the author of the draft. We were a congenial team, but for this occasion everyone sharpened his wits to detect flaws, omissions, loose statements, unestablished inferences, inadequacies of any kind. We were all jealous of the accuracy and quality of our reports. But the writers of the drafts sometimes took it rather hard. A series of consultations and processing stages followed before we had a report ready for submission.

Many of our recommendations were disregarded, a number were adopted sooner or later, and a few quite important ones are still being fought over. I had organized a strong committee of citizens who were of great help in advancing our public relations. I was well aware how reports molder on official shelves unless strong pressure groups can be brought to bear on public inertia and opposing interests.

I could tell many tales of our encounters with officials, tough ones and easy ones, pleasant ones and not so pleasant, during these years of devoted investigation, but that would overweight this cursory narrative. A case or two will indicate the kinds of problems we faced.

Within the public school system we had quite a variety of experiences. We issued four reports on school operations. One was on the

All Day Neighborhood Schools, a very promising and well-thought-out development for the service of seriously disprivileged children, another was a broad assessment of programs for the behavioral and vocational guidance of pupils, and two others were devoted to the special "600" day schools for refractory or particularly difficult youngsters. Our first report on the "600" day schools was highly critical, of the screening process for admission, of the programs for the educational advancement and the social training of these severely retarded pupils, of the method of selecting the specially qualified teachers they needed, in short of the whole system, although one or two of these schools were decidedly better than the others.

This report aroused a storm of protest at Board of Education headquarters. We were charged with gross misrepresentation. Complaints were made to city hall that we didn't know our business. Journalists were inspired to write favorable accounts of these schools. I felt sure of our ground and decided on a follow-up investigation. Our first had concentrated on the administration, the day-to-day procedures, the curriculum, and the services these schools provided. Now we made a thorough study of what happened to the children who were discharged or dropped out from the schools and also of the scholastic and behavioral attainment that pupils who entered in a particular year displayed at the stage of "graduating." It took us many months to collect and check these statistics—incidentally, a job the schools ought themselves to have done. It made a sorry exhibit. We fully realized how tough and uphill a task it was to arouse interest and evoke incentive in these rebellious and often cynical boys, and we certainly did not expect a miracle of redemption. But other experiments had shown that with patient, persistent, and well-guided effort significant improvement could be achieved. It was therefore very discouraging to find that on leaving the "600" schools the boys were practically all still greatly retarded educationally, especially in reading. The schools had served as a "containing" system rather than a rehabilitating one. It was therefore no wonder that after entering high school, mostly vocational school, they began to drop out in a continuous stream and that not one of those who had left the "600" schools in 1954 was reported as completing the high-school curriculum.

We strongly urged that no expansion of the "600" school system be made until its programs and policies were thoroughly overhauled in the light of the research and experience relevant to the education of troubled and troublesome youth. Our reports drew the attention of Commissioner Allen of the State Department of Education. He arranged for his own report, which duly corroborated our findings. Now instead of outraged protests there were announcements of improvements already planned and being put into effect. The need for reform was taken seriously and further advanced by a later, reconstructed Board of Education.

There has been a curious sequel to this affair. Some six years after these happenings and only a few months before this writing, a deputation visited me in my new office (which implies a story belonging to a later chapter), a deputation that included the principal of a "600" school and a gentleman with some connections at city hall, and invited me to undertake one more study of the "600" schools. I was unable, however, to get it financed. To write a very different report from our former ones would be a most pleasant task.

The second case I take concerned our investigation of the probation services of the city courts, at that time consisting of the Domestic Relations Court (with the Children's Court), the Magistrates Court, and the Court of Special Sessions. This was before the reorganization of the state judicial system. Each had its separate cohort of probation officers. The system had many shortcomings. The officers were poorly paid, inadequately trained, carrying too heavy case loads, and too dependent on the presiding judge to develop any initiative of their own. The service itself was perfunctory, offering little protection or guidance to the troubled youngsters under its almost nominal charge. In addition to recommendations on all these counts, we urged the amalgamation of the three services. The change would make for economy as well as efficiency, permitting unified recruiting and in-service training. The combined services, we claimed, should be headed by a chief probation officer of high quality and experience. Thus the probation function would acquire a more professional character, and there would be more freedom to develop plans for improved procedures and better supervision.

Two of the three presiding judges rejected our proposal for a unified service. But I determined to fight on, since we had considerable outside support for our proposals. One of the two opposing judges had not taken kindly to our investigation from the outset. I had several encounters with him. The first time was when I asked his permission to interview probation officers and obtain certain other evidences. His opening gambit was: "Have you ever been a probation officer?" When I said no, he flatly refused my request. It was a quaint bit of reasoning on the part of His Honor. My request was a courtesy one, since I had the authority to proceed without his approval. I intimated as much. "I'll call the mayor myself," he replied. He never did, and he reluctantly allowed me to make the necessary inquiries.

A good arena for the contention that followed was provided in the form of a monthly meeting of city officials, which was presided over by the director of the Youth Board, Ralph Whalen. I brought the proposal before this group, which included the presiding judges. It was argued for and against through several sessions, and in the end we obtained a good majority. One presiding judge was with us from the beginning, and the less obdurate of my two major opponents, with whom I had several private sessions, modified his objections and admitted there was something to be said for as well as against the proposal. So it was accepted and a bill drafted for the unification of the probation system, which was duly passed. Presently a highly competent probation chief, John A. Wallace, was appointed and important reforms are being gradually achieved.

In the course of our five and a half years, we issued eighteen "interim" reports, each dealing with a specific service or institution or group of institutions, followed by three "final" reports of broader range and concerned with major policies. There were some services we found to be well conceived and well executed; there were some fine officials and more than a few devoted and intelligent workers. But we found many lacks, and shortcomings, and we made many recommendations. Many of them met no effective response. Not infrequently the reform we proposed was fully endorsed by the agency under consideration, but the funds necessary to effect it were not granted. In other cases the reform was not dependent on additional funds, and the failure to implement it was due to the inertia or the objection of those in control. In such situations any success we achieved was usually the result of pressures and appeals on the part of interested citizen groups or a sequel of press reports of our findings. In the case of one major department, we had no effect whatever except when a popular evening newspaper cited a recommendation we had made respecting it.

Back of all our efforts was a feeling that rankled in me. We had been asked by the mayor to inquire what the city should do to reduce the menace of delinquency, but our recommendations, the result of considerable research, drew no kind of response, no real effort at implementation, from city hall. I sometimes wondered who at city hall ever read our succinct reports. A partial explanation for our very limited success is that the agency with the broad commission to co-ordinate and organize the city's activities in this area, the Youth Board, did not possess the power—or in our judgment the type of organization—this task called for. It was heavily engaged in subsidiary activities. Moreover, the Youth Board was itself an agency we evaluated, and it was not happy about our recommendations concerning it.

These conditions gave point to the most far-reaching of our recommendations—that a new supervising and planning authority be set up, exclusively devoted to this objective, composed of citizens of top rating in relevant achievement and experience, and directly responsible to the mayor. Had such an authority been in existence it would already have corrected, or prevented from developing many of the shortcomings to which our recommendations were directed. It would have established a system of priorities, based on experiment and experience. For example, all indications showed that the chances of successful treatment are much better for the incipient delinquent or the near-delinquent vulnerable youth than for the delinquent who is already inured to law-breaking behavior. While both types should be given the most promising treatment, it was a fact that the attention devoted to the earlier stages by our City agencies was minimal. To emphasize this need, we were able, with the assistance of a leading city official, Abe Stark, to set up our own program for the discovery, protection, and care of early offenders in a high delinquency neighborhood of the South Bronx, and it was beginning to show good results when we had to relinquish it because our project had come to its end.

We made a strong plea for the establishment of the kind of supervising and planning bureau we had projected but were defeated by the opposition of potent interests. For one thing, our plan would have deprived the Youth Board of its highest function. But the fight was not ended, nor is it to the time of writing. A later report has reinforced our recommendation. In one form or another this essential reform will yet be realized.

No other investigation captivated me so wholly as did this one. None presented me with such a variety of problems or with so many harassments and bureaucratic obstacles. For this kind of evaluative study the main problem is to get below the official surface, below the published reports, the information provided by the administration, the guarded statements of staff members, in order to attain adequate evidence of the effectiveness of the treatment, of the actual responsiveness of the beneficiaries of the service. We tried to sound out directly the views of the pupils or inmates, but that was not easy or always to be relied upon. We found that the interrogation of former officials, workers, and inmates was sometimes helpful.

I have left to the last a brief account of the chief impediments the city bureaucracy put in our way. I could not complain of the resistance exhibited by a few agency heads. It was natural enough that executives should dislike to have outsiders nosing into their affairs, though actually most of them did co-operate with us. But it was a genuine grievance when high members of the administration that had invited me to undertake this important task kept on making it needlessly difficult for me to accomplish it.

From the first I was stymied because our project was mistakenly put on a "provisional" basis. This meant that my staff and my secretaries were not eligible for the increments other city agents and civil service secretaries regularly receive. The budget director admitted to me it was an error—he was not aware it was planned as a five-year program! But he made out it might take a year and a half to get our status changed, and he took no step in that direction. So I had to carry on with secretaries who were disadvantaged and with a research staff which from the beginning was underpaid and could expect no redress. It had been arranged that the then deputy mayor would be my go-between when I had requests to make to the mayor. I poured out my woes to him, and he told me in sweet, sympathetic tones he would see what could be done. But nothing happened. I was sure that if I could get directly to the mayor he would salvage his own project. But I repeatedly failed to reach him since he was engrossed in one crisis or another. Sometimes I was informed at city hall that the budget for the following year was, owing to financial stringency, "frozen."

During the second year my pleas were still unheeded, and there were additional aggravations. I could not expect to retain my secretaries and some of my research staff were restless. I was determined not to carry on under these conditions. After a vain effort to get assurance at city hall, I went into a huddle with a few friendly officials, told them I was resigning and would see that my indignant letter of resignation was given publicity. They begged me not to resign. "You could approach a foundation," they said, "and we guarantee that next year your needs will be met." I was most loathe to disrupt the work we were all devoted to. So I yielded and was fortunate indeed that the New York Foundation agreed for the sake of the enterprise to provide the modest increments we should be receiving, on the understanding that the city would thereafter meet its own obligation. I also stipulated that in future I must have direct access to the mayor, since my go-between had been so unhelpful.

Thereafter the project went well for a time. I had opportunitites to speak to the mayor, who seemed entirely sympathetic and little aware of the difficulties we had experienced. I was assured of the budget addition we needed for the following year. The budget director was so informed, but he took the occasion to berate me for violating city ordinance number so-and-so, which forbade outside supplements for work the city was paying for!

Even then my troubles were not all over. For our final year I needed increments for our still underpaid research staff. I had already had to make one or two replacements, and one or two others had made a sacrifice to stay with us when they had more rewarding offers elsewhere. Besides, when we set up our early-discovery program in the South Bronx, the budget director had reduced the sum we decided was necessary to complete the staffing of the experiment. I failed to reach the mayor this time until it was too late. But again I was lucky. At short notice my good friend Stephen Currier, who had recently established the Taconic Foundation, realized the significance of our undertaking and came to my rescue. It came as a great shock to me when I learned, while completing this work, that Stephen and his wife, two such dedicated and still young contributors to great causes, had been lost in a little plane flying between Puerto Rico and the Virgin Islands.

From the whole experience I learned much about the city and how the city was run. I became deeply impressed by the hopelessness of its many submerged areas overpopulated by untrained, badly educated, frightened, and exploited minority groups. The war against delinquency could achieve some results, could rescue some of the youth of these areas, but the breeding ground of a mass of social pathology, including high delinquency, would still be there until these conditions were abolished. And I had learned what a vast enterprise it would be to stay the spreading rot of these areas, and what devotion, what massive well-guided expenditure, and what courage it would take to achieve their redemption.

I have been recounting the resistances and thwartings that beset my work as a municipal employee, but I would not want to leave the impression that I did not enjoy the effort and the struggle. For me the experience was rewarding and well worth while. Our successes were indeed limited, but it was a stage in the continuous fight for social advancement.

There was another very satisfying aspect of our project. I got together a most loyal and warmly co-operative staff. This statement applies equally to its secretarial and its research members. When we disbanded it was like the breakup of a big devoted family. Most of them have remained in more or less close association with me. The first recruit for the project, Jerome Liblit, a first-class man in every respect, became the program director of my latest enterprise. Another research member, Jeanette Gevov, gave me timely help in my recently published study of delinquency across the country. Sophia Robison, who was "assistant to the director," is teaching in the institution in which I have been playing an important role. William Thomas, now a professor at Columbia, has given a course of special lectures in the above-mentioned enterprise and is a consultant in a major research project we have established. Judith Greifer (now Benjamin) is occupied in a line of research closely related to the juvenile delinquency activities, on the National Committee for the Employment of Youth, with which I am also associated. William Goldsmith, now professor at Brandeis, has remained in consultation with me in various matters of common interest. My very able and companionable assistant director, Monsignor Paul Furfey, has returned from Washington to visit us on several occasions. Ernest Smith, now a professor at Hunter College, has been a regular attender of our parties, and Bonnie Wilkinson, now at Columbia, comes when she can. Our whole team, excepting one or two who have left the city, have held reunions on particular occasions—my own birthdays, an engagement, a wedding, a promotion, whatever it might be. These have been cheery festive occasions, where twelve or fourteen of us have foregathered around the table, recalling incidents of our days together, laughing over minor misadventures of that time, discussing new developments along the line of our recommendations. Some of our fine, devoted secretaries have always been present at these parties, usually Virginia, Lola, Dorothy, and Louise. A smaller group, whose place of work is not very far away from mine, has met together for lunch more frequently. Nobody could have had a finer or more congenial team than I possessed while in the service of the city.

24

I End Up as an Administrator

When the Juvenile Delinquency Evaluation Project came to an end in August, 1961, I looked forward to enjoying a somewhat less strenuous life. I could combine a bit of research, which would eke out my income beyond my tiny pension and the precarious returns from writings, with free-lance literary work. I always had the feeling I could write a better book than any I had written. I was like the golfer who thinks his last score, or his top score, did not do him justice. Next time he would know better how to play his chip shots, and he was losing some quite unnecessary strokes on the greens. I was approaching my eightieth birthday. I had no time to lose. I was in very good health, as eager as ever for the pursuit, and feeling quite capable of accomplishment.

My plan worked out pretty much as I had hoped. It was suggested to me that the National Institute of Mental Health might approve a grant for a country-wide conspectus of juvenile delinquency, following up our New York City study. The grant was approved, and I accepted it on condition that I could undertake the research on a half-time basis, so as to have ample time for my own writing. Such grants usually require an academic sponsorship, and I requested the New School for Social Research to act in this capacity, since I was associated with it as a member of its board.

For the next year and a half I followed this course with much contentment. The kind of writing that appealed to me at this stage was reflective commentary on the human lot, my philosophy of living, so to speak. I had been able to produce one little book in my bits of leisure during the previous five years, *Life: Its Dimensions and Its Bounds,* which appeared in 1960. It was the only book I wrote in the form of a dialogue, so that I could present the contrast between the prosaic matter-of-fact viewpoint of the plodding biologist, who was content to think of life as a product of organic chemistry, and the more imaginative outlook of the thinker, who claimed that to trace the emergence of a new phenomenon that has qualities not possessed by the constituents from which it has emerged is no explanation of the emergent—no explanation of what life is, no explanation of what life does or of how it is capable of development from a unicellular virus-like germ to man himself. It was a thoroughly controversial little book, alight with the true joy of battle. In the eighteen month interlude after the J.D.E.P. I found time to write another little book more directly concerned with the philosophy of living. It was published under the title *The Challenge of the Passing Years,* though my own preference was *Encounter with Time.* The problem it sought to face is perennial and universal.

My spell of occupied leisure was then abruptly ended, in a way I could never have anticipated. I found myself thrust into the presidency of an institution of learning.

For a great many years I had been a member of the board of the New School for Social Research, arising out of my friendship with Alvin Johnson, its first president. Alvin was one of the group of distinguished Columbia professors who had founded the institution at the end of the First World War, a galaxy including Beard and Robinson, Wesley Mitchell and John Dewey. Other outstanding figures came to give lectures there; among them were Franz Boas, Maynard Keynes, Harold Laski, Robert Frost, T. S. Eliot, Walter Lippmann, and Alfred Adler. It was founded in a spirit of protest, to give full range to scholarly freedom, a college for adults, without academic routines and with freedom to experiment while maintaining the highest quality of scholarship. Among those who joined the teaching staff at the outset were Thorstein Veblen and Horace Kallen. It began its career as a unique institution for the "continued education of the educated."

Its early years, however, were rifted with crises, because of financial troubles and divided opinions over policy. But its first president, Alvin Johnson, took firm grasp of the reins. It surmounted its difficulties owing to his ingenuity and his ability to make the effective last-moment appeal for funds. The school grew and flourished and moved to its present headquarters on Twelfth Street. Alvin's most notable exploit was the establishment of the "University in Exile," an academic asylum for leading European scholars expelled under the Nazi terror from the universities of Germany and later from Italy, Austria, and Spain. This great enterprise was made possible mainly by the timely offer of support by a then unknown friend, the philanthropic Hiram Halle of Hart, Schaffner, and Marx. The accession of these scholars gave a new academic standing to the institution, and they became its graduate faculty.

When Alvin at length resigned, the school ran into new troubles, but steadied itself again when Hans Simons took command. After his resignation there was the not uncommon difficulty of finding the kind of president this distinctive but quite unorthodox institution needed. There were delays and a last-minute disappointment in the process, and when a president was finally elected, he was a good man for other types of position but miscast for this one. There was disgruntlement and dissension on every hand, and the generous donors who had over the years met our operating deficits were alienated. The financial position became most precarious. When under these stresses our new president resigned, the board was at a loss to find another head under such unpromising conditions. Presently I came under pressure from my fellow board members. They urged me to take over in the hope that with their strong support I could bring the school back to its lost equilibrium.

The appeal came as an unmitigated surprise. I had never had any desire to become an administrator. During my professional career I had on four occasions been approached to allow my name to be presented for the presidency of a college or university, and I had always refused. With the myriad calls and distractions of office I would no longer have been able to sink myself deeply into some subject of absorbing interest, nor would I have possessed the leisure for free writing. It was not for me. But now I felt a special obligation. I was devoted to the school. I believed in its unique educational mission. I began by saying no, and my wife was strongly against it. But I yielded, not without apprehension. In April, 1963, I took over as president. I put on ice my other commitments, particularly the study I had in hand for the National Institute of Health—I was grateful for the courteous way in which they agreed to my request.

My apprehension soon vanished. The challenge became uppermost. With the warm support I received from staff and administration and board, the task became more pleasant than I had dreamed it could be. I also had the advantage of having as presidential aide, a lady, Mrs. Lillie Froelich, who had an unrivalled and discerning knowledge of the background of all the school's affairs. There were of course problems to be overcome. A few disgruntled staff members had to be reassured. A few who were making excessive demands had to be kept in line. One particularly troublesome case had to be firmly disposed of. It would be invidious to go into details on these matters, and in any event they were merely symptoms of an inadequacy of leadership that had had more serious consequences.

In the last resort the major problems were financial. The original and dominant sector of the enlarged institution, the School for Adults, had admirably maintained its standards through all vicissitudes. Its students had greatly increased, and when I took over they approached ten thousand, the majority of whom were college graduates who attended because they were interested in the rich spread of courses in literature, the fine arts, the performing arts, the humanities in all their aspects, social and economic movements, philosophical systems, and so forth. The lecturers were part-time members of the school, most of them giving only one or two once-a-week courses. This system made it possible for the school to enlist artists, authors, architects, and specialists across the arts and the sciences, who were quite ready to spend one evening a week at the school holding forth on their field of major interest and thus providing the remarkable range and quality of the school's offerings. But troubles had devel-

oped, in the first instance because of the poor remuneration a majority of the lecturers received. In the hand-to-mouth style that had
characterized the struggling institution in its earlier years, the lecturer was paid 50 per cent of the fees. The system worked exceedingly well for the few lecturers who attracted classes running into
several hundreds, but those who had minimum classes got the
scantiest of remuneration. Shortly before I took office, the then dean,
William Birenbaum, abolished this undignified and dubiously equit-
able system for fixed stipends, graded according to length of service,
reputation, and the attractiveness of the course. The transition was
difficult, it raised the lowest rates of pay and reduced the highest.
There was a good deal of complaining and protesting, but Dean
Birenbaum was resolute. He was an effective and imaginative administrator and had done as good a job as was possible with the very
limited funds at his disposal. Obviously, to maintain standards in
this as in other areas, we had to improve our financial status. The
task was of high priority.

It was eminently so for our graduate faculty. When it was simply
the "University in Exile," the rescued European scholars had been
happily content with the modest comfort and security the school
provided. Now that it had become a regular graduate faculty, it had
to compete for qualified scholars against other institutions at a time
when the greatly increased demand for them was accompanied by
considerable rises in the salary scales. I felt that the fine spirit of
liberal scholarship that had characterized the "University in Exile"
was no longer maintained. A few weeks before my incumbency, we
lost three of our best men, one in sociology and two in psychology,
because we could not meet the offer of other institutions. I was able
to prevent further losses of that type by obtaining a promise from
one of the school's best friends that he would make up the difference
when a more lucrative offer elsewhere threatened the loss of a really
good man. But the school's resources had to be greatly augmented
to put it on a sound basis, if we were not only to maintain but to
enhance its standards and have any assurance for its future.

The school had no endowment of any kind. It was high time a
beginning was made. But first the general fund for everyday needs
must be increased, and to this task the board and the administration

bent their efforts. We were fortunate in having a remarkably large increase in registration, and our fees, which had been below the level set by neighboring institutions, were raised. Special appeals were made to former friends of the institution. A particularly interesting feature of the new drive was that our first president, the man who had done more than anyone else to give form and direction to the institution, was spurred by the situation to devote himself, with a return of his old vigor and efficiency, to the cause.

Within two years the school moved from the edge of insolvency to a modest security, with a more comfortable budget than it had possessed for quite a number of years. The first steps had been taken to raise salaries, especially in the graduate faculty. There was new hope and new promise.

During my third and last summer as president, the affairs of the school were so relatively comfortable that I was able to give some thought again to my postponed research for the National Institute of Mental Health, and I enlisted the aid of a former research associate (Jeanette Gevov) to collect some information I needed in that connection. The resulting work was finally published in the fall of 1966, as *The Strategy of Delinquency Prevention and Control.*

My expectation had been to serve as a stop-gap president for a year or so, when troubles would have quieted down and a new president been found. But it was two and a half years before the board settled on a new president, John Everett. For me these were years of enriched experience, of tasks more formidable in the distance than in the endeavor, of quiet adventuring. And in the process I made notable additions to the number of my friends.

During these years there were some episodes that remain bright in my memory. One of them I record here. In November, 1963, I paid my first visit to Israel, to participate in the inauguration of the president of the University of Tel Aviv. The new president, George S. Wise, had been one of the ablest students I ever had at Columbia, where he took his doctorate. He seemed marked out for an academic career. But his progress was interrupted by an arthritic ailment that meant a period of hospitalization. It was during the severity of the great depression, and he had to make shift to earn a living. His ingenuity saw him through. Persuading a stricken travel agency that he could get them out of the red, he succeeded so remarkably well that he soon became its senior partner. Now, possessed of a competence, he gave up business to return to the academic fold. He was minded to train to become a medical research specialist, and made arrangement to enter a medical college. But again his old trouble returned most inopportunely, and he was unable to register when the college opened in the fall. Everything conspired to send him back to the world of business. He found an opportunity in the export of pulp and paper to Mexico and Latin-America in general, and again, through foresightedness, fluent knowledge of Spanish, an ability to cultivate relationships, he rose to the top, becoming the leading exporter to Latin-America, among his other exploits building the first newsprint mill in Mexico. But he still yearned for the academic life. He became an authority on Latin-American affairs, writing books on leading *caudillos*. At last he succeeded, giving up his major business activities on his appointment as the president of the University of Tel Aviv.

I had kept in close contact and friendship with him across the years, and it was for me a delight to be present and to speak at his inauguration. Since then, in the space of two or three years, he has turned a small struggling institution into a modern university, already well equipped to provide the scientific, medical, social, and cultural expertise that is of such prime importance to the young state of Israel.

During my one week in Israel I was able under good guidance to see at first hand the remarkable changes in their ancient homeland that the skill and devotion of its people were achieving, the agricultural and horticultural experiments, the development of industries, the renewal of culture. The country is a geographical anomaly, an incredible makeshift, a patchwork between deserts, where no milk and honey flow, but it was beginning to flourish. It brought strange thoughts to one who had been bred on the Bible to stand in Jerusalem and look across the narrow border to the lost holy places in hostile Jordan or to walk the streets of Askalon, where the news was not to be published of how the mighty of Israel had fallen.

Following Through

By the end of 1965 the school was in a much healthier situation than at the beginning of 1963. Every organization has its own breed of life, and there are some that make a remarkable recovery from their ailments. Not only was the school's financial position greatly improved but most of its internal troubles had been alleviated. The urgent need had brought forth the requisite response. I felt somewhat like a doctor who is aware in his heart that the patient's betterment is mainly due to other forces than his own prescriptions. With the necessary stimulus, the potencies of the body, so to speak, had reasserted themselves.

It had been my original intention to resign as soon as a new president was established in office. But a program I had initiated and which I regarded as capable of making an important contribution to the school's development and to its role among our institutions of learning, the Center for New York City Affairs, was still in the making and I had a strong desire to see it well established before I said good-bye. There was a definite danger that it would get under the control of the wrong man, and though I gave emphatic warnings to avert the danger I was quite uneasy about it.

My desire was to remain in charge for one year more. I made no overtures to that effect, because of two considerations. One was that an incoming president might very naturally not care to have his predecessor around. I did not want to be put in that embarrassing position. The other was that after all I was now in my eighties, far and away beyond the age when retirement is normally required and when the capacity for administrative responsibilities is held to be tenuous and at best precarious. The board had taken a chance in appointing me president. Now with a vigorous young president in office they would see no need to take a further risk with me.

It is unwise to make needless concessions to the tradition of the calendar, to stop living an active life in submission to the general belief that after a certain age one ought to, that one is no longer qualified to undertake an important job. I was in very good health, and I did not believe my work was deteriorating—though of course I might be prejudiced on the latter score.

So it came to me as a pleasant surprise when the board followed up the election of our new president by my appointment as chancellor, a new title at the school. It meant that while I would presumably be consulted on major matters affecting the institution I could devote myself during the following academic year mainly to my nursling, the Center for New York City Affairs.

When I took charge at the school it was obviously in need of financial restoration and the mediation of certain internal dissensions, but to maintain its former quality it had also to move in new directions as well as build up some areas that were lagging in development. After some comments on the last-mentioned objective, I shall turn to the new enterprise of the school that was my main reason for remaining with it for one year more.

The major academic weakness was in the graduate faculty. It had a number of competent and scholarly teachers, and it turned out some excellent graduates. But it no longer had the distinction it possessed when the "University in Exile" brought to the school many of the most eminent scholars of Europe, a great galaxy of economists, sociologists, psychologists, political scientists, jurists. Now the facutly was struggling for survival. Its salary scale was too low to be competitive, and at the time I entered some of its best younger men were leaving for more attractive positions elsewhere. New incentives, new opportunities, new leaders were needed, but that would take time. All I was able to effect was a gradual but inadequate rise in the salary scale. In addition I initiated overtures to the Ford Foundation for aid in the establishment of a new M.A. program covering a wider range of subjects and better adapted to the intellectual aptitudes of our more mature student body. Under my successor the graduate faculty has already been enhanced, and the new M.A. program has been successfully negotiated and inaugurated. Furthermore, with the able co-operation of our new dean, Allen Austill, a superior type of Senior Day College has been set up.

There are two ways in which an institution of learning can maintain or achieve distinction in the highly competitive market for able scholars that has arisen from the great expansion of colleges and universities throughout the country. One is by being blessed with large endowments and a body of wealthy alumni or being a state institution with a legislature that is willing and able to vote munificent budgets annually, so that it can afford to attract and hold outstanding professors in every category. The other is by fostering some area of concentration within the wide field of learning so that the institution comes to be regarded as a leader in this area. The New School is remote from the likelihood of acquiring eminence in the former way. But from the outset it set itself to gain distinction from the quality and sophistication of its ever increasing range of courses in adult education. As I envisaged its prospects, its future depended on limiting its expansion in other directions, while selectively advancing standards and cultivating to the full the potentialities of its major field, the education of adults.

I had as a teacher always wanted, and always failed, to initiate programs for the exploration and teaching of the movements and trends of social life in the great city. Then, as president of the New School, I set my sights higher and worked on plans for a new area of scholarly activity within the institution, a whole division focused on the needs, special features, and problems of the metropolis. The scheme received wide approbation and encouragement alike from leading citizens and city authorities. But we craved more than "God speed you"—we wanted the resources to set it going. The school was in no position to launch projects involving new expenditures.

It was a gala day for me when in an enthusiastic letter my good friend and our most generous donor, J. M. Kaplan, pledged a sum of $100,000 as a priming fund. I enlisted in the cause my able former research associate, Jerry Liblit, and we went to work with a will. By February of 1965 we held our first classes on city affairs, given by leading erperts and drawing in a group of highly qualified students. We held the first of what has proven to be a very serviceable series of seminars by invitation, where we succeeded in bringing together, for the searching discussion of some major city problems, municipal authorities, planners, participants in the field of operation, critics, opponents, and others intimately acquainted with the subject. The record of these seminars is then, whenever funds are available, handed over to a skilled writer for the preparation of a succinct volume providing our citizens with the best available information on the issue. We devised special training programs for city employees, potential employees, and volunteer workers. We planned a series of fundamental researches on the larger and more controversial problems that beset the city and were particularly gratified when the Samuel Rubin Foundation came forward with the funds for our first such project, a scrutiny of the public health services of the city. We were also much indebted to the New York Foundation for enabling us to set up the Metropolitan Information Service, so that we could send out regular bulletins on city operations, movements and developments, as well as special reports on significant current situations. We acquired a very able administrator, Sol Markof, who has unearthed much unavailable information and skilfully presented it in the regular bulletins of the service. For the first time the citizens of New York City are beginning to be provided with a wide range of timely, tested knowledge concerning its many-sided affairs, the challenging questions they raise, the steps that are being taken to resolve its troubles, and the further developments of policy that may be requisite. The whole program was a new development in the area of adult education.

The new center, moreover, gave some needed justification to the title of our institution, The New School *for Social Research*. Research had hitherto had a minimum role within the institution. Ours was the kind of research that had a direct bearing on the well-being of society, an area of research on the whole neglected elsewhere, because of the vogue for quantitative studies. It was action research, no less scholarly on that account, research devoted mainly to the clarification and resolution of the complex problems of urbanization. The school was the most highly urbanized of our institutions of higher learning, since it drew the vast majority of its teachers and its students from the metropolitan area. It was therefore appropriate that it should aspire to be an independent research arm of our great city.

The inherent vitality of the center was shown in its steady progress. I had stayed on as chancellor mainly to be assured of its viability. Now I knew my mission was accomplished, and I sent in my resignation. It was pleasant to reflect that of all my post-retirement activities this New School episode was for me a new kind of challenge and had the richest reward in new experience.

The progress of the center exceeded my expectations, but I have never known of a new enterprise that did not run up against some obstacle or blockage. In our case the obstacle came from inside the institution. I had taken it for granted that the center was an integral part of the institution. However, the school was embarking at this time on a very considerable building program, and the administration apparently assumed that this precluded new expenditures in other directions, and that the new division would be self-supporting and not make calls on the general fund. We were running a modest deficit in our second year, largely owing to promotional activities, and I could obtain no promise that it would be met. This situation might have been a grievous threat to our future, but happily in the last few months of my tenure a most gratifying number of major researches for which we had sought funds were given the financing they needed. This development not only assured our role in metropolitan research, a major need in the complex and tangled economy of the city, but also provided funds sufficient to wipe out our deficit.

My period of administration put a stop to any serious writing, but before it began I had spent many absorbing hours pondering and making notes on the curious history of man's power over man and the resulting work, *Power Transformed*, was almost ready for the publishers when I took office. The subject of power in society had not in my judgment received any deep-searching treatment by political scientists. There were relatively few books addressed squarely to the subject, and few of the few were really significant. One thing that struck me was a direct relation between the degree of liberation of groups and peoples from powerlessness or sheer subjection and the amount of social violence and civil commotion. In other words, liberty in this context brought forth not peace but the sword. In the longer historical perspective there have occurred successive waves of social liberation, elevating subject classes from elite domination, abolishing slave classes, turning serfs into free workers or owners of land, raising workers from utter dependence on exploiting employers to membership in masterful unions, abolishing colonialism over the undeveloped areas of Asia and Africa and Latin-America, extending the right to vote to the very poor, emancipating women from legal and social subservience, asserting the rights of disprivileged minorities to equality of opportunity. Not only did this gradual process of liberation increase the amount of civil strife and social violence; it also, in our own age, the period in which these movements have been most fully advanced, culminated in the bloodiest holocausts of war in human history.

Some light is thrown on this unhappy relation between liberty and violence when we appreciate the fact that although many other attributes men prize can be distributed more or less equally between them power can never be divided in this manner. Society, if it so wills, can go very far to equalize opportunity, to equalize various human rights, even to equalize wealth. But not to equalize power. In fact the more you equalize other things, the more you must concentrate power to maintain the system. That is why communism in any strict sense must mean absolute rule, not the meaningless dictatorship of a proletariat but the sheer control of a potentate and his clique. Aside from that, the work of the world must be directed by the few; the many must always take the orders of the few, or else anarchy alone will reign. The best device the more advanced societies have found is to make the few who rule responsible in some sense to the many who obey. That is democracy, which is impossible without widespread civic education and the diversification of the economy into various foci of relatively autonomous power competing and conflicting and co-operating with one another and all of them bringing cross-pressures to bear on the central government. But even so, even under the form of democracy, the excercise of power still holds grave dangers to society. Human beings rarely choose the best qualified men, the true statesmen, to be their rulers. And the lesser men they choose are tempted to exploit their power. Power has an intoxicating effect, and the multitudes are easily gulled by rhetoric that panders to their prejudices. Political history is predominantly a history of misrule, under oligarchy and democracy alike.

These were the themes to which my new book was devoted. The first part of it was an exposure of the continuous series of gross errors and follies the governments of the West committed during the half-century ending in 1965, with the consequent train of evils that still continue to plague mankind.

Nor did the exhibits of the false calculations and the follies of ruling power cease with the end of the Second World War. The powers could not even make a peace, nothing better than the disruptive "cold war." And besides many other commotions and tensions there was the stupidly prolonged Korean War, and there is still at the time of writing the miserable drag-out of the unintended, undeclared, and confused war in Vietnam, escalated time and again beyond the assurances and expectations of our authorities, with all the perils of the bitter divisions it has created.

Most of my adult life had been lived under the shadow of great wars and threats of war. Through all these years I had been acutely conscious of the egregious unwisdom exhibited by so many of the men who rule over the nations. It was this thought that inspired what I thought then might be my last book, *Power Transformed*.

This present writing refutes that thought. Even before my retirement at the end of August, 1966, I had made the decision to write my own story. And before it was ready for the press, I became intrigued with a dramatic conception that held promise in my eyes. I have always regarded our greater novelists and dramatists as better social scientists than many professional contributors to that field. In all my later wanderings I have continued to engage in the study and presentation of the tangled social relationships of people.

In my final retirement I seem to be no less busy than when I was in academic harness. Nor is my work any less enjoyable. As every right-minded academician should sooner or later do, advisedly sooner rather than later, I resigned, with a sense of relief, from a number of committees, retaining, however, a rather exacting one I enjoyed, the research committee of the American Philosophical Society, whose chief function is to allot grants in aid of research to scholars across the whole field of the sciences and arts, and taking on a pleasant unexacting new one, in my role as president of an organization devoted to the rescue of some of the buildings that formed part of the unlamented New York World's Fair and the transformation of them into culturally recreational and broadly educational institutions.

There is one aspect of growing old that brings its sadness the more frequently as the years increase. I hear the bell toll for one after another of my associates, former colleagues, and friends. Even more desolating was the death of my two remaining brothers. Donald, my junior by less than two years, died peacefully in 1963 to end a peaceful life. In disposition he was utterly unlike me. He was so gentle, conservative, selfless, recessive, always dutiful, simply religious. He inherited my father's prospering business and carried it on routinely for a time; then at an early age he retired altogether, disposing of the business to a cousin, packed a minimum of articles he might need, locked up the house, and went to live with our good Renfrewshire cousins. He did not wait even to sell our house, and I never found out how it went into other hands. It was quite some time afterward before I learned about it. I was anxious to collect certain items from our old home, including photographs, a few books, and particularly the great Bible containing our family records, but before I began my inquiries they seem to have disappeared and I was never able to trace them.

Then in 1966 my brother Keith died. He had always been healthy, vigorous, and endlessly active. In his adventurous out-of-doors life, he had met with various accidents and recovered completely. Once on a lonely little dock in Argentina, while waiting for a ferry on his way to aid and comfort a sick and destitute wartime buddy—he had flown from Canada for the purpose—a bull suddenly appeared from nowhere, caught Keith on his horns, and threw him violently. After months of recovery in hospital Keith was able to return home, wholly restored. But a year or so before his death, while at home with the lady he married latish in life, he went out to repair a birdhouse and fell from a ladder into the snow. He broke a hip bone in the fall and was unable to move as the snow thickened into a blizzard. It was many hours later before anyone knew and came to his rescue. The exposure had weakened him, and though he rallied into his old cheerful self, it no doubt hastened the end.

The loss of my wonderful and most dear brother was the heaviest blow dealt me by the Last Enemy and Friend. Man is the most help-less, unprotected, unarmed, unself-fulfilled of all creatures, depend-ent in a multitude of ways on the service, co-operation, support, of his fellow men. As he moves through his brief spell on the neutral earth, his urgent need for assurance is sustained through the vicissi-tudes that befall him by the presence of friends, companions, asso-ciates. Partings and deaths increasingly strain the web of our belong-ingness. Keith's death created the biggest and most irremediable rent in the social fabric of my being.

26

My Credo

I call it my credo and not my creed, because "creed" suggests a system of religious doctrines and my struggling thoughts on religion contain no articles, nothing more than vague intimations. Instead I shall be speaking of my dominant attitudes, my way of responding to the problems of living, the offspring of the manner in which experience has tuned my native temperament.

We may learn much about ourselves, but there is one preliminary question probably all of us have asked, especially in our youth, without ever finding an answer, without any conception of what could be an answer: What am I? What is this "I" that is me, this insulated center of feeling and thinking, of hoping and fearing, a creature of nerves and moods, becoming a self at some moment of endless time, at this spot of endless space? My thoughts are mine, though others have thought them, though others have taught me to think them. My feelings are mine alone, even if they are responsive to the feelings of others. I cannot feel the feelings of others, the resonances within me cannot cross the barrier of the self. Nobody experiences *my* sorrows or *my* joys. Nobody else knows the quality, the tone, of my aspirations, of my loves and my lusts. My heart throbs pulsate in no other breast. They may matter nothing to others. They certainly matter nothing to the universe. But they matter much to me.

In this respect we are all self-enclosed beings, but we cannot live in our insulation. Every man is an island, but through his senses and perceptions he forms bridges to other islands, and the islands form archipelagoes, and they are all linked to a great mainland. Our feelings remain our own, but they yearn for contacts, closer and looser relationships, self-interested and outgoing relationships, transient or enduring ties. The deeps of nature demand the intimate relationship of sex, the priming ground of nearly all other relationships. Sex is the builder and breaker of a thousand bridges, the great source of inter-self involvements, the bringer of joy and of death.

We are social animals, of course, and I am a highly socialized one. In my youth nothing gave me so much delight as being invited to a party. The presence of friends is a comfort and an enlivener. To know that I have good neighbors, even if I should see them rarely, gives me a pleasant feeling. I love an evening of bright conversation and regret that it comes to me much more rarely than in earlier years. I am always ready to meet strangers. No two faces are alike, nor any two personalities, and the discovery of new ones intrigues me, even though there are some that I heartily dislike. But for me there is no quality in the world that can compare with the quality of personality. That is why a powerful drama thrills me more than any other work of art.

We grow up into an adult world that opens before us a web of new relationships, as we prepare for our occupation, as we are attracted to members of the opposite sex, who assume a whole array of new characteristics when our interest awakens, and as we cultivate our predilections and seek outlets for our energies. But the hungry "I" that cannot break through its insulation complicates and distorts the associations it forms. It associates and separates. Self-seeking asserts itself against the common cause. We override the obligations we have assumed. We compromise and we quibble, and the conflict is never wholly resolved. Here is the whole crux of morality. To be moral is to recognize and to respect one's obligations to others, while still regarding one's obligations to oneself.

It may be an impossible ideal. These antithetical obligations may at times be irreconcilable. Even when they are reasonably compatible, the self-interest is good at disguising itself as obligation to oneself, thus defeating the obligation to others. Each of us has one life to live, his own measure of fulfillment to seek. There have indeed been a few dedicated spirits who have found in service to others the road to their own fulfillment. My own brother Keith came very close to being one of them. He loved to help others without counting the cost, whether it was with money, even at times when he had little to spend, or, say, by cutting down a tree or repairing a roof or traveling a thousand miles to comfort a sick friend. But the majority of us are dominated by the urgency of private ambition and must struggle against the resistance of rivals and the limitation of lot and circumstance, so that we—at best—minimize our obligations to our society. The businessman, the politician, the professional, the scholar, the artist, the scientist, the soldier—not excluding the "man of God" —everyone after his kind, are in the pursuit of self-advantage, power or position or wealth or prestige. These motivations intrude even where men seek the less relative and more satisfying goals, the advance of learning, the pursuit of enlightenment, the achievement of significant expression in some art, the cultivation of some excellence, the complete participation in some form of communion, which may be, though rarely, the "communion of the saints."

Like everyone else, I have at times been disturbed by the conflict between what my nature demanded and social obligations that went counter to that demand. Like most other people, in later years I came to accept, with little or no compunction, a working compromise. For me the conflict was most intense, but also confused, in early youth. This was the consequence of the puritanic prescriptions in which I had been so solemnly indoctrinated at home. Gradually and uneasily I rejected as genuine obligations a number of these rigorous negatives and was troubled only by the distress my parents, but mostly my father, felt on that account. When I could conceal my transgressions from them, my conscience was perfectly at ease. I was concerned with distinguishing what I myself felt were social obligations from what my people held them to be. Here we touch on a permanent problem respecting social obligation; aside from legal requirements, we are free to decide what our social obligations are, whom they apply to and how far—to our kin, our near neighbor, friends in trouble, our fellow workers, and so forth—and under what conditions these demands should override our personal interests. My own mode of compromise is an obvious expression of my temperament. I am rather compassionate and like to come to the aid of people whose troubles I know about. I hate to do anything to hurt or offend those who put trust in me. But if I have a strong urge that persistently nags for satisfaction, I am not too mindful of imputed counter obligation so long as I can satisfy that urge without serious risk of grieving those I love.

It is practically impossible to conceive how there could be any full reconciliation between the claims our society makes on us and the degree and kind of freedom the personality claims for its own greater fulfillment. Even conscience demands a compromise, for in our multigroup society obligations themselves may be inevitably at war. Government demands that men violate their religious code to take up arms. Unions demand the sacrifice of family obligations. Businessmen can meet unscrupulous competition only by being unscrupulous in turn. And so it goes.

The ethic of the greater religions has been mainly directed to the solution of this conflict. They found the answer in the control or subjection of the self-seeking spirit in man. Oriental mystical religion sought the solution in the life of abnegation that counted earthly gain as vanity and vexation and found peace in the retreat from it all, the contemplation that culminates in Nirvana. Jewish religion took a very different route, impressing on the folk the awesome authority of an ever present God whose chosen people they were, a God who laid down with strong sanctions a precise code of law and ritual observance. But while it was a particularly potent influence in the promotion of group solidarity, this religion, with the priority assigned to the Jewish people, did little to cure the self-centered passions that found their locus in group aggrandizement. The great distinction of the Christian religion, itself an offspring of Judaism, was that it proclaimed a universal ethic that made no distinction between Jew and Gentile, bond and free. The service of one's neighbor was the service of a God of love, and every man who needed your aid was your neighbor. Its simple code of behavior was summed up in the commandment, "Whatsoever ye would that men should do unto you, even so do ye also unto them: for this is the law and the prophets."

This Hebraic-Christian maxim was a profoundly revolutionary principle, but mankind was wholly unready to accept it. So the not unprecedented phenomenon came about that a great area of the Western world became formally Christianized at the same time that the spirit of Christianity, the ardent faith of its early disciples, was dissipated. Religion was transformed into clericalism and orthodoxy. Its adherents and many of its high priests went their own way almost as if they had never heard the admonitions of the gospels. They persecuted and burned "heretics" and "unbelievers," and as sects arose they engaged in bloody "wars of religion." There were enclaves of noble and devoted men and women who sought to follow the teachings of their master, but their influence did not pervade their society.

The main thrust of Christianity was directed to the overcoming of the excesses of self-centeredness, but it tended to minimize the need for self-realization. Perhaps the strength of man's self-seeking drive was regarded as so great that it needed no ethical sponsorship. But the Christian ethic laid such stress on humility, on meekness, on turning the other cheek to the smiter, that it discounted the claim of self-fulfillment, the striving toward achievement, the demand of the creative urge in man that has widened his horizon, enriched his mind, built up his heritage of culture, and vastly improved the human lot in the march of ever advancing technology. The rewards Christianity offered to the faithful, for their sufferings and sacrifices, were otherworldly, the prophetic insubstantialities of paradise. Modern man has grown immune to this appeal and expectation. The downtrodden have come to regard such consolation as "pie in the sky." This limitation in the Christian ethic has been accented by rebels in earlier times, but modern iconoclasts have given it sharper emphasis. So Swinburne invoked the bright masculine Greek god Apollo by way of contrast and exclaimed: "Thou hast conquered, O pale Galilean; the world has grown gray from thy breath," and Nietzsche characterized Christianity as "the morality of slaves."

Nietzsche was inveighing against the moral prescriptions of Christianity, but the religious divisions that have racked the earth have not been motivated by ethical differences. Men argue and dispute over moral precepts, but they did not imprison and torture and burn their fellow men on that account or fight bloody wars under such banners. The rending divisions have been over theological abstractions, cosmogonies, rituals, cloudy symbols, and the diversities of names for a Godhead that conveyed nothing to the minds of men, sanctities without substance, effulgences in a vacuum. Under these signs men gave free range to their lusts and greeds. Actually there is a large core of moral prescription common to all the great religions, so that differences in moral valuation are more like variations on a universal theme than flagrant contradictions over which men might be moved to resort to violence and oppression. It was on no such ground that the Cross fought against the Crescent or that the mother church sought to extirpate "heresies" or that the divergent "heresies" persecuted one another. The embattled forces of the various faiths were not minded to ravage and destroy one another to defend or to advance their moral values, any more than they were minded to observe the moral values they professed.

We are all of us like debtors who cannot fully meet their commitments and make some sort of composition with their creditors. We have our standards, higher or lower, the values we live by, the goals we seek, as these are compromised by our special temptations and accommodated to the batterings of experiences. Under these promptings we form our likes and dislikes, attractions and repulsions, ways of thinking and ways of doing, the contours of developed personality. The orientation of these attitudes and habits becomes our philosophy of living, though we rarely spell it out. Presently I shall indicate what my own is by offering a list of my likes and special dislikes.

Philosophy in the broader sense has always been an interest of mine. I admire the enterprise of the free inquiring mind that probes beyond the findings of science to ask, What does it all signify. How does it all hold together? In my youth I read ardently the works of the great philosophers. But while I had regard for their insights and their ingenuity and sometimes their nobility, it became clear enough that none had reached the goal they sought. The greatest thinkers are still only beginners in nature's school. Since my Oxford days I have had some personal acquaintance with leading philosophers—not the very modern ones, who seem to me to have deviated from philosophy into the calculus of symbols.

My favorite is Bertrand Russell, with his probing, baffled quest for the reality behind appearances and his untrammeled, incisive commentaries on the problems of man and of the cosmos. My attraction to him was enhanced by my own very sporadic acquaintance-ship, beginning in London when I was invited to a meeting of the Aristotelian Society and ending some fifty years later in a chance ride with him on the London underground. He was so utterly sincere, unpretentious, intellectually valorous, and after his fashion morally dedicated, with an impish wit that neatly exposed the shallowness of much that passes for thinking. He made me feel, as I have never felt for anyone else, that he was curiously greater than he was wise.

In more recent years I have ceased to tease myself with the unanswerable problems of metaphysics, but I still enjoy dabbling in the middle ranges of philosophy, the theories of physics and biology and social science. My training and experience incline me to be particularly concerned with the most practical of philosophies, the philosophy of living.

Having taught on the average some two hundred students a year over a lifetime of teaching and having received the confidence and discussed the personal problems of more than a few of them, I had good opportunity to assess many aspects of adolescent behavior. At a later time I conducted a lengthy series of studies of young teenagers who had got into one or another form of trouble with the law, many of them dwellers in city slums. In a number of researches I undertook I made contact with the officials of many agencies, politicians, city and state employees, professional workers. I have been active also in various professional and welfare organizations. So wide a sampling of persons and programs helped to form my philosophy of living and to confirm my list of likes and dislikes.

There are, however, a few categories of persons with whom I have tended to stay on more formal terms, not because of having any less interest in them, but because of being inhibited by a sense of "social distance"—in particular, high officials. If occasionally one of them for whom I had a liking indicated a readiness to welcome my visits, I rarely followed it up. They had so many preoccupations in areas remote from my own that I was too conscious of the danger of intrusion. Again, I have reached the stage of friendship with a few very wealthy persons but generally refrained from developing it. This compunction proved strongest in my relations with wealthy women.

This tendency may be the relic of a lack of self-assertion that characterized my earlier years but was to a considerable extent overcome. Though reasonably self-sufficient, I have been slow to make advances where I was not sure of my reception. I have reached the conclusion that bashfulness is a vice and modesty an overrated virtue. We approve modesty, especially in men, not so much as a grace, but as giving us a competitive advantage over them. If you hesitate to make overtures, another will win favor ahead of you. If you are unready to stake your claim, another will pre-empt the location. If you fail to put forward your achievements, your quiet murmurs will be drowned in the clamor of the less inhibited.

Which brings me to the last of these preliminary remarks. I have painfully discovered that I am less secure in sizing up women than men. My early assessments of them suggest a bias in a particular direction. For example, I have had scores of secretaries over the years. More than once, on appointing a new one, I have thought, Now I have found the perfect secretary! But as the weeks go by a flaw appears and grows—say, too frequent absences on account of putative headaches or a laxness in filing or a forgetfulness to remind me of telephone calls or dates or a decreasing lack of interest in the job. They appeared at first like bright new-minted coins, but the freshness and lustre faded. On the other hand, I have had one or two who at first sight were less responsive or prepossessing but later revealed a growing devotion and a steady efficiency. With the male members of my staff, I have rarely indeed had any reversal of expectation.

My likings for people and things are compulsive and far-ranging.

For people, I am not merely tolerant of difference, whether it be difference of "creed, color, or national origin," but appreciative. My dislikings are specific and quite limited. They are mostly directed against doctrines I repudiate and the people who preach them. I wish I could separate my detestation of certain doctrines from my dislike of their promoters, but I cannot do it.

Through a long lifetime I have noticed relatively little change in the character and diversity of my appreciations and enjoyments, except that I perforce abstain from a few more athletic and tempestuous activities. Books of all kinds are indispensable. I take much pleasure in works of art, and music most of all—except the more outrageous extravagances of ultramodernists. I take particular delight in a good stage play, old or new, I can drop into a movie for a spare hour or two and not notice the passage of time. I love to bask in the sun on a summer beach and dip into the waves. I still enjoy, but in abbreviated form, outdoor sports, pitching approach shots on our big summer lawn, scouting the woods for mushrooms, and an infrequent trip in a sailboat or canoe. I delight to stroll in my garden and observe the changing wonder of growing things. Indoors we play for an hour after dinner some kind of game—at present it is Scrabble —and I like a keen game of bridge with players who are not too much better than myself. But my chief enjoyment is and always was to sit in the seclusion of my study, employed in the toilful effort of shaping thoughts into appropriate words.

Perhaps my philosophy of living is best exposed in the list of my detestations—they are strong and unqualified.

I detest exhibitions of arrogance, with its insufferable demand for unearned privilege. I dislike bland doctrinaires, with their naïve assertions that God is on their side, whether it be the Southern Baptist who thinks God put the Negroes where they belong, to be hewers of wood and drawers of water for the higher race, or the well-heeled, cultivated reactionary who links his notions on true-blue economics with the eternal verities; and I have no love for the smooth prelate who never probes any problem, is always ready with unctuous words of consolation, bestows his easy blessing with lavish generosity and takes good care to be aligned with the powers that be. I despise the affluent empty-headed women who trumpet their undying patriotism while, with snobbish zeal, preening themselves on their putative descent and uttering chauvinistic war whoops against "appeasers" and intruding aliens.

I dislike people who would impose their own standards and conformities on others. There is a rigor of complacent middle-class righteousness I find very disagreeable. I dislike censors and the censorious. I dislike pompous jacks-in-office and the corresponding jills. I dislike politicians who betray their function by catering to every serviceable prejudice. I dislike the folk who want to "cure" prostitutes by putting them in jail and would apply the same prescription to homosexuals. I dislike intolerance of every kind and the overbearing and sadistic promoters of it. I am a liberal in the literal sense of the word. I believe in a society where all men are free to go their own ways, to enjoy their own styles and customs, to find their own salvation if haply they can—so long as in doing so they are not causing positive injury to others.

I have a special detestation for all forms of unnecessary violence, whatever its motivation. Violence is a total disruption of social relationships. It is the coarsest and bluntest and most indiscriminate instrument to serve any purpose, for it crushes or destroys many things besides the object at which it is directed. What an incredibly better place this earth would be if people in general and rulers in particular gave up the notion that violence solves any problem! Violence is an unhappy necessity when it is resorted to solely to defeat or control violence initiated by others. This is a function of the police force and in a wiser world will be the function of an international police force. But even so the necessary resort to counterviolence effects no cure, no settlement of any international dispute, no rehabilitation of the criminal or wrongdoer The presence of violence is an indication of social illness, and you don't cure illness by damaging the patient.

A society is sustained by its traditions, but it can also be destroyed by them. How the sanctity of outworn traditions can put blinkers on the mind is testified by the amazing complacency with which men of good intelligence accept the resort to war as the final arbiter of disputes between states. In earlier times a people consisted of a small elite, possessing all the power and practically all the wealth, and the subject masses, illiterate, impoverished, henchmen, laborers, serfs, expendable in the wars of their masters. In such wars conquests could be made, triumphs won, heroes acclaimed, territories annexed, captives enslaved. All that is of the past, dead or dying, but the traditions it established live on. Now any war can embroil the great powers, and that portends the death of civilization. But we feverishly prepare for such wars at prodigious cost. We still assume that the "final solution" is to send millions of youth into the flames, while millions of men, women, and children at home are consumed in the hell-fire that descends from the skies.

Finally, I have my dislikes within my own world of scholarship—in this area, not dislike of people but of viewpoints or assumptions, not detestations but repudiations. I particularly deplore the assumption that you can interpret organisms or organic evolution or the working of the mind in terms of mechanism. A machine is a fabricated device of man to increase his efficiency and to economize his labor. It is a means and nothing but a means, a structure of parts put together in a factory. An organism, on the other hand, is not constructed; it grows as a unity. Its form is there from the first and evolves. Above all, organisms *live* and mechanisms are devoid of life. The organism is infinitely more subtly composed than any mechanism. What I dislike is the tendency of some biologists to minimize the difference between organism and mechanism, to treat life, consciousness, mind, as having no dynamic role in evolutionary development and to regard these primary principles as merely resultants of the quasi-mechanical action of natural selection operating on the chance variations of heredity. In a similar fashion some psychologists try hard to ignore the psyche and to reduce mental operations to a stimulus-response mechanism. They are in turn the blood brethren of the sociologists who refuse to be concerned with qualities unless they can reduce them to quantities—and thus "attitudes" become merely percentages of favor or disfavor for or against some person or institution—and who refuse to deal with relationships, the stuff of society, and limit themselves to counting the numbers related this way or that.

These stubborn heresies of mine lead up to a major tenet of my faith. I believe in the open-endedness of all human thinking, feeling, experiencing, expressing, and achieving. The actualized is only a mite of the potentially actualizable. The future stretches beyond all horizons. No one has said or will yet say the final word on anything. The only thing that is finished is the history of the past, but the past itself is never finished. It is germinal of every future. Ten thousand years is insignificant in the ever ongoing time expanse during which man may still flourish on this earth and stretch his wings far beyond it. But what visionary prophet of ten millenia ago could have foretold the triumph of science, the prosperity of our greater civilization, the attainments of the arts, and the richness of our many-faceted cultural heritage?

We have intimations in the exploratory fantasies of dreams, in the strange perceptive powers elicited under the influence of hallucinatory drugs, in the experiences of persons who, suddenly faced with a grave crisis, exhibit a flash of valorous insight that normal life never evoked in them, and in the conceptions of great thinkers, poets, and artists that skirt the edges of fresh understandings and a sublimer art.

Some other intimations come in those rare hours when our perception is quickened and our vision clarified, beyond the limits of our normal range. There is unevoked capacity we cannot reach at will. It lies latent in us, in our humanity. A not dissimilar phenomenon, also rare enough, is the manner in which a group of associates can all at once experience a heightened rapport, each achieving a new empathic understanding of and with the others. This can occur on various levels. It is most often recorded as a religious manifestation. On some special occasion an afflatus spreads over the group, and they thrill to the immediate presence of the divine, and departing, they say, with fervor, "It is good for us to have been here." But it may also occur on an everyday occasion that is thus rendered memorable. I recall, for example, how once at our Chilmark cottage a party foregathered whose members had never before all come together. It included Bob Merton and Ted Abel, and there were three girls who were visiting the Mememsha Inn: Illa, the remarkable wild animal photographer who was eventually killed by a lion, Mura, who had been a distinguished dancer in Vienna, and Iliana, who had a poetic quality of her own. There was a bit of chatter, and then Mura contributed a delightful series of dance caricatures of some of us. Then somehow a glow pervaded the group, a sense of high undifferentiated joyousness, a new feeling-tone that transcended time and place. Among the potencies humanity may yet realize, we must include the capacity for finer and richer emotional experience.

As a nineteenth-century poet has put it, man is an infant "still in the go-cart"—his coming-of-age is not yet in sight. Barbarity and dark superstition still entrap great multitudes. The liberation of inclusive community is only slowly being approached. The art of government is still rudimentary. Gross blunderings, the insolence of power, dim-sighted nationalisms, retard every advance. But there are strong counterimpulses that must sooner or later win out.

There will be science that goes beyond measurement in the exposition of the great categories that are now little more than names for identified unknowns, energy, electromagnetism, life, consciousness, thought, time and space, and that form of energy that maintains in eternal balance the whole of the infinite universe, gravity. There will be philosophy that gives more significant interpretation of the relationships between man the thinker and the cosmos that does not think. The range of studies we call the humanities will grapple more thoroughly with the depth of experience that finds expression in the great authors of the past. There will be scholarship that transcends laborious commentaries, critiques, recordings, tracing with fresh insight the response of cultural change to a changing world, analyzing the formative forces of history, the rise and supersession of civilizations. There will be religion that is redeemed from crude cosmogonies and anthropomorphic deities, to satisfy the yearning of the heart for communion with the divine as it is intuited in the contemplation of the grandeur and wonder and beauty and mystery and terror of a universe that forever fulfills eternal law.

Man is in the toils of becoming. It may be eons before he is the evolutionary fulfillment of man-ness—if that should ever come. He is fettered by self-imposed and group-imposed chains. He suffers from the impulses and inhibitions of immaturity. Even at best he is still poorly educated. We are so much better at drilling the memory than at evoking the imagination. Rarely does youth receive the mode of upbringing that would call out and sustain whatever talent is within its range. We fall into the complacency of make-do habits. We regulate our times and seasons by an outmoded calendar and become old before our time because a traditional chronology so prescribes. We have still to conquer the disabling diseases of middle age that cripple our prime and shorten our lives. Three-quarters of the earth's inhabitants are still prevented from developing their capacities by abject poverty, although the resources to end it are now abundantly at our command. The culture the race has acquired, the marching sciences and the aspiring arts, has been produced by a small minority of those who could have enriched it still more except for their "birth's invidious bar." Some roads to the future are slowly being opened, but the way is long and the farther we travel the longer looms the untravelled way.

Vignettes

Having set my mind and pen to the recording of events lived through and experiences undergone, I hoped to give some impression thereby of the rhythm of living, the feeling-tone, of the particular person who was caught up in these events and enjoyed or suffered these experiences. But on surveying the account I recognize that the ambience of everyday existence has to be conveyed in a different mode. This final chapter is therefore devoted to incidents and fleeting situations that may illustrate characteristic moments in the flux of my days.

The memory has a seemingly capricious quality. Certain glimpses of the long ago remain imprinted on it when all the context is buried beyond recall, like instantaneous flashes coming through a great darkness. And for the years beyond that early phase, certain episodes stand out in the details of their setting, like a frame of a moving picture the rest of which is blurred and barely recognizable. I have referred to the early glimpses in chapter 2, and after adding a few more, I shall recount a series of the clearly etched episodes, or vignettes, that have punctuated the various stages of my life.

First, I am standing at a window listening to the blasts of wind and watching with absorbed eyes the raindrops dash against the pane and run slanting down and stop and run again till they reach the window frame and vanish; I press my nose against the exposed glass and feel its coolness in contrast with the sensuous comfort of my own warmth. Next comes my recollection of toddling down the back stairs and into the yard, sniffing the acrid, tangy smell of drying skate hung on triangular racks, and peering over the garden wall beyond, where I savored particularly the smell of wet cabbage.

I remember the rasp of my father's light-brown whiskers as he picked me up in his arms. I have a vision of him as a brownish, roughish figure dressed in Harris tweeds that had a pleasant peaty odor.

I have a stronger remembrance of two first occasions. The earlier, when I was four, is of being washed and primped and combed for my first attendance at our Free Church. It took so long that I fretted and my mother shook me into patience. Then there was the walk across town to the church, with the air full of bells and the good folk all moving in the same direction making a straggling procession along the street. I had to be shown off to every passing acquaintance. I have a somewhat later recollection of sitting in our gallery pew, while the parson's voice resounded interminably through the church, observing the folks sitting in the opposite pews, and then dreamily staring at the rose window high up at the back, the only concession our austere church made to beautification, watching its changing lights and shadows.

The second occasion was the most exciting event of my early years, the sendoff for my first day's schooling, precisely on my fifth birthday. I have described it in chapter 2.

Of my earlier school days memories still remain only as glimpses, and I shall end this series with an account of the event that bit most deeply into my consciousness. It was not associated with any of my early school successes but with a situation that shocked alike my dignity and my sense of justice. I would have been in my seventh year at the time.

One bright day of spring our grouchy and erratic headmaster strode into our classroom in one of his black moods. As usual in those undisciplined days the pupils were sprawling in their seats, inattentive and chattering. He looked round rheumily for a victim and his eye fell on me, though I was one of the less troublesome members of the class. He pulled me out roughly, holding me by the scruff of the neck, made me stand in front of the class, berated us all, and especially me, in mocking angry tones with an occasional stutter, and then produced, I don't know from where, a fool's cap, put it on my head, and bade me sit on a stool in a far corner all through the afternoon.

As I turn now to the well-remembered episodes I am calling vignettes, my problem is to decide which arrows of remembrance to pull out of the full quiver.

(1) *Schoolboy Incident* (ca. 1894). I liked to be one of the boys. I joined them in all sorts of escapades, however rude or dirty they might be. I could not bring myself to use the forbidden words with which some of them interlarded their speech, but I had no objection to their doing so. Sometimes we formed into sporadic gangs from different neighborhoods and each gang would try with a bit of roughhouse to capture some member of the opposing gang. With the gang I was ready to do things I would never have done by myself.

One day a few of us were wandering along the sea front when we spied a wounded seagull drifting on the tide within easy distance. The boys gleefully began to hurl stones at it. The gull fluttered its ineffectual wings and made short dives. A stone or two would find its mark, and the gull would utter a whining gurgle. That cry struck home in me. I felt a sudden compassion. It was no longer fun. I hated what we were doing. And I rejoiced when the gull made a frantic effort and was able to swim out of range.

The incident dated a change in my outlook. I began to detest wanton cruelty. I began to feel a vague affinity with other living creatures. "The pity of it" began to dawn.

(2) *Causerie in Aberdeen* (1908). During my earlier years at the University of Aberdeen my chief associates were a group of young lecturers, all Highland scholars steeped in classical studies. I was the maverick among them who had abandoned that ancient and honored discipline for a subject that only by courtesy could be entitled a "discipline."

In these days when movies were yet undeveloped and television was far in the future, we had no problem with vacant hours. A frequent evening occupation was to talk late into the night in the rooms of one or another of the group. We did not assemble to discuss a particular topic; it was always the casual give-and-take of the moment. Our range of common interest was rather circumscribed. We rarely talked politics, except for an occasional uncomplimentary comment on the antics of some politician. We rarely mentioned the fine arts. We often dwelt on the foibles of our professor bosses and the deviant devices of students. We freely indulged in observations on the ways of mankind and especially of womankind, illustrated by cases whether within the university circle or in the outside world.

On this occasion we were met in the rooms of John Fraser, an untidy, hunched, stocky scholar, somewhat unprepossessing in appearance except for his fine dark eyes, who liked to assume the role of the cynic but who was very goodhearted. He had been playing golf that afternoon at Deeside with a student, and someone asked about his game. "Deplorable," he answered with a comic grimace, "I could have done as well if I had used my umbrella handle instead of my clubs." "I can see some advantage in that, Fraser," said the incisive, quiet-spoken Calder—he and Fraser were our ablest scholars—"at least you would have spared the turf." "Don't you know Fraser's principle?" interjected burly, shy Michie, "Spare the turf and spoil the game." "What made it worse," continued Fraser, "is that this chap I was playing with was no joker, and when I made a rotten shot, he would say, 'Bad luck, sir,' with a damned superior air. You remember the short hole across the ravine. I had the lead for once and sliced a big loop into the brush. There was a strong wind blowing at my back. Well, this chap took a number five, changed his mind, and pulled out——" "An umbrella," Calder interrupted. "Perhaps he found his umbrella gone," I added. This was one of the allusions to classical literature that figured so much in our talk. In a play by Aristophanes one of the characters constantly interrupts the conversation by interjecting that he's "lost his oil-flask," a reference to the ancient Greek habit of anointing the body with olive oil and carrying a little oilflask for the purpose slung at the side. Since this ending made no sense in an English version, Gilbert Murray substituted in his translation, "found his umbrella gone." The fourth member of our party, jolly, red-headed Petrie, recognizing the allusion, burst into a loud guffaw.

Presently Calder began mimicking the inflated manner in which our somewhat pompous professor of Greek translated passages to his class. He cited as an example a passage from the *Odyssey*. "Yea, verily in good sooth, the deviltry of Agamemnon would have foully encompassed my doom in mine own halls, were it not that——" "he found his umbrella gone." It was Petrie with another guffaw. For the rest of the evening the phrase became a sort of refrain that every member waited his opportunity to drag in. We chatted about problems of translation and the impossibility of conveying the style and idiom of foreign poetry to an English reader.

The hour was getting late when Michie shook himself and launched into a thoroughly naughty story—which I remember to this day. Somehow it acted as a signal for the group to disband.

(3) *An Evening with Music* (ca. 1910). It happened during a Christmas vacation. I was spending it in Edinburgh with the family of a good friend who had been my classmate at the university there. The house next door was occupied by a stiff-backed retired rear admiral, a bit of a martinet, who had an only daughter living with him. I had met Lilith, as I shall call her, on one or two previous occasions when I visited my friend's home. She was a tall, pale, dark-eyed, dark-haired lady, quietly dignified, seemingly rather impassive, but she could break into a most engaging slow smile. She was somehow very attractive, but had shown no interest in any of the numerous young men who fell in love with her. I should judge she was in her middle twenties. I had never met her except in company, and as she was very fond of music, I invited her to a symphony concert at MacEwen Hall, the splendid, colorful edifice where the university held its convocations. She accepted with good grace and chatted in low pleasant tones as we drove there. I do not remember the earlier music, but after the interval the orchestra played Strauss's *Death and Transfiguration*. As the music soared Lilith gently took my hand and kept holding it as though to communicate her enjoyment. Suddenly her grip tightened, and for the first time she turned to face me. Her eyes were lustrously afire as

she looked straight into mine. A thrill passed through me and kept reverberating. There was no longer orchestra or domed hall. There was only the music of transfiguration, no longer coming from outside. When the last chord ended, she suddenly withdrew her hand and sighed. I turned to her and the light seemed to die in her eyes. She gave me a sudden, fleeting kiss, a kiss that had in it the benediction of parting. We spoke scarcely a word on the way back. She was not for me nor I for her, and we both knew it. I never met her again.

(4) *The Beaver Dam* (1921). For twenty years we had happy summer months at our Lake Muskoka cottage, and in the course of our roaming over that lake system and far beyond it we ran into an adventure now and again. This is the story of a little episode in the earlier days before I was as good a woodsman as I wanted to become.

A neighbor farmer had told us of a beaver dam in the brush about a mile and a half from our cottage, saying it was quite a sight to see the great swarm of ducks that swooped down on to it at nightfall. I found my way there once in broad daylight. It lay some distance up from the farther shore of a bay that opened out beyond our nearest headland. The track to it was very faint and ended in bushes about twenty yards short of the pond. I decided one September afternoon to visit the pond and wait for the coming of the ducks. I took a canoe to the shore of the bay above which the dam was situated and found my way to it with little trouble. The sun went down, but no ducks arrived. I watched for them in vain till it grew quite dark. When I started homeward, I could not strike the trail. It was a perfectly calm night, and the sky was a thick blanket of uniform dark gray. None of the nighttime indicators of direction could be discerned as I wandered through the scrub. I sounded everywhere for the slightly softer feel of the trail underfoot. I tripped over fallen logs, and as I passed under a tree a branch caught my face and ripped off my glasses. It was no use trying to find them, and besides I might in the effort trample on them. So I took some old letters from my pocket and by sticking bits of them on twigs made a paper trail, the direction being shown by the ascending level at which I attached them as I proceeded. In the course of my wanderings I twice found myself stepping into water. I had circled both times back to the beaver dam. Where there are no landmarks the tendency to bias under the controlling influence of the dominant hand, whether the right or the left, is not corrected, and one unwittingly circles around. After I touched the edge of the pond for the third time, I was already weary and scratched by thorny vines.

I would gladly have settled for the night on a bed of pine needles. The air was pleasantly warm, and I was used to makeshift camping during our canoe trips into the wilds. But I was already very much concerned about the anxiety my wife and family must be feeling over my failure to return. I sat on a log to think out some plan. I decided it was useless to try for that elusive trail again. I knew there must be other trails somewhere in the area. They would probably all lead down to the water's edge, since the deer and other animals would go there to drink. At the other end of the dam from that at which I had approached it, the beaver had cut some saplings and laid them across an outlet to the pond, from which a small trickle of water spilled. I found that spot and followed from there a line I judged to be roughly parallel to the shore, correcting the circling tendency by a pace at right angles after every ten paces. Presently I hit a spot where the ground seemed smoother to the tread. I felt around, and there was one direction in which the softer tread continued. It was a trail, and it led slowly downward. With immense relief I cautiously followed on, losing it and picking it up again, and after about three-quarters of a mile could sense the shore ahead. It was quite some distance from where I had beached the canoe, but walking was easy along the shore, and after a spell of paddling I was at our dock.

I found everything in commotion when I landed. Ethel had been organizing a search party, and it had taken quite some time to muster our widely scattered neighbors. They were just about to set off. The rest can be imagined.

Next morning I set out again for the beaver dam, found my paper trail and recovered my glasses intact.

An Unusual Kind of Canoe Trip (*ca.* 1924). In the late summer, when the heyday of the mosquitoes was ended, I knew no greater pleasure than to join with a congenial companion or my brother

Keith on a ten-day or longer canoe trip that circled through stream and lake within the great mesh of waterways in northern Ontario. It was a lonely area, where we might travel for weeks without seeing any other human being.

One summer we had as a visitor at our Muskoka cottage a young man who had been a student of mine in the very first class I ever taught, at the University of Aberdeen. He was an American who was spending that winter in Aberdeen doing some work for his father, who was engaged in the granite trade. A very able student, he had now become a teacher of government at a first-class college. He was a burly, pleasant, outgoing fellow, and we were happy to have him as a guest.

But we soon discovered he had not the remotest interest in or knowledge of the great world of the out-of-doors. His only sport seemed to be hunting. Rather reluctantly we let him have a .22 rifle we used occasionally for target practice. He went out in the later afternoon with it, shot a flicker thinking it was a pheasant, and later on shouted to us to come and see his big catch. He was holding a skunk by the tail and asking "What have I bagged?" But his main wish was to sit on the verandah and talk with me about problems of government.

In desperation I proposed a short canoe trip—two days going down the Musquash River to Flat Rock and back. It would be a new experience for him. He nearly upset the canoe when he stepped into it. His paddling was so clumsy I asked him to sit back and let me do it all. We left the lake and portaged into the river. I pointed out nature scenes as we went along. "Do you see that scrub pine overhanging the bank? Watch the kingfisher sitting on it. He may plunge in any minute after a fish." "Yes. By the way, what do you think of the unicameral system they set up in Greece?" "Look Herbert, do you notice how the cardinal flowers are reflected in that dark pool?" "Yes. I suppose we need a bicameral system since we're a federal state. But do you think it serves any good purpose to have bicameral legislatures in the constituent states?" So it went. I was trapped. Then I remembered that my good friend was keen about arithmetical and mathematical puzzles. Perhaps he didn't know this one. "Do you know the problem about the ages of Mary and Ann?" He didn't. "Well, here it is. The combined ages of Mary and Ann are forty-two years. Mary is twice as old as Ann will be when Ann is three times as old as Mary was when Mary was three times as old as Ann. How old is Ann?" Something like that. He asked for a piece of paper and silence reigned—all the way to Flat Rock, while we set up our tiny tent and I made a fire, during our supper, and so into the quiet night. And all next morning and into the early afternoon. Just as we arrived back at our own lake, he shouted, "I have it." He had.

(5) *Night Ride* (*ca.* 1925). It was early that midsummer evening when I returned from my roaming in the Muskoka woods. As I approached our gate Ethel was waiting for me, with a look that intimated something bad had happened.

The elder son of our nearest neighbors and very good friends, the Bretts, had fallen from high up on a pine tree. He was lying unconscious, suffering from concussion. The doctor, reached by telephone, had said it was essential he be taken without delay to the Toronto General Hospital, some hundred and twenty miles away. I was the only person at hand to drive him there. No ambulance could be procured without a grievous loss of time.

While I snatched a hasty meal, the back of our car was filled full of cushions and blankets to form a level bed on which the boy could be laid. I was given strict instructions that there must on no account be any jolting of the patient. I must drive slowly and avoid swerving or any sudden motion. It was about eight in the evening when I set off. The first twenty miles to Gravenhurst were the worst, bumpy with rough-cut, loosely laid stone, and the time it took to crawl over it seemed interminable. Emerging into the highway I made a little more speed, alerted by headlights to oncoming cars and thus able to avoid any swerving. I had not gone far before I felt the ominous drag of a flat tire. I dared not try to change tires by the roadside, the chance of a jolt was too great. Fortunately I observed the sign of a filling station some little way ahead; I snailed ahead on my flat till I reached it and was able to get efficient and careful service. The rest of the way was uneventful, but I had to be ceaselessly watchful until at length I drew up at the hospital and saw my patient taken in charge.

I started back around two in the morning, enjoying the freedom to put on speed at last. I ran into a wild thunderstorm that accompanied me until I was only a few miles from home. Then the clouds broke, and as I descended toward our cottage, a rosy aura of dawn spread out over the eastern sky. I welcomed it as a good omen, and so it proved to be.

The boy lay in a coma for a day or two, but recovered and gradually was fully restored.

(6) *Farewell to the Toronto Skating Club* (1927). It was the last Saturday evening dance session of the season, and my last winter before we left for New York. All through the winter and into the spring I had been a faithful attender of these sessions. Figure skating had transformed my attitude to the long Canadian winter. Before I took it up I wearied for the time when the earth would be green again. Now the snowbound season was welcome in its due course. I practiced diligently the "school figures" and took lessons regularly from the pro. But it was the dance sessions I really enjoyed. Floor dancing is a mild pleasure compared with the swift, free gliding motions of the waltz and the mazurka and the ten-step on ice. I was transported to another world when the orchestra struck up and I could swing to its rhythm in harmony with an accomplished partner. We were a very friendly group, and although we all had favorite partners, we mixed quite freely and usually found our dancing companions in the course of the evening.

This windup session was always a special occasion. The balcony was crowded with observers. To open the event an exhibit in free dancing was given by our most expert pair. Thereafter the prizes were distributed to the winners of the club competitions. I had no pretensions as a competitor, but I did get a quite minor award as a member of the winning quartet.

Everybody seemed particularly gay that evening. The dancing was exuberant and whirling. There were a number of spills as pairs unguardedly clashed, but no one minded. On with the dance—we end with a bang.

But for me there were premonitions of finality. Would I ever again belong to a club like this one, share in a pastime that would mean so much to me? In leaving Toronto I was cutting myself off from many happy associations. I would learn to establish new ones, but this was a way of relationship that might be ending forever. Would I ever again skate to the strains of the *Dance of the Flowers* from the *Nutcracker Suite* or *Tales from the Vienna Woods* or the lilt of a favorite Brahms waltz until the band put its seal on the evening by striking into *Auld Lang Syne?*

As we grow older and as transitions come, there is one last time and then another, the last time we play tennis, or occupy a seat of office, or subscribe to a concert or opera series, or visit Europe, one after another last times. Usually we don't know it is the last.

My foreboding was prophetic. I never danced on ice again. The New York Skating Club was of that date both inconvenient and of little account. It was one joy I owed to Canada alone.

(7) *The Rosy Leptonia* (ca. 1930). It was a humid overcast day in mid-August. The ground was well soaked in the freshened woods from the heavy rainstorm of the day before. It should be a good day for the mushroom hunter. I wandered rather further afield than usual. I had picked up a number of good edibles and was about to turn back when I observed what looked like pink flowers growing in a nook between some spruces ahead. Could these be wild roses growing so close to the earth and so solitary? No, they were mushrooms, delicate, slender-stemmed, rose pink, smooth capped, with a tiny depression in the center. The leading authority of the time, Kauffman on the *Agaricaceae of Michigan,* said it was "rarely seen." I held five perfect specimens of it in my hands. Every year thereafter, while we had our Muskoka home, I searched that wood again, but never did it reappear. Nor have I ever seen a specimen anywhere since.

One of the allurements of the mushroom hunt is the hope of finding something rarely found or something never identified before. Mushrooms are remarkable that way. Some kinds are exceedingly finicky. They are found only once in a very long time or once within a whole great area. The famous mycologist Charles H. Peck reported many kinds he found only once, some kinds that were only once discovered anywhere. One remarkable instance was that of a large-sized scarlet mushroom (*Pluteus coccineus*) that was discovered once in the fork of a tree in Ohio and never seen before. It was a single specimen.

The assiduous amateur searcher is sure to run into surprises, to spot a species he has never seen before or some quite unusual specimen of a species he knows. I recall, for example, how once near the shore of Lake Muskoka I saw what in the distance looked like a man's straw hat sitting on a log. It was an unusually fine specimen of the lovely edible *Volvaria bombycina,* the greatest of the pink-spored mushrooms and one I have found only once again. And among other finds there was a magnificent five-tiered example of the sulfur polypore, all golden and coral in delicately tinted beauty, spotted on a dry ditch one late October day at the end of a long and empty search. Other interesting forms have been brought to me by neighbors, in Palisades or on the Vineyard, who have come to look on me as a local authority. But the rosy Leptonia was my first and greatest prize.

(8) *Incident in Vienna* (1932). I had been in Vienna in earlier days, when it was the easygoing cultural capital of western Europe. Now it was shorn of its power and prosperity, but it still showed a brave front to the casual visitor, and it was still the abode of *Wein, Weib, und Gesang.* I had been spending some time in Munich, where I watched with the gravest misgivings the Hitlerian bid for power. But for Vienna the writing on the wall was still invisible.

One morning I was strolling along the Ring when a brief summer shower broke, and I took shelter in a convenient portico. As the rain was clearing a tall brunette approached me and asked in bad, halting German: "Can you please tell me how to get to the Kantgasse?" She was obviously American and relieved when I replied in English. I consulted a pocket map I carried and offered to guide her there. The way was a bit complicated; she seemed somewhat troubled— and she was trig and good-looking. It was the post office she was seeking. I waited while she visited it. She came out looking very unhappy. "Nothing, nothing," she murmured as though speaking to herself.

I did not wish to intrude on her troubles but suggested it was time for a bit of lunch. She seemed not to hear me but accompanied me anyhow. Over some wine and lunch she broke into her story. It was another instance of what can befall too naïve and trustful young ladies.

She was on the road to becoming a professional dancer and, after a spell at a well-known establishment in Paris, had been paying short visits to famous dancing masters in Berlin and Munich, ending in Vienna. At Paris she had fallen in love with a dancing instructor, a bizarre, flamboyant character from all I could make out, and well —he had gotten her into trouble. But he had sworn he would make early arrangements for their marriage as soon as she returned to Paris and meantime would send her frequent letters and tell her about his plans. But no letter reached her in Berlin, and none in Munich, and now her last hope was gone. Her money was going, too, and no alternative was left except to return home to her folks in Cincinnati. She had her passage booked. It would be awful. "I can't look them in the face any more."

Her simple sincerity was as obvious as her distress. I felt in no position to offer any counsel. She planned to leave next day, but I might be able to distract her melancholy for a few hours. I asked her to spend the evening with me at the City-Bar. These Viennese "bars" were rather distinctive, cosy retreats where you could sit at a little table and dance in a pleasant atmosphere to the music of an accomplished fiddler and occasionally also a cellist. With so fine a partner, the evening sped pleasantly, and I was surprised how well she could give pause to her worries. It was long after midnight before we took our last farewell. "I wish tomorrow would never come," she said in a husky voice.

Three weeks later, a postcard from her reached me. It was written on board her liner. It contained the sentence: "The weight has been strangely lifted from me."

(9) *The Bridge Quartet.* I put no date to this entry. Over many years, at least every second Saturday, our foursome met for its own special brand of bridge. I shall describe the way we characteristically behaved at one of these sessions.

I was always rather fond of bridge. In my early years at Columbia

Ethel and I had been members of a group we called the Poison Oak and Ivy Club. It met every few weeks more for entertainment than for the rigor of the game. There were two deans, Lee McBain and Will Russell, and their wives, my political science colleague, Lindsay Rogers, and his wife, a professor of engineering, Kip Finch, and his wife, and his colleague Walter Slichter, with his wife. But the competition was not so much over bridge scores as over the excellence of the dinner that the wives of the various pairs in turn provided at the club's monthly meetings. Having eaten and drunk well we settled down to two or three hours of go-as-you-please bridge, freely interspersed with bantering conversation. The awards of a winner's prize and a booby prize brought the gay proceedings to a close.

Our quartet was a very different affair. We played for modest stakes and were serious about it. Bill Casey was a delightful kind of individualist. His students spoke of his classes in sociology as Caseology. He taught a subject that wasn't in the books, but he was a most remarkable if wholly unorthodox teacher. While the rest of us played more or less according to Goren, Bill had no use for any conventions. Bill was a law to himself in all his ways. If he opened with a three bid, it was not pre-emptive, as with the rest of us. "When I open with a three bid, I mean *three*," he would say, though we were never sure what strength that indicated. Theodore Abel was his opposite number, a cautious and unadventurous player with a tendency to understate his hand. He was constantly arguing with Bill, who was his old-time pal, and Bill always had what seemed to him, but often not the rest of us, a perfectly logical reason for doing exactly what he had done. The fact that his choice of a card had unfortunate results was for him no argument. The third player was my son Donald, who was superior to the rest of us, a real student of the game and shrewd at drawing inferences. As for me, I was a rather mediocre exponent, but I enjoyed the competition, the vagaries of the company, the endless variations of the deal, and the ups and downs of luck.

I can produce one bit of evidence that falsely suggests a higher rating of my game. I was once invited by the great Ely Culbertson to join with him in a foursome that included General Eisenhower.

I prudently declined the honor. Culbertson aspired to other achievements besides his dominance in bridge. In fact he devoted a sizable portion of the big royalties he received from his books on bridge to promote a plan for world order and world peace. He remarked to me on one occasion that he was "the kept man of twenty million women," believing the women to be the chief buyers if not the readers of his popular bridge books, "but that's my road to an end." His first wife, Josephine, was herself one of the finest of bridge players. His beautiful second wife, Dorothy, took some courses with me at Columbia and interested me in his ideas, which were by no means without significance. I did some revising for him of a memorandum on the subject that he submitted to the United States Senate, and it was in recognition of that service, regardless of my bridge capacity, that he rashly invited me to play with him.

To return to our quartet, there was often a great amount of wrangling over our bridge table. Donald was a faithful critic, and Ted Abel sometimes growled at my play, a liberty I reciprocated. Sometimes our voices would become emphatic, and Ethel, resting upstairs, would grow apprehensive and occasionally would call down to me. I would hasten to explain it was only our argumentative way. When we took a brief recess from the game, we would argue, not quite so noisily, over the political situation or the deplorable state of education. Bill tended to a kind of aristocratic conservatism and was always claiming they ran things better in England. Ted would take one side or the other, according to his mood, and I would raise objections to Bill's more sweeping pronouncements. The whole affair would last till midnight or beyond. Ted was always ready to stop, and Bill was always eager to go on.

Even after these many years there comes a now rare occasion when the old quartet is reunited for another wrangle over the green table.

(10) *A Kind of Symposium* (ca. 1952). Throughout my career I have taken sporadic pleasure in participating in one or another free-lance discussion group. In Aberdeen it was the casual meetings of a group of kindred scholars. In Toronto it was a group of leading businessmen, with a political figure included, and one or two Uni-

versity colleagues. In New York I was associated with an occasional causerie of some kind. One of these had a hostess-leader who was likely to propound a topic for the evening, usually with a philosophical ring to it. It is one of these affairs I shall now describe.

Our attractive hostess had a capacious house in the east eighties. She planned and edited various series of books on great themes and was highly successful in enlisting as their writers the most distinguished authorities over the whole expanse of science, scholarship, philosophy, and religion.

On this occasion, when after the dinner hour a circle was formed in the living room, there were two protagonists, both philosophical theologians, Paul Tillich and Jacques Maritain. The subject was— heaven help us!—the relation of "existence" and "essence." I was a sceptic when metaphysicians discoursed on such elusive abstract concepts, wondering whether they were dealing with mental apparitions or the properties of reality. I listened for a time in a querulous half-spell while Tillich, who mostly had the floor, expounded the thing-in-and-for itself. The gentle Maritain contented himself with an occasional comment or demurrer. Except for one German scholar very few of the members intervened in the discussion. I was sitting between two Columbia friends for whom I had a great regard, the Italian scholar Arthur Livingston and the down-to-earth philosopher W. P. Montague. In my irreverent way I whispered an occasional acrid comment to one or the other, to which they duly responded. Very properly our hostess looked reprovingly at me and put her finger to her lips. The dialectic went on, flowing over most of us, with an occasional probing question from some member of the group. A foreign scholar raised the issue of existentialism, which Tillich proceeded to put in its place.

Finally our hostess, summing up in a few gracious words for the protagonists, suggested adjournment, and ushered us into the dining room, where the table was richly laden with tidbits and drinks. On the way in I said to Livingston: "Would you call this existence or essence?" "I'd call it delicatessence," was his reply.

28

Footnote Finale

To man nothing human—or subhuman or unhuman—is alien.
The capacity to form relationships is the source of man's major joys
and most vexatious problems. Life itself, from the lowest organic
form to the highest, is a ceaseless process of sustaining and modifying
relationships.

Man is related, willy-nilly, to everything in the heavens and on
earth. To the earth itself with its cornucopia of products, with the
flux of its seasons as they determine the rains and the droughts and
the storms, with all its forms of teeming life from the virus and
bacillus and the insects and the worms and the snakes and the fishes
and the birds to the other mammals, whether they serve or disserve
the rapacious animal that strives to master them all. He is related
to the reaches of space, with the pull of the forces that direct the
earth's path in its cosmic motions and with the beat of the radiations
that flow from the sun and the stars and galaxies unthinkably remote.
And finally he is related, in ways he is mostly unaware of, to his fellow men from near kin to the peoples in the far corners of the planet.

Life is a miracle of relationships, the continuity of a mesh of relationships that began before any living thing began. I call it a miracle
because I know no other word for what lies beyond understanding,
in the contemplation of which we can well get lost in wonderment.

Man himself is a great spinner of new relationships, as well as an untiring tinkerer with existing relationships. The threads of his spinning stretch further and further within and now beyond earth's bounds. And who knows whether some future day they may not link with the threads from another kind of conscious life on some planet no telescope can ever see.

Life is the richer and the more abundant where the web of relationship is freely and co-operatively spun, with no invidious barriers against expansion. The widening of the range of actual and potential community is an index of civilization. The capacity of the individual to accept and to share in the widened circle is an index of his culture. The primitive that dwells in us resists and seeks to disrupt the process of expansion.

History is dominantly the record of the making, remaking, and unmaking of group relationships. It is a piebald tale, in which achievement and high enterprise are crossed by disaster and retreat and the ruin of peoples through the muddled folly of power and the impassioned credulity of the multitude. It accents the contrast between the remarkable prowess of scientific man in establishing new relations with the physical environment, making it more serviceable to his needs, and his lamentable shortsightedness in his relations with his fellow men.

I have lived through two generations of vast suffering and brute passion, in which the resurgent primitive mind has shattered the promise of the greater community. We live in the aftermath of confusion and in an era of new promise, the promise of the greater society when for the first time abject poverty will cease to oppress great numbers and decent justice will be extended to disprivileged minorities; but the promise is beclouded by the perilous stupidities that still beset the resort to force.

My own career has been occupied in learning, lecturing, and writing about social relationships. It has been an engrossing occupation.

Thus I have lived the fullness of days. I have "warmed both hands before the fire of life." My dominant feeling is one of thankfulness.

And I still indulge myself in the thought that one more chapter may be added before the tale is wholly told.

Appendix One

Vita

Birth

    Stornoway, Scotland, April 17, 1882

    To Donald and Christine Morrison MacIver

Marriage

    To Ethel Marion Peterkin, August 14, 1911

Children

    Ian Tennant Morrison (deceased), Christine Elizabeth (Bierstedt), Donald Gordon

Education

    1903 M.A. Edinburgh, first-class honors in classics

    1907 B.A. Oxford, double first in "Greats"

    1905 D. Ph. Edinburgh

Honorary degrees

    1929 Litt. D., Columbia

    1936 Litt. D., Harvard

    1947 Litt. D., Princeton

    1950 Litt. D., Jewish Theological Seminary

    1950 D.Sc., New School

    1951 L.H.D., Yale

    1952 LL.D., Edinburgh

    1957 LL.D., Toronto

Professional positions

    1907-15 Lecturer on political science, Aberdeen University

    1911-15 Lecturer on sociology, Aberdeen University

    1915-22 Professor of political science, University of Toronto

    1917-19 Vice-chairman, Dominion of Canada War Labor Board

1922-27 Head, Department of Political Science, University of Toronto

1927-36 Head, Department of Economics and Sociology, Barnard College, Columbia

1929-50 Lieber professor of political philosophy and sociology, Columbia

1951-56 Successively, director of research projects on the Jewish Defense Agencies, the Assault on Academic Freedom, the Nations and the United Nations

1956-61 Director, City of New York Juvenile Delinquency Evaluation Project

1963-64 President, New School for Social Research

1965-66 Chancellor, New School for Social Research

Fellow

Royal Society of Canada

American Academy of Arts and Sciences

American Philosophical Society

World Academy of Arts and Science

British Academy (Corresponding Fellow)

Member

American Sociological Society

Institut International de Sociologie

Phi Beta Kappa

American Political Science Association

Honorary Member, Instituto de Estudio Politicos, Madrid

Awards

Woodrow Wilson Memorial Award

Kurt Lewin Award, Society for the Psychological Study of Social Issues

Founders Medal, New School for Social Research

Commander of the Royal Order of Phoenix (Greece)

Books

Community — a Sociological Study (1st ed.; London: Macmillan, 1917; New York: St. Martin's Press, 1917)

Labor in the Changing World (Toronto and London: Dutton, 1919)

Elements of Social Science (1st ed.; London: Methuen, 1921)

The Modern State (1st ed.; Oxford: Oxford University Press, New York: 1926)

Relation of Sociology and Social Work (New York: Columbia University Press, 1931)

Society—a Textbook of Sociology (1st ed.; New York: Farrar Rinehart, 1937), rewritten and enlarged, with Charles Page, as *Society: An Introductory Analysis* (New York: Rinehart, 1949)

Leviathan and the People (Baton Rouge: Louisiana State University Press, 1939)

Towards an Abiding Peace (New York: Macmillan, 1935)

Social Causation (1st ed.; Boston: Ginn & Co., 1942)

The Web of Government (1st ed.; New York: Macmillan, 1947; rev. ed. and paperback, 1965)

The More Perfect Union (New York: Macmillan, 1949)

Democracy and the Economic Challenge (New York: Knopf, 1952)

Academic Freedom in Our Time (New York: Columbia University Press, 1955)

The Pursuit of Happiness (New York: Simon & Schuster, 1955)

The Nations and the United Nations (New York: Manhattan Publishing Co., 1959)

Life: Its Dimensions and Its Bounds (New York: Harper & Bros., 1960)

The Challenge of the Passing Years (New York: Trident Press, 1962; Pocket Books, 1963)

Power Transformed (New York: Macmillan, 1964)

The Prevention and Control of Delinquency (New York: Atherton Press, 1966)

Clubs

Century Association, Harvard Club of New York City

Home

Heyhoe Woods, Palisades, New York

Appendix Two

My Private Game
of Patience

My patience game is the ordinary Canfield, described in every book on card games, but it is no longer a matter of making a coup or nothing. Every deal counts. You start with 1,000—we'll call it dollars, and the object is to turn the thousand into a million. You put a stake on every play. The stake must not be greater than a fifth of the total you possess. Thus the first stake must not be more than 200. If on the hand you score 10 points, you neither win nor lose. If you score nothing, you lose the amount of your stake. If you score 5 points, you lose half your stake. If you score 15 points, you make a profit of half your stake, 20 points, you double the amount, and so forth. If you get a coup, you get 5 times your stake. For example, if your stake is 100 and your total is 1,000, 20 points gives you 1,200, a coup gives you 1,500. There is one exception. On the first deal of every bracket of 25 deals, you double your regular take. That is why it is preferable to put the maximum stake on the first deal of a bracket.

The counting of points goes as follows:

Points made	Score
0–2	0
3–7	5
8–12	10, and so forth.

Your stake must always be 10 or a multiple of 10. You may increase your stake when your total score permits a higher multiple. If your score falls below 4 times your stake, you must lower your stake so that it is not more than a fifth of your total score.

To make the system clearer I present an example of a game that was won—$1,000,000—in 119 hands. (My best win—51 hands.)

My Private Game of Patience

	Scores					Stakes					Totals
$1,000	100^1	120^1	110^1	100^1	140^1	20^1	—	—	—	—	1,400
	130^1	110^1	100^1	100^1	90^1	—	—	—	—	—	900
	190^1	200^1	220^1	210^1	210^1	—	—	—	—	30^1	2,100
	225^1	240^1	225^1	375^1	350^1	—	—	—	—	50^1	3,500 (1)
	325^1	375^1	375^1	375^1	400^1	—	—	—	—	—	$4,000 (2)
$3,000	350^1	325^1	300^1	375^1	375^1	—	—	—	—	—	3,750
	375^1	400^1	430^1	405^1	405^1	—	—	—	—	—	4,050
	555^1	510^1	565^1	510^1	510^1	—	90^1	—	—	—	5,100 (3)
	510^1	960^1	910^1	910^1	910^1	—	—	10^2	—	—	9,100
	960^1	910^1	810^1	910^1	960^1	—	—	—	—	—	$9,600
$9,600	195^2	188^2	165^2	175^2	195^2	—	20^2	—	—	—	19,500 (4)
	185^2	185^2	165^2	185^2	185^2	—	—	—	—	—	18,500
	285^2	285^2	265^2	245^2	265^2	—	40^2	—	—	—	26,500
	225^2	245^2	465^2	415^2	415^2	—	—	—	—	—	41,500
	415^2	395^2	395^2	375^2	375^2	—	—	—	—	—	$37,500
$27,500	335^2	365^2	365^2	335^2	395^2	—	—	—	—	—	39,500
	395^2	365^2	335^2	365^2	425^2	—	—	—	—	—	42,500
	725^2	675^2	625^2	775^2	825^2	—	10^3	—	—	—	82,500
	755^2	755^2	755^2	705^2	705^2	—	—	—	—	—	70,500
	120^3	170^3	170^3	210^3	250^3	—	—	20^3	—	—	$250,000
$20,000	200^3	230^3	200^3	170^3	320^3	30^3	—	—	—	—	320,000
	320^3	470^3	440^3	410^3	470^3	—	—	60^3	—	—	470,000
	470^3	470^3	440^3	740^3	740^3	—	—	—	—	—	740,000
	800^3	800^3	800^3	$1{,}000{,}000$		40^3	—	—	—	—	$1,000,000 (5)

1. Coups are given in italics, double coups in boldface.

2. At end of each bracket "interest" is deducted unless the total for each line of five exceeds the initial score for each line. The deductions are as follows:

End of first bracket	1,000
End of second bracket	5,000
End of third bracket	10,000
End of fourth bracket	50,000
End of fifth bracket	100,000

If you proceed to a sixth bracket you must make your million before it ends. The remaining score after deduction must be not less than the deduction or the game is ended.

3. A larger stake than I usually make (a seventh of the score).

4. No deduction is made for a bracket if the score for the first line is higher than the starting score and if the scores of the other four lines are each higher than that at the end of the previous line. If I had had to make a deduction for

the second bracket the game would have been over. The first score on the third bracket was a double coup, that is, 5 times the stake, multiplied by 2.

5. Stake reduced because a coup would have given a million with this stake.

I have introduced a few frills in my mode of playing the game but will not complicate this statement with them.

The play is by no means automatic. Practice will suggest ways in which you can improve your chances. In Canfield, cards are turned over in threes. Before you play from the seven cards showing on the table, you should turn over your first three and if the face-up card is playable, don't play until you have looked at the top card of your second three. (You're not allowed to riffle through the unexposed cards.) Try and avoid using up the whole three of any turn unless you know that you have a playable card in a lower three. It is desirable to remember the previously exposed cards as you play on. The reason for these and various other precautions will become obvious in practice.

I play only two or three hands in intervals of writing, so that a promising game will run on for several weeks.

Appendix Three

The Island Revisited

(In the middle thirties I paid my last visit to the island of my birth. My parents were no more, my brothers were scattered, my acquaintances had passed beyond my ken. I was a stranger among the folk, but their ways and their speech and the earth and the shore awakened thoughts the more sharp-edged because I felt so much alone. I did not belong any more. Perhaps had it not been for the writing of this book I would never have unearthed from old records the forgotten memento I wrote on that occasion. Since it conveys a fuller impression of my boyhood home than I have offered in the text, I give it below.)

The train journey had seemed interminable, but at last I embarked on the little steamer that would take me to the far island of my birth. Already these unknown faces on the boat, my fellow travellers, awoke the now unfamiliar sense of home. The quiet voices, the patient eyes, in fact every form and motion, witnessed to a common origin. We were all struck from the same mint, my fellow travelers and I, and we were going home, back to our place of coinage.

Through the long northern evening I watched the low dark coastline of the island as it rose imperceptibly from the west, until passing the lighthouse we entered its wonderful harbour and slowed down to the little pier. The coming of the steamer is always the event of the day, an occasion faithfully observed by the townspeople. To many of them the assembling on the pier is a kind of ritual, the necessary conclusion of the day, establishing the sense of the outer world while they watch with curious eyes the returning voyagers. To this

255

remote island few strangers penetrate. With scarcely an exception the travelers are returning, some of them from distant shores, for the island sends forth many wanderers over the face of the earth to follow fortune on every frontier. Whether they find it or fail, most of them cherish the desire to see once more, not in dreams, the Hebrides. So they cross the Minch in the little *Sheila,* and the waiting crowd passes round the word. There's Alick or Norman or John, adding surname or (as is more common in the islands) nickname, back from Calgary or Seattle, from West Australia or the Malay States. A few return after so many years that, unwelcomed by friends or relatives, they pass unknown through the inquisitive throng.

How unchanged the little town seems, especially to those who come from the changeful world without. The same kippering sheds, the same barrels and herring troughs, the same quays, the tides still ebbing and flowing between the same walls, the little boys still fishing off the same stone steps, the same gulls still calling in the bay, the same houses in their sleepy lines of grey and brown. Some new signs are painted over the shopfronts; the number of automobiles signalizes the irreverent triumph of mechanism; and on a neighboring hill stands a war memorial. But otherwise, in all essentials, the aspect of the town seems little touched by the hand of time or that hastier hand which the traveler knows as "progress."

The outer aspect is the same, and the same manner of life still prevails beneath it, the same rhythmic speech, the same bustle round the docks, beyond it the same quiet coming and going, the same somber religion, just as the same tides come up the bay. The traveler feels, perhaps with surprise, how deep are the roots of that life and custom from which he has gone apart. He has changed, but it abides. To it he can return, though not to that old self he was when he made part and parcel of it. And then, beyond the sameness, he comes to comprehend the poignant difference. Time is not so easily cheated. The river remains, but the water is always flowing to the sea. The community remains, but life has been flowing on. Babes have married, and their babes are now where once their mothers were. The boys he knew, those who stayed faithful to the place, are perhaps town councilors, perhaps—strangest of contrasts—elders of the little church. And the older men, once the stalwarts of the town, where are they? Their names are cut in the stones of the churchyard. Yes, they tell him, there's been a sad thinning of the ranks these last years. X had gone to his rest, and Y, and poor Z is in bad shape. He's the last of the band, a great fighter he was, but the spirit's out of him. It won't be long ere he join the others.

It almost seems, as one hears the tale, as though death too had a season for reaping, and was just finishing his harvest.

In the morning I looked from my window down the quiet street. The houses seemed so empty, because I could no longer name their unseen inhabitants. In that corner house Mrs. A used to live, with her brood of daughters. I half expected to see them running out, to hear their young voices. But the voices are no longer young, and the brood has flown, the nest is empty. I look across the bay, the unchanging bay, with the dark-sailed boats still moving slowly out to sea. I breathe the smell of the sea, the tang of the seaweed, the odor of nets drying in the sun. What is the subtle relation between the memory and the smell of things, that this should evoke more vividly than sight or sound these early recollections, so vividly that it rolls back the intervening years and I seem to stand again on the threshold of youth? Imagination can recall the scenes we have once known or evoke the echo of once familiar sounds, like the noise of screaming sea gulls, but it is powerless to share in the lost world of the smells of earth and sea. In compensation, when in actuality we sense them again, nothing intervenes between us and the past which they restore. They belong only to the present, so that the present and the past are one. And themselves undimmed by remembrance, they vivify all memories. So I found it on this native heath, savoring the forgotten smells of the seashore, of the dark heather roots, of the wet banks along the stream where once we fished for trout, of the weedy lines between the crofts, and of the blue peat smoke that drifted through the evening air.

Here it was, along those quays and across that bay and among the heather-clad hills beyond, that I dreamed and played, and woke to the inquisitive hopes and fears of boyhood. Here, in this little town which only a moment ago I saw with different objective eyes, that

I first felt the uncanny wonder of life, and yearned to understand, and believed with the confidence of inexperience that the key of knowledge would unlock its mystery. Here the spur of ambition first urged me to strive toward dawning goals. Here I was nursed in the strong uncomfortable language of heaven and hell, offering the oppressive alternatives of lurid damnation and meaningless bliss, and shook myself free at length, with vast relief, from their ancient spell. Here I learned, from the silent starry nights, the immutable eternity of law that rings about our little lives. Here I heard the secret voices of nature, borne through the winds and the waves, telling of life and death. Here lived my comrades and first friends, my rivals and boyish foes. Here was my home, where a father toiled for me and a mother watched over me with indomitable love. And here the light shining in the eyes of a girl first stirred profounder deeps, as an angel might descend to trouble the pool, and left me alone and wondering, subdued by a breathless, fearful joy.

I knew all the moods of this island, knew its age-old influence on the spirit of the people, of whom also I was. I could feel once more the long drifting lines of southwestern rain, when day after day the leaden skies sought the sodden heather and the steaming mists of the brown peat bogs mingled with the soft smirr of the dissolving clouds. I could hear the elemental wailing of the winter storms, now rising to a shriek, now sinking to a whisper through which the persistent crash of angry waters arose. I felt the solitude of the moor, monotonous and bare save where some desolate loch spread its peat-brown surface. I knew the bleak and stony wastes that stretch out to the northern seas, the bold hills, sacred to the deer, that rise from the long inlets of the southern shore, the dark streams where salmon and sea trout run, and the white sands that lie open to the waves. I knew also the beauty of its morning and the glory of its sunset, and the great calm that falls on its shimmering lochs and bays.

Such a land has bred its own people. Where the earth yields so little to their toil, men must follow the sea as well. A grave and patient race, they are content with little. They wring meager crops of oats and potatoes from the thin patches of their crofts, and eke them out with the precarious harvests of the sea. Precarious in another sense as well, for the sea is never to be trusted and every village nurses the tragedy of the men and the boats that do not return. On this coast nothing intervenes between man and the elemental forces. Everywhere the land is naked to the winds and to the skies, for there are no kindly trees to interpose their protective screen. The wind and the rain and the sun sweep freely over the moors and the hills, over the low huddled thatched houses that scarcely detach themselves from their surroundings, suggesting a pathetic mimicry. They live too close to nature, the people of this inclement northern coast, to achieve light-heartedness. They are too much with it, riding the waves through the night watches, guarding their spare highland cattle on the desolate moors, or cutting their peat from out of the bogs. And the women are subdued by more incessant toils, for in the intervals of domestic work and much child-bearing they are hoeing the stubborn crofts or carrying the dried peat blocks in creels across the moor or carding and spinning and dyeing and "waulking" to make the island tweeds.

Is it, then, small wonder that this people is much-enduring and somber-minded. They have few comforts and few recreations, and even the latter incline to melancholy. Their native songs are for the most part minor and plaintive, telling of far dreams and ancient yearning, of parted love and eternal farewell. Their tales are of the lost heroic days, of old adventurers and uncanny prophets, of omens and portents, of banshees and ghosts. They live close to nature, but save when in exile, they can scarcely be said to love it; they do not even know it. They people it with insubstantial forms but are curiously ignorant of its flowers and ferns and mosses, its herbs and fungi, its birds and beasts. They have the dangerous gift of imagination, making the dream a substitute for the reality. They are evasive and moody, vaguely romantic and sternly fatalistic. They are exceedingly fond of gossip and argument, and in the long winter nights they love to join the *ceilidh* round the flickering, heartless peat fire that is built in the center of the clay floor. A kettle hangs above it, and they drink strong tea from the pot that is always brewing at the side; as the storm rages without, the talk turns gradually from local concerns to those melancholy reflections on life and death in which their spirit takes a sad delight.

The most potent support, as it is also the expression, of this spirit is their religion. No doubt even in this land of Thule the times are slowly changing. Just as slate roofs are ousting thatch, just as the car is banishing the jolting cart, just as the steam-drifter is taking the place of the old wherry, so also the conditions which produced this island temperament are in some measure undergoing change. The sea is not so perilous as it was, and swifter travel disturbs the fairies of the roadside. Poverty is less extreme, and health insurance and old-age pensions may be prejudicial to the attitude of fatalism. I do not belong to those who always deplore the decline of the ancient spirit and regret the passing of its former superstitions. Why should my native people remain mournfully picturesque to please the anthropologist or the romantic traveler? They, too, have their lives to live and must obey the law of life, prepared to accept its demands and seize its occasions under penalty of being left to molder among lost causes and obsolete faiths. Better that customs should pass and that institutions should change than that a people should preserve them in its own decay. Better the risks of purposive change than the false security of an outworn tradition. Better, yes, perhaps even less dangerous in this always risky business of living, better the hope of the young than the faith of the old. And here is the problem of that grim aspect of religion which reflects the temperament created in this people by the centuries of elemental life. For though all things change, a religion such as this, invoking all the mysterious powers of hell and heaven to guard its dread anathemas, resists change more stubbornly and more blindly than anything else on earth.

It is indeed an impressive occasion to observe the great "festival" of this religion, when the "communion season" has come round; to watch the set faces of the folk, the men in their clumsy dark Sabbath clothes, the black-shawled women, the resigned young people, the trailing children, as they gather from miles around to the bare white-washed church, bereft within and without of adornment or grace, or to the green beyond the church where sometimes, on account of the multitude, the "table" is spread; to hear the long shrilling unison as they follow the "precentor" in penitential psalm or in some Israelite song of deliverance; to see them bowed in prayer while the preacher wrestles long and mightily with his God on their behalf or settled in tense ranks of silence while he reiterates, in the hypnotic rhythm of his Gaelic eloquence, the strong words of damnation and salvation; then to advance to the culminating act of the sacrament, when after the ministers have broken bread and tasted the cup the elders pass the "elements" to the elect. The solemn occasion may last five days, from the Thursday "fast day" to the Monday "thanksgiving." Perhaps the most curious feature of it all is the Saturday observance, when the men, being the old stalwarts of the congregation, rise in turn to "speak to the question," in other words to expound a selected subject or text, exemplifying their doctrinal soundness and testifying to the saving power of the "word."

This is the regular form of Highland communion, but it is to be witnessed in all its rigor only on the western fringe, and nowhere more than in this Isle of Lewis. It holds the quintessence of this religious spirit, which has none of the boisterous joy in salvation evinced, for example, by the east coast fishermen or the blithe sense of liberation from sin that, for example, the Salvation Army proclaims. It has little appreciation of divine fatherhood or human brotherhood but remains gloomy, repressive, bitterly orthodox. There is no beauty in its holiness or gladness in its praise. If it reflects the bleak and often tragic existence lived in an environment that inspired gloom and fatalism, by its dread sanctions it has impressed this attitude on minds whose secret need might well be to find an antidote, and not a confirmation, of their prevailing melancholy. Instead, it seeks to close every avenue of escape. It abhors dance and gaiety. It regards art and beauty as lures of the devil or at best as profane pursuits unworthy of the seriousness of life. It includes the most natural diversions under the formidable and unarguable name of sin. It is the enemy of youth, making men and women old before their time.

One of the most unhappy aspects of this religion, as of some ancient and modern derivatives of Christianity, is its gross separation of the interest of the soul and of the body. Consequently, its devotees take no healthy delight in themselves but look upon the body furtively, "like a guilty thing, afraid." Their hardy open-air life has given this people a fine physique (though tuberculosis is far too common), and the women, in youth, have a quiet gracefulness. But the association of the body with sin poisons the mental atmosphere. The effects are of course most obvious in the relationship of man and woman. People avoid the direct mention of sex as far as possible, and when they refer to it at all, it is generally in an uneasy and constrained manner. Love-making is no doubt part of the necessary order of things. It is natural that John should be courting Janet, but they must conceal the fact as much as possible. In His own mysterious way God has appointed the union of the sexes, and we must accept the mystery, humbly and fearfully. Sexual relation is viewed in the murky light of the unpleasant story of the Fall. The body is thought of under the incongruous and foolish name of the "flesh," and the flesh is the central fact of the unholy trinity, the world, the flesh, and the devil.

It might be expected that among a people so environed, so subject to influences which tend to depress and restrict the spontaneity of the feelings, there would occur violent revulsions. Sometimes the flesh takes its revenge in secret orgies or rapelike debauches after a drinking bout. Often, when he visits the town, the countryman drowns his melancholy in liquor, knowing no limit short of utter drunkenness. He is the desperate drinker who drinks, not to enjoy himself, but to feel free. Then, by the law of reaction, his reserve gives place to the noisiest exhibitionism, and he shouts his liberty to the four winds, in language so starkly indecent that a London docker might hear it with envy. In former days many a patient pony jogged back with its master lying stupefied in the wooden cart, and there were occasions when the master died from exposure on the way or, falling by the roadside, never reached home at all. They closed the public houses of Stornoway, but there are nights when these wild outbursts may still be heard in its streets.

I should be sorry to overestimate the part played by repression and reaction in the life of this island people. There are brighter scenes that live in memory. I can see the fishermen casting off cheerily on a clear morning, and the fishergirls chattering gaily over the herring troughs. I know the warmth of hospitality which is everywhere displayed, even to strangers, and the social merriment which attends a homecoming or a wedding or some other event which makes permissible the expression of natural feeling. I recall, too, the delight in argument which fills the hours round many a peat fire in the wintry days. But the insistent voice of melancholy always returns, as surely as the Atlantic rains. And always it mingles with that other voice, the voice of this religion which bids man "think of his latter end," which bids him abjure the "works of the flesh" and warns him of the fearful final penalty for sin.

I well remember, here in my own youth, how my spirit protested within me against these mighty and oppressive claims and how, with much pain and travail, it sought to resist them, I remember the growing sense of relief, of spiritual emancipation, as I came to learn that this ghostly doctrine was no more the eternal verity than any other belief which has been bred in the darkness of our suffering and ignorance. Liberal as my parents were in other ways, we were immersed nevertheless in the prevailing influences. Of all freedoms which the human mind can find, this still seems to me, from that early experience, the first and the greatest, this which rests in the faith that we belong, not to others, not to some power whose will is not our will and whose ways are not our ways, but to ourselves. Of course there is a real sense in which we belong to one another, to our society, to our race. It is most obvious that as individuals we owe everything to our race, which through the age-long vicissitudes of its faith in life has borne us to our appointed hour and place. But even to our race we cannot owe—in the other sense of that confusing term —the denial of what it has bequeathed us, the sense of the true and of the desirable which is inbred in us. And if its priests and prophets, in its name or under some mightier sign, bid us deny it, we must protest that our inheritance is within us, far more surely than in any tradition that calls us from without, that our nature is a truer guide than their word. *Nos qui vivimus,* we the momentary heirs of all the ages, must carry on this marvellous adventure of our race, trusting to our inheritance—in other words, to ourselves—trusting at once our instinct and our vision, believing that life is deep and complex beyond our understanding, but believing at least in life, and above all refusing to accept any purposes with which we cannot identify our purposes and any goals that are not our goals.

And now, looking backward, I perceive that the thing which was hard to struggle against was not this creed itself. As soon as one permits oneself to think freely, its hold relaxes. The difficulty was with that which checked one's thought, the compulsion of the social influences which guard the creed. For it is most jealously guarded. Its devotees view with profound disapprobation those who do not bow to its claims. A kindly good-natured folk, in this they are bitter and inexorable. He who denies the faith is outcast, but he who deserts it is anathema. Far less heinous, in their view, to break all the commandments than to doubt one jot or tittle of their theology. They have in full measure the curious conviction of all tradition-bound people, that the whole scheme of the universe has been "revealed" to them. And they cling tenaciously to their own stern doctrines, separating themselves into their narrowing fold from every heresy that may arise in the world without.

They are in truth, in their interests as in their thoughts, still remarkably remote from the world. The spirit of industrialism has never touched this island. When a great industrial magnate, who had purchased the island from a poverty-stricken laird of the old school, came forward with a series of magnificent schemes, in which he sought to play the part of the benevolent autocrat, he was foiled by the dour obduracy of the countryfolk. His wealth and power were nothing to them. So Lord Leverhulme retired vanquished, abandoning his canneries and his model houses and his roads and his railway. As a last gesture he gave the land over in his will to the people themselves. The townspeople accepted the offer, including the responsibility of a castle and a large estate which they soon found to be an expensive burden to maintain. But the countryfolk refused to own their land! What did they care for ownership when the only real difference was that they would then be liable for taxes from which they were otherwise exempt? To such a folk what do the great names of capitalism and socialism matter? These come to them as the empty sounds of alien strife. And in the assurance of their ancient ways they think to themselves: "Why do the heathen rage, and the people imagine a vain thing?"

Index

Index

Index